STRUGGLES IN THE DAWN

THE STORIES OF

THE GREAT INDIAN EPICS

STRUGGLES IN THE DAWN

THE STORIES OF

THE GREAT INDIAN EPICS

THE

RAMAYANA AND MAHABHARATA

JOHN CAMPBELL OMAN

GYAN

Published by

Gyan Publishing House
5, Ansari Road
Daryaganj, New Delhi-110002
Phone: 011-47034999, 9811692060
E-mail: books@gyanbooks.com

Distribution Network
gyanbooks.com
India, USA, Canada, UK, Australia

ISBN: 978-93-6920-403-8 (PB)

First Published, 1893

2nd Impression 2025

Printed at: Gyan Press, Delhi.

STRUGGLES IN THE DAWN
THE STORIES OF THE GREAT INDIAN EPICS
Author: JOHN CAMPBELL OMAN

STRUGGLES IN THE DAWN

THE STORIES OF

THE GREAT INDIAN EPICS

THE

RAMAYANA AND MAHABHARATA

BY

JOHN CAMPBELL OMAN,

PROFESSOR OF NATURAL SCIENCE IN THE GOVERNMENT COLLEGE, LAHORE,

AUTHOR OF INDIAN LIFE, RELIGIOUS AND SOCIAL; &c.

LAHORE:

PRINTED AT THE "MITRA VILASA" PRESS.

1893.

ERRATA.

Page	71	line	24	for	ather	read	at her.
„	80	line	27	„	gandy	„	gaudy.
„	81	„	8	„	gandy	„	gaudy.
„	179	„	35	„	fined	„	find.
„	18C	„	11	„	hosts	„	host.
„	211	„	10	„	a interior	„	anterior.
„	„	„	23	„	anordinary	„	an ordinary.
„	216	„	21	„	vehicles	„	vehicle.
„	231	„	26	„	halucination	„	hallucination.

CONTENTS.

PAGE.

General Introduction 1

PART. I.—*THE RAMAYANA.*

CHAPTER I.

Introductory Remarks 15

CHAPTER II.

The Story of Rama's Adventures 18

CHAPTER III.

The Ram Lila 78

APPENDIX.

Legend of the Descent of Ganga 91

Notes 95

PART II.—*THE MAHABHARATA.*

CHAPTER I.

Introductory Remarks 99

CHAPTER II.

The Story of the Great War 104

CHAPTER III. PAGE.

The Sacred Land 209

APPENDIX.

(1) The Bhagavatgita or Divine Song 221

(2) The Churning of the Ocean. 233

(3) Nala and Damayanti 237

Notes 250

Concluding Chapter 253

PREFACE.

The Indian Epics are precious relics of the spring-time of Eastern thought, introducing one unacquainted with the life and aspirations of the Orient into a new and singularly fascinating world, differing very remarkably from that depicted in the epic poetry of Western lands. But although these epics are extremely interesting, and although they are accessible in English translations, more or less complete, they are such voluminous works that their mere bulk is enough to repel the ordinary English reader, and even the student, in these days of feverish occupation.

I may, no doubt, be justly reminded that every Indian History, written within recent years, contains abstracts of the two epics ; but these abstracts, I would observe, are skeletons rather than miniatures of the poems ; they are the dry bones, on which the historians try to support a fabric of historical inferences or conjectures, and they are necessarily deficient in the mythological, romantic and social elements so important to a proper comprehension of the Ramayana and Mahabharata. Besides, when the structures are so colossal, so composite and in many respects so beautiful, their can be no harm in having yet another view of them, taken probably from a new stand-point.

In Europe the Homeric poems are very extensively studied in the original Greek, they are productions of very moderate size in comparison with the Indian Epics, many and excellent translation of them, in both prose and verse, are always issuing from the Press, and yet condensed epitomes of the Iliad and Odyssey are welcomed by the reading public, by whom also prose versions of the poetical narratives of even English poets, as Chaucer, Spenser, Shakespeare and Browning, are favourably received.

Such being the case I make no apology for the appearance of this little volume, in which I have not only tried to reproduce faithfully, *in a strictly limited space*, the main incidents, and more striking features of those gigantic and wonderful creations of the ancient Bards of India,—the Ramayana and Mahabharata—but also to direct attention to the abiding influence of those works upon the habits and conceptions of the modern Hindu.

As they are often very incorrectly cited in support of views for which there is no authority whatever in their multitudinous verses it has been my especial aim to give as accurate a presentment as possible of the Indian Epics, taken as a whole ; so that a fair and just idea—*neither too high nor too low*—of their varied contents and their intellectual level might be formed by the readers of this volume, be they Europeans or Indians. And from what I have recently learned, I have good ground for believing that both classes of readers will, after perusal of this little book, be in a position to see the erroneous character of many ideas in regard to life in ancient India which are current in their respective circles.

Where, for any reason, I have especially desired that an event recorded, or an opinion expressed, in the epics should be reproduced without the possibility of misrepresentation on my part, I have thought it best to quote *verbatim* the translations of them made by Hindu scholars, although, unfortunately, their versions are by no means elegant, and, indeed, often quite the reverse. But as they, no doubt, reveal the structure and texture of the poems in a way that no more free or polished English rendering could possibly do, I fancy the citations I have made will probably not be unwelcome to most readers.

My book is divided into two distinct parts dealing separately with the Ramayana and the Mahabharata, and at the end of each part I have given, in the form of an Appendix, one or two of the more striking legendary episodes lavishly scattered through these famous epics, and which, though not essential for the comprehension of the main story, are too beautiful or important to be omitted. Of these episodes I should say that they are the best-known portions of the Ramayana and Mahabharata, having been told and retold in all the leading Indian Vernaculars and having, most of them, been brought before the European world in both prose and verse.

A general *introduction* to the two poems and a *concluding chapter*, containing remarks and inferences based on the materials supplied to the reader in parts I and II, complete the scheme of this little volume, which,

I trust, will be found to be something more than a mere epitome of the great Sanskrit epics; for, in its preparation, I have had the advantage of considerable local knowledge and an intimate acquaintance with the people of *Aryavarta*.

LAHORE:
1st July 1893.

J. C. O.

STRUGGLES IN THE DAWN.

GENERAL INTRODUCTION.

Foremost amongst the many good things in the old-world literature of India, stand the two famous epics, the Ramayana and the Mahabharata, which are loved with an untiring love by the Hindus, for they have kept alive, through many a dreary century, the memory of the ancient heroes of the land, whose names are still borne by the patient husbandman and the proud chief.* These great poems have a special claim to the attention even of foreigners, if considered simply as representative illustrations of the genius of a most interesting people, their importance being enhanced by the fact that they are, to this day, accepted as entirely and literally true by some two hundred millions of the inhabitants of India. And they have the further recommendation of being rich in varied attractions, even when regarded merely as the ideal and unsubstantial creations of oriental imagination.

Both the *Ramayana* and *Mahabharata* are very lengthy works which, taken together, would make up not less than about five and twenty printed volumes of ordinary size. They embrace detailed histories of wars and adventures, and many a story that the Western World would now call a mere fairy tale, to be listened to by children with wide-eyed attention. But interwoven with the

* " No other work in India at the present day possesses the attraction which these opics have for the majority of the people." Life in an Indian village by T. Rama Krishna B.A.—(T Fisher Unwin, 1891.)

narrative of events and legendary romances is a great bulk of philosophical, theological and ethical materials, covering probably the whole field of later Indian speculation. Indeed the epics are a storehouse of Brahmanical instruction in the arts of politics and government; in cosmogony and religion; in mythology and mysticism; in ritualism and the conduct of daily life. They abound in dialogues wherein the subtle wisdom of the East is well displayed, and brim-over with stories and anecdotes intended to point some moral, to afford consolation in trouble or to inculcate a useful lesson. To epitomize all this satisfactorily would be quite impossible, but what I have given in this little volume will, I hope, be sufficient to show the nature and structure of the epics, the characteristics that distinguish them as essentially Indian productions and the light they throw upon the condition of India and the state of Hindu society at the time the several portions were written, or, at any rate, collected together. The narrative, brief though it be, will reflect the more abiding features of Indian national life, revealing some unfamiliar ideas and strange customs. Even within the narrow limits of the reduced picture here presented, the reader will get something more than a glimpse of those famous Eastern sages, whose half comprehended story has furnished the Theosophists of of our own day with the queer notion of their extraordinary *Mahatmas*; he will learn somewhat of the wisdom and pretensions of those sages and will not fail to note that the belief in divine incarnations was firmly rooted in India in very early times. He will incidentally acquire a knowledge of all the fundamental religious ideas of the Hindus and of the highest developments of their philosophy; he will also become familiar with some primitive customs which have left unmistakable traces in the institutions of modern social life in the East as well as in the West; and will, perhaps, be able to track to their origin some strange conceptions which are floating about the intellectual atmosphere of our time.

Woven out of the old-time *sagas* of a remarkable people, "the ancient Aryans of India, in many respects the most wonderful race that ever lived on Earth,"* the Sanskrit epics must have a permanent interest for educated people in every land; while all Indian studies must have an attraction for those who desire to watch, with intelligent appreciation, the wonderfully interesting transformations in religion and manners, which contact with western civilization is producing in the ancient and populous land of the Hindus. Not less interesting will such studies be to those who are able to note the curious, though as yet slight, re-action of Hindu thought upon modern European ideas in certain directions; as, for example, in the rise of Theosophy, in the sentimental tendency manifested in some quarters towards asceticism, Buddhism and Pantheism; in the approval by a small class in Europe of the cremation of the dead, and in the growing fascination of such doctrines as those of metempsychosis and *Karma*.

Although it is difficult for the Englishman of the nineteenth century to understand the intellectual attitude of

* Professor Max Muller's Hibbert Lectures 1878, page 50.

modern India in respect to the wild legends of its youth, it may help towards a comprehension of this point if one reflects that had not Christianity superseded the original religions of Northern Europe, had the Eddas and Sagas, with their weird tales of wonder and mystery, continued to be authoritative scripture in Britain, the religious faith of England might now have been somewhat on a par with that of India today—an extraordinary medley of the wildest legends and deepest philosophy. It is a subject for wonder how the gods of the real ancestors of the English people, the hardy Norsemen, have entirely faded from popular recollection in Britain, how Sagas and Eddas have been completely forgotten, leaving only a substratum of old superstitions about witchcraft, omens, &c., (once religious beliefs) amongst the more backward of the populace. How many Englishmen ever think, how many of them even know, anything about Thor or Odin and the bloody sacrifices (often human sacrifices)* with which those deities were honoured? How many realize that this worship and these rites had a footing in some parts of Europe as recently as 800 years ago?†

The almost complete extinction of the ancestral beliefs of the European nations is a striking fact to which the religious history of India presents no parallel. In Europe the great wall of Judaic Christianity—too often cemented with blood—has been reared, in colossal dimensions, between the past and the present, cutting off all communication between the indigenous faiths and modern

* Prisoners of war of all ranks were sacrificed in numbers.

† Du Chaillu's "The Viking age," Vol. I, Chapter XX *et seq.*

speculative philosophy of the Western nations; while diverting the affectionate interest of the devout from local to foreign shrines; from Stonehenge and Iona to Jerusalem and Galilee.

No barrier of nearly similar proportions has ever been raised in India. Islam, it is true, has planted its towers in many parts of the country and has, to some restricted extent, blocked the old highways of thought, causing a certain estrangement between the old and new world of ideas; but the severance between the past and the present has nowhere been as complete as in Europe, for many an Indian Muslim, though professing monotheism, still lingers upon the threshold of the old Hindu temples and still, in times of trouble, will stealthily invoke the aid of the national deities, who are not yet dead and buried like those of the Vikings. Hence it may be asserted of the vast majorty of the Indian people that their vision extends reverentially backward, through an uninterrupted vista, to the gods and heroes of their remote ancestors.

And who were those remote ancestors, those Aryan invaders of India in the grey dawn of human history? We have had two answers to that question. A few years ago the philologists assured us, very postively, that the Aryans were a vigorous primitive race whose home was in Central Asia and who had sent successive waves of emigration and conquest westwards, right across the Continent of Europe, to be arrested in their onward march only by the wide waters of the Atlantic. We were also assured, by these learned investigators into the mysteries of words and languages, that one horde of Asiatic Aryans instead of following the usual westward course adopted by their brethren, had turned their thoughts towards the sunnier climes of the South, and, scaling the north-western barrier of India, had conquered the aborigines and settled in the great Indo-Gangetic plain at the foot of the Himalayas. These conclusions find a place in all our text-books of Indian or European History. The school boy, who has read his Hunter's brief history* of India, knows well that "the forefathers of the Greek and the Roman, of the English and the Hindu, dwelt together in Central Asia, spoke the same tongue, worshipped the same gods" and that "the history of ancient Europe is the story of the Aryan settlements around the shores of the Mediterranean." However, these conclusions have recently undergone revision and radical modification: Within the last decade a theory, which originated in England with Dr. Latham and which met with contemptuous disregard when first propounded, has been revived by certain German *savants* and scientists.† Supported by the latest results of craniological and anthropological investigation, Latham's theory, in a modified form, has, under the erudite advocacy of Dr. Schrader and Karl Penka, gained all but universal acceptance. The theory now in favour, which is founded more on inferences from racial than linguistic peculiarities, differs from the one referred to above in a very important respect. The home of the Aryans, instead of being found in Central Asia, is traced to Europe, so that

* A brief history of the Indian people by Sir William Wilson Hunter, K.C.S.I. Trübner & Co.

† The world has recently been informed by Dr. Brinton that the theory attributed to Dr. Latham was really first advanced by Omalius D'Halloy in the *Bulletins de l'Academie Royale de Belgique* in May 1848.—*Nature July 21st 1892.*

the Aryan invaders of India, many centuries before Christ, were men of *European* descent who pushed their way *eastward* and gradually extended their dominion first over Iran and subsequently over Northern India, having scaled the snowclad Himalayas, literally in search of "fresh fields and pastures new." When they reached India, after a long sojourn in Eastern countries, they were a mixed European and Asiatic race, with probably a large share of Turanian blood,* speaking a language of Aryan origin.† A strong, warlike, aggressive race, these Aryans won for themselves a dominant position in ancient India, and have left to this day the unmistakable traces of their language in many of the vernaculars of the land.

The decision of the question of the origin of the Aryans and the locality of their primitive home is not one of purely antiquarian interest, it is one of national importance, as any one will be prepared to admit who knows, and can recall to mind, the effect upon the educated Hindus of the announcement that their own ancestors had been the irresistible subjugators of Europe. Whether the Norman conquerors of England were of Celtic or, as the late Professor Freeman insisted, of Teutonic stock, is not unimportant to the Englishman for the true comprehension of his national history and not without some influence even in practical politics; but of far greater moment will it be for the Hindu whether he learn to regard the Aryans of old as an Asiatic or a European race, cradled on the "Roof of the world" or in the flats of the Don.

* As is maintained by Dr. Hermann Braunehoffer. Journal of Royal Asiatic Society, 1890—pp. 687—689.

† The Origin of the Aryans—by Isaac Taylor M.A., LL.D. (Walter Scott) Prehistoric Antiquities of the Aryan Peoples by Dr. O. Schrader translated by F. B. Jevons M. A. (Charles Griffin & Co.

Although all Hindus look upon the Aryan heroes of the Indian Epics as the *ancestors* of their race, and fondly pride themselves in their mighty deeds, the claim, in the case of the vast majority, is, of course, untenable ; since the great bulk of the Indian population has no real title to Aryan descent. Yet Rama and Arjuna are truly Indian creations, enshrined in the sacred literature of the land. And the pride and faith of the Hindus in these demigods has, perhaps, sustained their spirits and elevated their characters, through the vicissitudes of many a century since the heroic age of India.

What genuine facts, or real events, may underlie the poetical narratives of the authors of the Ramayana and Mahabharata will never be known. The details naively introduced are often such as to leave an irresistible impression that there is a substratum of substantial truth serving as a foundation for the fantastic and airy structure reared by the poets and we now and then recognise, for instance in their despairing fatefulness, a distant echo of ideas which have travelled with the Aryan race to the Northern seas. But the too fertile imagination of the Indian poets, their supreme contempt for details and utter disregard of topographical accuracy, leave little hope of our ever getting any satisfactory history out of the Sanskrit epics, or even of our establishing an identity in regard to localities and details of construction such as has been traced, in our own day, by Schliemann between the buried citadel of Hissarlik on the Hellespont and vanished Ilion. For those who do not share these opinions there is a wide and deep field for industrious research ; but I confess that I am somewhat indifferent regarding the extremely doubtful history or the very fanciful allegory that may be laboriously extracted from the Indian epics by ingenious historians and mythologists. Indeed I would protest against these grand epics being treated as history, for then they must be judged by the canons of historical composition and would be shorn of their highest merits. They are *poems* not *history*, they are the romantic legends and living aspirations of a people, not the sober annals of their social and political life.

Like the other great poems created by the genius of the past, the Indian epics have a value quite independent of either the history or the allegory which they enshrine. They appeal to our predilection for the marvellous and our love of the beautiful, while affording us striking pictures of the manners of a bygone age, which, for many reasons, we would not willingly lose.

Being religious books the Ramayana and Mahabharata are, more or less, known to the Hindus; but it is a noteworthy fact that even educated Indians are but little acquainted with the *details* of these poems, although both epics have been translated into the leading vernaculars of the country and also into Euglish. I have known educated young men, with more faith in their ancient books than knowledge of their contents, warmly deny the possibility of certain narratives having a place in these books, because to their somewhat Europeanized ideas, they seemed too far-fetched to be probable. The more striking incidents are, however, familiar to every Hindu, for Brahmans wander all over the country, reciting the sacred poems to the people. They gather an audience of both sexes and all ages and read to them from the venerable Sanskrit, rendering the verses of the dead language of the Aryan invaders of India into the living speech of their hearers. Sometimes the Brahmans read and expound vernacular translations of these poems of Valmiki and Vyasa. Often-times these recitations are accompanied with much ceremony and dignified with a show of religious formalities.* Day after day the people congregate to listen, with wrapped attention, to the old national stories, and the moral lessons drawn from them, for their instruction, by the Pandits. To this day a considerable proportion of the people of India order much of their lives upon the models supplied by their venerable epics, which have, moreover, mainly inspired such plastic and pictorial work as the Indian people have produced ; being for the Hindu artist what the beautiful creations of Greek fancy, or the weird myths of the Middle ages, have been for his European brother.

Impressed with the importance of some knowledge of the Indian epics on the part of every one directly or indirectly interested in the life and opinions of the strange and highly intellectual Hindu race, which has preserved its marked individuality of character through so many centuries of foreign domination, I have written, for the benefit of

* The preparations for a recital of this kind in a village in the Madras Presidency are thus described. "People came pouring in from Kelambakam and from neighbouring villages to the house of the village headman. On the *pial* of his house was seated the preacher. Before him was placed the picture of Krishna playing the flute and leaning on a cow. The picture was profusely decorated with flowers. There were also two small vessels. In one there were camphor and some burning incense, in the other were flowers and fruits. The people swarmed about like bees." Life in an Indian Village by T. Rama Krishna B. A. page 144.

those, whether Europeans or Indians, who may be acquainted with the English language, the brief epitomes of them contained in the following pages; deriving my materials not from the original Sanskrit poems, which are sealed books to me, but from the translations, more or less complete and literal, of these voluminous works, which have been given to the world by both European and Indian scholars. On all occasions where religious opinions or theological doctrines are concerned I have given the preference to the translations of native scholars, as I know that Indian Sanskritists have a happy contempt for western interpretations of their sacred books, and it seemed very desirable, in such a case, to let the Hindus speak for themselves. Besides, I am of opinion that the English versions of the Ramayana and Mahabharata, now being given to the world by Indian scholars, have a unique value, which later translations will, in all probability, not possess. The present translators are orthodox Hindus possessing a competent knowledge of English and their aim has been to produce English versions of their sacred poems, as understood and accepted by themselves and by the orthodox Indian world to-day, their renderings, no doubt, reflecting the traditional interpretation handed down from past times. Hereafter we shall have more *learned* translations, in which European ideas will do duty for Indian ones, and the old poems will be interpreted *up to* our own standard of science and philosophy. In wild legends we shall discover subtle allegories veiling sober history, in license and poetry we shall find deep religious mysteries and in archaic notions shall recognise, with admiration, the structure of modern philosophy. Something of this has already come about and that the rest is not far off is evident; for we have only recently been told, that "in "the *Shlokas* of the Ramayana and Mahabharata we have "many important historical truths relating to the ancient "colonization of the Indian continent by conquering in-"vaders * * all designedly concealed in the priestly "phraseology of the Brahman, but with such exactitude "of method, nicety of expression and particularity of de-"tail, as to render the whole capable of being transformed "into a sober, intelligible and probable history of the "political revolutions that took place over the extent of "India during ages antecedent to the records of authentic "history, by any one who will take the trouble to read "the Sanskrit aright through the veil of allegory cover-"ing it."*

While regretting my shortcomings in respect to the language of the bards who composed the Sanskrit epics, since I am thereby cut off from appreciating the beauty of their versification and the felicities of expression which no translation can possibly preserve, I derive consolation from the reflection, that with sufficiently accurate translations at hand—similar to our English versions of the Hebrew and Greek Scriptures—a knowledge of Sanskrit is certainly not essential for the production of a work with the moderate pretensions of this little volume.

* The Ethnography of Afghanistan by Dr. H. W. Bellow C.S.I. in the Asiatic Quarterly Review, October 1891.

PART I.

THE RAMAYANA OR ADVENTURES OF RAMA.

CHAPTER I.—Introductory Remarks.

Once every year, at the great festival known as the *Dasahra*, the story of the famous Hindu epic, the *Ramayana*, is, throughout Northern India, recalled to popular memory, by a great out-door dramatic representation of the principal and crowning events in the life of the hero, Rama. The Ramayana is not merely a popular story, it is an inspired poem, every detail of which is, in the belief of the great majority of the Indian people, strictly true. Although composed at least nineteen centuries ago, it still lives enshrined in the hearts of the children of Aryavarta and is as familiar to them to-day as it has been to their ancestors for fifty generations. Pious pilgrims even now retrace, step by step, the wanderings, as well as the triumphal progress, of Rama, from his birth-place in Oudh to the distant island of Ceylon. Millions believe in the efficacy of his name alone to ensure them safety and salvation. For these reasons the poem is of especial value and interest to any one desirous of understanding the people of India ; affording, as it does, an insight into the thoughts and feelings of the bard or bards who composed it and of a race of men who, through two thousand eventful years, have not grown weary of it.

In this paper I shall first give a brief summary of the leading events narrated in the Ramayana and then proceed to link, as it were, the past with the present, by describing the annual play as I have often witnessed it in Northern India.

The Ramayana, written in the Sanskrit language, embraces an account of the birth and adventures of Rama. The whole poem, which is divided into seven books or sections, contains about 50,000 lines and occupies five goodly volumes in Mr. Ralph Griffith's metrical translation,* which is, to a certain extent, an abridged version. To Valmiki is attributed the authorship of this famous epic and a pretty story is told of the manner in which he came to write it. A renowned ascetic, a sort of celestial being named Narada, had related to Valmiki the main incidents of the adventurous life of Rama and had deeply interested that sage in the history of the hero and his companions. Pondering the events described by Narada, Valmiki went to the river to bathe. Close at hand two beautiful herons, in happy unconsciousness of danger, were disporting themselves on the wooded bank of the stream, when suddenly one of the innocent pair was laid prostrate by the arrow of an unseen fowler. The other bird, afflicted with grief, fluttered timidly about her dead mate, uttering sore cries of distress. Touched to the heart by her plaintive sorrow, Valmiki gave expression to his feelings of irritation and sympathy in words which, to his own surprise, had assumed a rythmic measure and were capable of being chanted with an instrumental accompaniment. Presently, Brahma himself, the creator of all, visited the sage in his hermitage, but Valmiki's mind was so much occupied with the little tragedy at the river-side, that he unconciously gave

* The Rámáyan of Válmíki translated into English verse by Ralph T. H. Griffith M.A., Principal of the Benares College,—London, Trübner & Co.

utterance to the verses he had extemporised on the occasion. Brahma, smiling, informed the hermit that the verses had come to his lips in order that he might compose the delightful and instructive story of Rama in that particular measure or *sloka.* Assuring Valmiki that all the details of the stirring tale would be revealed to him, the Supreme Being directed the sage to compose the great epic, which should endure as long as the mountains and seas exist upon this earth. How Valmiki acquired a knowledge of all the details of the story is worth remembering, as being peculiarly Indian in its conception.

" Sitting himself facing the east on a cushion of *Kusa* grass, and sipping water according to the ordinance, he addressed himself to the contemplation of the subject through *Yoga** And, by virtue of his *Yoga* powers, he clearly observed before him Rama and Lakshmana, and Sita, and Dasaratha together with his wives in his Kingdom, laughing and talking and acting and bearing themselves as in real life."†

* Of Yoga and Yognism I have given a brief account in a previous work. " Indian Life, Religious and Social" p.p. 11—47.—(London, Fisher Unwin).

† The Ramayana, translated into English prose from the original Sanskrit of Valmiki by Manmatha Nath Dutt. M. A., Deva Press, Calcutta. If not otherwise stated, all prose quotations from the *Ramayana* included in the following pages are derived from this work.

CHAPTER II.—The Story.

The story of the Ramayana, in brief outline, is as follows :—

In the ancient land of Kosala, watered by the river Surayu, stood the famous Ayodhya,* a fortified and impregnable city of matchless beauty and resplendent with burnished gold, where every one was virtuous, beautiful, rich and happy. Wide streets traversed this city in every direction, lined with elegant shops and stately palaces glittering all over with gems. There was no lack of food in Ayodhya, for "it abounded in paddy and rice and its water was as sweet as the juice of the sugar-cane." Gardens, mango-groves and "theatres for females" were to be found everywhere. Dulcet music from *Venas* and *Panavas* resounding on all sides, bore evidence to the taste of the people. Learned and virtuous Brahmans, skilled in sacrificial rites, formed a considerable proportion of the population; which also included a crowd of eulogists and "troops of courtezans." The pride of ancient families supported a large number of genealogists. Hosts of skilled artizans of every kind contributed to the conveniences and elegancies of life, while an army of doughty warriors protected this magnificent and opulent city from its envious foes. Over this wonderful and prosperous capital of a flourishing kingdom, ruled king Dasaratha, a man some

* "The ruins of the ancient capital of Rama and the children of the Sun may still be traced in the present Ajudhya near Fyzabad. Ajudhya is the Jerusalem or Mecca of the Hindus" Note Vol. I, page 35 of Mr. Griffith's translation of the Ramayana (Trübner & Co., London.)

sixty-thousand years of age, gifted with every virtue and blessed beyond most mortals. But, as if to prove that human happiness can never exist unalloyed with sorrow, even he had one serious cause for grief; he was childless, although he had three wives and seven hundred and fifty concubines.* Acting upon the advice of the priests, the Maharajah determined to offer, with all the complicated but necessary rites, the sacrifice of a horse, as a means of prevailing upon the gods to bless his house with offspring. The accomplishment of such a sacrifice was no easy matter, or to be lightly undertaken, even by a mighty monarch like Dasaratha, since it was an essential condition of success that the sacrifice should be conducted without error or omission in the minutest details of the ritual of an intricate ceremony, extending over three days. Not only would any flaw in the proceedings render the sacrifice nugatory, but it was to be feared that learned demons (Brahma-Rakshasas), ever maliciously on the look-out for short-comings in the sacrifices attempted by men, might cause the destruction of the unfortunate performer of an imperfect sacrifice of such momentous importance. However, the sacrifice was actually performed on a magnificent scale and most satisfactorily, with the assistance of an army of artizans, astrologers, dancers, conductors of theatres and persons learned in the ceremonial law. Birds, beasts, reptiles and aquatic animals were sacrificed by the priests on this auspicious occasion, but the sacred horse itself was dispatched, with three strokes, by the

* What a terrible thing it is for a Hindu to be childless can be understood, and then only partially, by bearing in mind that, without a son to perform the complex funeral rites and ceremonies for a deceased father, the dead man's soul must undergo ages of trouble in the next world.

hand of Kauçalya, Dasaratha's queen. When the ceremonies had been conducted to a successful close, Dasaratha showed his piety and generosity by making a free gift of the whole Earth to the officiating priests; but they were content to restore the magnificent present, modestly accepting in its stead, fabulous quantities of gold and silver and innumerable cows.

The Gods, Gandharvas and Siddhas, propitiated by the offerings profusely made to them, assembled, each one for his share,* and Dasaratha was promised four sons.† While these events were transpiring, a ten-headed Rakshasa named Ravana was making himself the terror of gods and men, under the protection of a boon bestowed upon him by the Creator (Brahma), that neither god nor Demon should be able to deprive him of his life. This boon had been obtained by the Rakshasa as the reward of long and painful austerities.‡

The hierarchy of minor gods, in their own interest and for the sake of the saints who were constantly being dis-

* According to Hindu belief the gods and the spirits of departed ancestors are actually nourished and sustained by the aroma of the burnt offerings made by pious persons. Hence the vital importance of these sacrifices upon which the very safety and continuance of the Universe depend.

† This incident introduces us to an important Hindu idea, that the *exact* performance of certain prescribed rites and sacrifices leads to the attainment of definite objects, as, for example, purification from a particular sin, the destruction of a hated enemy or the discovery of a friend. The gods themselves performed sacrifices, and Indra is commonly addressed as "the performer of a hundred sacrifices."

‡ The Indian ideas respecting austerities are very peculiar and as they pervade their religion and literature are specially note-worthy. "According to the Hindu theory the performance of penances was like making deposits in the bank of heaven. By degrees an enormous credit was accumulated, which enabled the depositor to draw to the amount of his savings, without fear of his drafts being refused payment. The power gained in this manner by weak mortals was so enormous, that gods as well as men were equally at the mercy of these all but omnipotent ascetics; and it is remarkable, that even the gods are described as engaging in penance and austerities, in order, it may be presumed, not to be outdone by human beings. Siva was so engaged when the god of love shot an arrow at him" (Note to page 4 of Professor Sir Monier William's "Indian Epic Poetry.") In the course of the following pages of this book we shall meet with ascetics very often and become familiar with their doings.

turbed in their devotions by this Ravana and his fellows, appealed to the Supreme Deity to find some remedy for the evil. Brahma, after reflecting on the matter, replied.

" One only way I find
" To stay this fiend of evil mind.
" He prayed me once his life to guard
" From demon, God and heavenly bard,
" And spirits of the earth and air,
" And I consenting heard his prayer.
" But the proud giant in his scorn,
" Recked not of man of woman born,
" None else may take his life away
" But only man the fiend may slay.

(Griffiths).

On receiving this reply the gods petitioned Vishnu to divide himself into four parts and to appear on earth, incarnate as the promised sons of Dasaratha, and thus, in human form, to rid the world of Ravana. Vishnu consented. He proceeded to the earth and appeared amidst the sacrificial flames of Dasaratha's offering, in an assumed form " of matchless splendour, strength and size"—black, with a red face, and shaggy hair—apparelled in crimson robes, and adorned with celestial ornaments, holding in his hands a vase of gold, containing heavenly nectar, which he handed to the king, with instructions to make his three queens partake of the sacred draught, in order that they might be blessed with sons.

Dasaratha distributed the nectar amongst his wives, though not in equal proportions. In due time the promised sons were born, *viz.*, Rama, Lakshmana, Bharata and

Satrughna. Rama possessed the larger share of the divine nature and decidedly excelled his brothers in prowess. To him, especially, was alloted the task of destroying Ravana. And countless hosts of monkeys and bears were begotten by the Gods, at Brahma's* suggestion, to aid him in his work.

Whilst yet a mere stripling, Rama was appealed to by the sage Vishwamitra to destroy certain demons who interrupted the religious rites of the hermits.

The boy was only sixteen years of age and Dasaratha, naturally solicitous for his safety, declined to let him go to fight the dreadful brood of demons who had an evil reputation for cruelty and ferocity; but the mighty ascetic waxed so wrath at this refusal of his request, that "the entire earth began to tremble and the gods even were inspired with awe.". Vasishta, the King's spiritual adviser, who had unbounded confidence in Vishwamitra's power to protect the prince from all harm, strongly advised compliance with the ascetic's request, and Dasaratha was prevailed upon to allow Rama and Lakshmana to leave Ayodhya with Vishwamitra.

The incidents of the journey reveal a very primitive state of society. The princes and their guide were all of them on foot, apparently quite unattended by servants and unprovided with even the most ordinary necessaries of life. When they reached the river Sarayu,† Vishwamitra communicated certain *mantras* or spells to Rama by the knowledge of which he would be protected from fatigue and fever‡ and from the possibility of being surprised by the

* The belief in divine incarnations, for the benefit or salvation of the world, is a common and familiar one in the Hindu religion.

† The modern Gogra.

‡ Protection against *fever* would be specially desirable in a country covered with forest and jungle as the India of the Ramayana evidently was.

Rakshasas against whom he was going to wage war.

The land through which our travellers journeyed was sparsely inhabited. A goodly portion of it seems to have been covered with woods, more or less pleasant, abounding in the hermitages of ascetics, some of whom had been carrying on their austerities for *thousands of years.* Beside these pleasant woods there were vast, trackless forests, infested by ferocious beasts, and grim *Rakshasas,* and it was not long before the might of the semi-divine stripling, Rama, was tried against one of these terrible creatures, Tarika by name, an ogress of dreadful power, whom Rama undertook to destroy "in the interests of Brahmans, kine and celestials." When the ascetic and the two princes arrived in the dark forest where the dreaded Tarika ruled supreme, Rama twanged his bowstring loudly, as a haughty challenge to this redoubtable giantess. Incensed at the audacious sound of the bowstring, Tarika uttered terrible roars and rushed out to attack the presumptuous prince. The ascetic raised a defiant roar in response. That was his entire contribution to the combat in which Rama and his adversary were immediately involved, Lakshmana taking part in it also. This, the first conflict in which Rama was engaged, may be taken as a type of all his subsequent battles. Raising clouds of dust, Tarika, "by help of illusion," poured a shower of huge stones upon the brothers, but these ponderous missiles were met and arrested in mid-air by a volley of arrows. The battle raged fiercely, but the brothers succeeded with their shafts in depriving Tarika of her hands, her nose and her ears. Thus disabled and disfigured,

Tarika changed her shape* and even concealed herself from view, while still continuing the fight with unabated fury; but Rama, guided by sound alone, assailed his invisible foe with such effect that he eventually laid her dead at his feet, to the joy of Vishwamitra and the relief of the denizens of the great forest over which she had terrorised.

After this successful combat, the ascetic, Vishwamitra, conferred on Rama a gift of strange weapons, which even the celestials were incapable of wielding. How very different the magic weapons received by Rama were from those familiar to the sons of men, will be apparent from the poet's statement that the weapons themselves made their appearance spontaneously before Rama, "and with clasped hands, they, well pleased, addressed Rama thus: These, O highly generous one, are thy servants, O Raghava. Whatever thou wishest, good betide thee, shall by all means be accomplished by us."

Such wonderful and efficient weapons, endowed with a consciousness and individuality of their own, needed, however, to be kept under strict control, lest in their overzeal or excitement they might effect undesigned and irreparable mischief. The sage accordingly communicated to Rama the various *mantras* or spells by which they might, on critical occasions, be restrained and regulated in their operations.

In their woodland wanderings amongst the hermitages the brothers and their guide came across many sages

* The power of assuming a multiplicity of forms at will and of passing from a huge to a minute size, or the reverse, to suit the exigencies of the moment is enjoyed by a great number of personages in the Hindu epics.

whose laborious austerities were constantly being hindered by wicked, flesh-eating Rakshasas. Indeed the world, outside the cities and villages,—which it would seem were very few and far between—as pictured by Valmiki, is a very strange one, mostly peopled by two sets of beings, *hermits* striving after supernatural power through the practice of austerities, and *demons* bent on frustrating their endeavours by unseasonable interruptions of their rites, or impious pollution of their sacrifices. Sometimes, as in the case of Ravana, the demons themselves would practise austerities for the attainment of power.

Very prominent figures in the poem are the great ascetics, like Vishwamitra himself, who a Kshtriya by caste and a king by lineage, had obtained, through dire austerities prolonged over thousands of years, the exalted rank and power of *Brahmanhood*. A single example of his self-inflicted hardships and the consequences resulting therefrom may not be out of place. He once restrained his breath for a thousand years, when vapours began to issue from his head, "and at this the three worlds became afflicted with fear." Like most of his order, he was a very proud and irate personage, ready, upon very slight provocation, to utter a terrible and not to-be-escaped-from curse.* Once, in a fit of rage against the celestials, Vishwamitra created entire systems of stars and even threatened, in his fury, to create another India by "the process of his self-earned asceticism."

The life led by the princely brothers in their pedes-

* We shall in the course of the development of this story have frequent opportunities of learning the awful and irrevocable character of curses uttered by Brahmans and others, rejoicing in the possession of stores of power acquired by the practice of austerities.

trian wanderings with this mighty sage was simplicity itself. They performed their religious rites regularly, adoring the rising sun, the blazing fire or the flowing river, as the case might be. Their sojourn in the forests was enlivened by pleasant communion with the hermits to whose kind, hospitality they were usually indebted for a night's lodging, if such it can be called, and a simple fare of milk and fruits. Vishwamitra added interest to their journeyings by satisfying the curiosity of the brothers in regard to the history of the several places they visited. Here, as he informed them, the God Rudra had performed his austerities—for even the gods were not above the necessity and ambition of ascetic practices—and blasted the impious Kama into nothingness with a breath. There, the great god Vishnu of mighty asceticism, worshipped of all the deities, dwelt, during hundreds of *Yugas*, for the purpose of carrying on his austerities and practising *yoga*.* At one time Vishwamitra would relate the history of the origin of Ganga and of her descent upon the earth, as the mighty and purifying Ganges, chief of rivers. At another time he would himself listen complacently, along with his princely companions, to the history of his own wonderful asceticism and marvellous performances, as the wise Satananda related it for the special edification of Rama.

So passed away the time in the forests, not altogether peacefully, however, for the object of the journey would not have been fulfilled without sundry fierce and entirely successful encounters with the *Rakshasas*, those fiendish interrupters of sacrifice and persistent enemies of the an-

* Vide M. N. Dutt's Ramayana, page 75.

chorites. Eventually the wanderers came to the kingdom of Mithila, whose king, Janaka,* had a lovely daughter to bestow upon the worthy and fortunate man who should bend a certain formidable bow which had belonged to Siva and which he had once threatened to use in the destruction of the gods.

Janaka's daughter, the famous Sita, whose matrimonial future was thus connected with Siva's bow, was of super-human origin, having sprung from the Earth in a mysterious manner ; for, while Janaka was ploughing the ground in the course of a child-conferring sacrifice, the lovely maiden had, by the favour of the gods, come to him out of the furrow.

Allured by the fame of Sita's beauty, suitor after suitor had come to Mithila and tried that tough bow of Siva's, but without success ; and Rama's curiosity was awakened about both the mighty weapon and the maiden fair.

Having been introduced by Vishwamitra to the king of Mithila, Rama was allowed to essay his strength against the huge bow, and huge it was indeed, for it had to be carried on an eight-wheeled cart which "was with difficulty drawn along by five thousand stalwart persons of well developed frames." To Rama, however, the bending of this gigantic bow was an easy matter, and he not only bent but broke it too, at which event all present, over-whelmed by the noise, rolled head over heels, with the

---

* "The remains of the capital founded by Janaka and thence termed Janakapur are still to be seen, according to Buchanan, on the Northern frontier at the Janeekpoor of the maps" (Note to Professor H. H. Wilson's translation of the Uttara Rama Charitra.)

exception of Vishwamitra, the "king and the two Raghavas." The lovely and much coveted prize was Rama's of course. Arrangements for the wedding were carried out in grand style. Dasaratha and his two other sons were invited to Mithila and brides were found, in the family of Janaka, for all the *four* brothers. Upon a dais covered with a canopy, and decked with flowers, the happy brides and bridegrooms were placed, attended by the king and the priests of the two families. Water-pots, golden ladles, censers, and conchs, together with platters containing rice, butter, curds and other things for the *Hom* sacrifice, were also arranged for use on the platform. The sacrificial fire was lighted, the appropriate *mantras* repeated and the four bridegrooms led their brides first round the fire, and then round the king and the priests. At this stage of the proceedings showers of celestial flowers rained down upon the happy couples, now united in the bonds of matrimony.* After these marriages the return to Ayodhya was accomplished with rejoicings and in great state; but Vishwamitra took his solitary way to the Northern Mountains.

As the years went by and Rama was grown to man's estate he was endowed with every princely virtue; the people idolised him and his father, desirous of retiring from the cares of government, determined to place him upon the throne. But, although apparently simple of execution, this arrangement was beset with difficulties. Rama was the son of the Raja's eldest and principal wife; but Bharata was

* I have had the good fortune to be present at a marriage ceremony, carried out professedly in accordance with Vedic rites, which closely resembled the wedding of Rama and his brothers, as described by Valmiki.

the son of his favourite wife, the slender-waisted Kaikeyi. The suffrages of the people and Dasaratha's own wishes were entirely in favour of Rama, but, apparently unwilling to face the grief or opposition of his darling Kaikeyi, the king took advantage of Bharata's absence on a visit to a distant court, to carry out the rather sudden preparations for Rama's installation as *Yuva-Raja*, hoping, it would seem, to keep Kaikeyi in complete ignorance of what was being done. The whole city, however, was in a state of bustle and excitement at the approaching event. The streets were being washed, and watered, flag-staffs were being erected on every side, gay bunting was floating about and garlands of flowers adorned the houses. Musicians played in the high ways and in the temples, and, notwithstanding the seclusion of the women's appartments, it was impossible to conceal from the inmates of the *zenana* what was going on in the great world outside. A deformed and cunning slave-girl, named Manthara, found out and revealed the the whole plot to Bharata's mother. At first Kaikeyi received the intelligence with pleasure, for Rama was dear to every body; but the slave-girl so worked upon her feelings of envy and jealousy, by artfully picturing to her the very inferior position she would hold in the world's estimation, the painful slights she would have to endure and the humiliation she would have to suffer, once Kausalya's son was raised to the throne, that, in a passion of rage and grief, she threw away her ornaments and, with dishevelled hair, flew to the "*chamber of sorrow*" and flung herself down upon the floor, weeping bitterly. Here the old king found her "like a sky enveloped in darkness with the stars hid" and had to endure the angry reproaches of his disconsolate favourite. Acting upon a suggestion of the deformed slave-girl, the queen reminded her husband of a promise made by him long previously, that he would grant her any two requests she might make. She now demanded the fulfilment of the royal promise, her two requests being that Rama should be sent away into banishment in the forests for a period of fourteen years and that her own son Bharata should be elevated to the dignity of Yuva-Rajah. On these terms, and on these only, would the offended and ambitious Kaikeyi be reconciled to her uxorious lord. If these conditions were refused she was resolved to rid the king of her hated presence. Dasaratha, poor old man, was overwhelmed by this unexpected crisis. He fell at his wife's feet, he explained that preparations for Rama's installation had already commenced, he besought her not to expose him to ridicule and contempt, he coaxed and flattered her, alluding to her lovely eyes and shapely hips, he extolled Rama's affectionate devotion to herself. He next heaped bitter reproaches upon Kaikeyi's unreasonable pride and finally swooned away in despair. But she was firm in her purpose and would not be shaken by anything, kind or unkind, that this "lord of earth" could say to her. The royal word she knew was sacred and had to be kept, at any cost.

As soon as it came to be known what a strange and unforeseen turn events had taken, the female appartments were the scene of loud lamentations and the entire city was plunged in mourning. Rama of expansive and coppery eyes,*

* In this description of Rama and in other places I have borrowed the epithets I find in Dutt's translation of the Ramayana, in order to preserve something of the peculiar character of the original.

long-armed, dark-blue like a lotus, a mighty bowman of matchless strength, with the gait of a mad elephant, brave, truthful, humble-minded, respectful and generous to Brahmans and having his passions under complete control, was the idol of the zenana, the court and the populace. The thought of his unmerited banishment to the forests was intolerable to every one. But he himself, with exemplary filial devotion, prepared to go into exile, at once, without a murmur. The poet devotes considerable space to a minute description of the sorrow experienced by the prominent characters in the story on account of Rama's banishment. Each one indulges in a lengthy lamentation picturing the privations and sufferings of the ill-fated trio and nearly every one protests that it will be impossible to live without Rama. With affectionate regard for Sita's comfort, and loving apprehension for her safety, Rama resolved to leave her behind with his mother; but no argument, no inducement, could prevail upon the devoted wife to be parted from her beloved husband. What were the terrors of the forest to her, what the discomfort of the wilderness, when shared with Rama? Racked with sorrow at the proposed separation, Sita burst into a flood of tears and became almost insensible with grief. At the sight of her tribulation Rama, overcome with emotion, threw his arms about his dear wife and agreed to take her with him, come what may.

Lakshmana, with devoted loyalty, would also accompany his brother into exile.

Kaikeyi, apprehensive of delays, hurried on their preparations and herself, unblushingly, provided them with the bark dresses worn by ascetics. The two brothers donned their new vestments in the King's presence.

> But Sita, in her silks arrayed,
> Threw glances, trembling and afraid,
> On the bark coat she had to wear
> Like a shy doe that eyes the snare.
> Ashamed and weeping for distress
> From the queen's hand she took the dress.
> The fair one, by her husband's side
> Who matched heavens minstrel monarch, cried:
> 'How bind they on their woodland dress,
> Those hermits of the wilderness?'
> There stood the pride of Janak's race
> Perplexed, with sad appealing face,
> One coat the lady's fingers grasped
> One round her neck she feebly clasped
> But failed again, again, confused
> By the wild garb she ne'er had used,
> Then quickly hastening Rama, pride
> Of all who cherish virtue, tied
> The rough bark mantle on her, o'er
> The silken raiment that she wore.
> Then the sad women when they saw
> Rama the choice bark round her draw,
> Rained water from each tender eye
> And cried aloud with bitter cry.*
>
> (GRIFFITHS).

After giving away vast treasures to the Brahmans the ill-fated trio took a pathetic leave of the now miserable old King, of Kausalya who mourned like a cow deprived of her calf, of Sumitra the mother of Lakhsmana and of their "other three hundred and fifty mothers."

* Here is a pretty subject for a picture by any artist, Hindu or other.

With an exalted sense of filial duty the exiles also bid a respectful and affectionate farewell to Kaikeyi, the cruel author of their unmerited banishment, Rama remarking that it was not her own heart, but "*Destiny* alone that had made her press for the prevention of his installation."

When Rama and his companions appeared in the streets of the capital, in the dress of ascetics, the populace loudly deplored their fate, extolling the virtues of Rama while giving vent to their feelings of disapproval at the King's weak compliance with his favourite's whim. Sita came in for her share of popular pity and admiration, since she "whom formerly the very rangers of the sky could not see, was to-day beheld by every passer by."

A royal chariot conveyed away to the inhospitable wilderness the two brothers and faithful Sita, torn from stately Ayodhya, their luxurious palaces and the arms of their fond parents. All they carried with them, in the chariot, was their armour and weapons, "a basket bound in hide and a hoe." Crowds of people, abandoning their homes, followed in the track of the chariot, resolved to share the fate of the exiles, And such was the grief of the people that the dust raised by the wheels of the car occupied by Rama and his companions was laid by the tears of the citizens. They drove at once to the jungles and rested there for the night. During the hours of slumber the exiles considerately gave their followers the slip and hurried off, in the chariot, towards the great forest of Dandhaka. When they arrived at the banks of the sacred and delightful Ganges the charioteer was dismissed with tender messages to the old king from his exiled children. After the departure of the charioteer Rama and his companions began their forest wanderings on foot. Their hermit life was now to commence in earnest. Before entering the dark forest that lay before them, the brothers resolved to wear "that ornament of ascetics, a head of matted hair" and, accordingly, produced the desired *coiffure* with the aid of the glutinous sap of the banian tree. Thus *adorned* and clothed in bark like the saints, the brothers, with faithful Sita, entered a boat which chanced to be at the river side and began the passage of the Ganges. As they crossed the river the pious Sita, with joined hands, addressed the goddess of the sacred stream, praying for a happy return to Ayodhya, when their days of exile should be over. Having arrived on the other bank the exiles entered the forest in Indian file, Lakshmana leading and Rama bringing up the rear. Passing by Sringavara on the Ganges, they proceeded to Prayaga at the junction of the Ganges and the Jumna. Here they were hospitably entertained by the sage Bharadwaja who recommended them to seek an asylum on the pleasant slopes of wooded Chitrakuta. On the way thither Sita, ever mindful of her religious duties, adored the Kalindi river—which they crossed on a raft constructed by themselves—and paid her respects to a gigantic banyan tree, near which many ascetics had taken up their abode. On the romantic and picturesque side of Chitrakuta the exiles built themselves a cottage, thatched with leaves, "walled with wood, and furnished with doors." Game, fruits and roots abounded in the neighbourhood, so that they need have no anxiety about their supplies. So much did they appreciate the quiet beauties of their sylvan retreat, the cool shade, the perfumed flowers, the sparkling rivulets and the noble river, that they became almost reconciled to their separation from their friends and the lordly palaces Ayodhya, in which city important events were happening.

The exile of Rama, had been too much for the doting old Maharajah.* Weighed down by sorrow, he soon succumbed to his troubles, and Bharata, who was still absent at Giri-braja, was hastily summoned to take up the regal office. He, accompanied by his brother Satrugnah, hurried to the capital and finding, on his arrival, how matters really stood, heaped reproaches upon his wicked, ambitious mother, indignantly refusing to benefit by her artful machinations. In a transport of grief Bharata "fell to the earth sighing like an enraged snake," while Satrugnah, on his part, seized the deformed slave-girl Manthara and literally shook the senses out of her. In Rama's absence, Bharata performed his father's obsequies with great pomp. The dead body of the late king, which had been preserved in oil, was carried in procession to the river side and there burnt, together with heaps of boiled rice and sacrificed animals. A few days later the *sraddha* ceremonies for the welfare of the spirit of the departed king were performed, and, as usual, costly presents,—money, lands, houses, goats and kine, also servant-men and servant-maids were bestowed upon the fortunate Brahmans.

* Dasaratha himself attributed these misfortunes to his having when a youth unwittingly killed, with a chance arrow, a young hermit in the forest. The boy's father, himself a hermit, cursed Dasaratha and the effects of the malediction were apparent in the troubles attending the kings declining years.

When this pious duty, which occupied thirteen days, had been fulfilled, affairs of state demanded attention. Bharata, although pressed to do so, resolutely declined to accept the sceptre, and resolved to set out, with a vast following, on a visit to Rama in his retreat, hoping to persuade him to abandon his hermit-life and undertake the Government of the realm. Great preparations had to be made for this visit to Rama, which was a sort of wholesale exodus of the people of Ayodhya of all ranks and occupations. A grand army was to accompany Bharata and the court, with all the ladies of the royal family, including the no-doubt-reluctant Kaikeyi, were to swell the procession. A road had to be made for the projected march of this host; streams had to be bridged, ferries provided at the larger rivers and able guides secured. When the road was ready and the preparations for the journey completed, chariots and horsemen in thousands crowded the way, mingled with a vast multitude of citizens riding in carts. Artificers, of every kind, attended the royal camp. Armourers, weavers, tailors, potters, glass-makers, goldsmiths and gem-cutters were there; so also were physicians, actors and shampooers, peacock-dancers and men whose profession it was to provide warm baths for their customers. Of course the Brahman element was strongly represented in this great procession from the flourishing city to the solitudes of the forest. Bharata's march is described at great length by the poet; but only one incident need be mentioned here. On the way the hermit Bharadvaja, desirous of doing Bharata honour, and probably not unwilling to display his power, invited him and his followers, of whom, as we have seen, there were many thousands, to a feast at his hermitage. At the command of the saint the forest became transformed into lovely gardens, abounding in flowers and fruits. Palaces of matchless beauty sprang into existence. Music filled the cool and perfumed air. Food and drink, including meat and wine, appeared in profusion :—soups and curries are especially mentioned and the flesh of goats and bears, deer, peacocks and cocks; also rice, milk and sugar. In addition to all this, a host of heavenly nymphs from Swarga descended to indulge in soft dalliance with the ravished warriors of Bharata's army.

> "Then beautious women seven or eight
> "Stood ready by each man to wait.
> "Beside the stream his limbs they stripped,
> "And in the cooling water dipped.
> "And then the fair ones sparkling-eyed
> "With soft hands rubbed his limbs and dried
> "And sitting on the lovely bank
> "Held up the wine-cup as he drank."
>
> (GRIFFITHS.)

For one day and one night the intoxicating enjoyment continued; and then, at the word of command, all the creations of the Sage's power vanished, leaving the forest in its wonted gloom.

Having taken a respectful leave of the mighty ascetic, Bharata and his followers threaded their way through the dense forests towards the mountain Chitrakuta and the river Mandakini. After a long march they at last found the object of their desire, the high souled Rama, "seated in a cottage, bearing a head of matted locks, clad in black deerskin and having tattered cloth and bark for his garment." When Rama heard of his father's death he was deeply moved and fell insensible upon the ground, "like a blooming tree that hath been hewn by an axe." The loving Vaidehi (Sita) and the brothers Lakshmana and Bharata sprinkled water on the face of the prostrate man and restored him to animation, when he at once burst into loud and prolonged lamentations. Presently Rama pulled himself together and duly performed the funeral rites, pouring out libations of water and making an offering of *ingudi* fruits to the spirit of his departed father. These offerings were not worthy of being presented to the manes of so great a man as Dasaratha; but were justifiable, under the circumstances of the case, on the accepted principle that "that which is the fare of an individual is also the fare of his divinities."* Bharata and the rest, respectfully sitting before Rama with joined hands, entreated him, with the greatest humility, to undertake the reins of Government; but he was not to be persuaded to do so. He would not break the resolution he had made, nor would he be disloyal to his dead father's commands. Then Javali, a Brahman atheist, insisting that there was and could be no hereafter, that Dasaratha, once his sire, was now mere nothing, advised the prince to yield to the reasonable wishes of the living and return with them to rule over the kingdom of his ancestors. Rama, however, warmly rebuked the atheist for his impiety, and all that Bharata could accomplish was merely to

* This significant passage from the Ramayana ought to clear away the doubts that may linger in any ones mind regarding the fact that animal food was commonly eaten in ancient India, since animal sacrifices are constantly referred to. Of course there is abundant positive evidence on the subject as in the preceding page.

induce him to put off from his feet a pair of sandals adorned with gold, which he (Bharata) carried back with him in great state to deserted Ayodhya—now inhabited only by cats and owls—as a visible symbol of his brother Rama, in whose name he undertook to carry on the affairs of the State, until the appointed fourteen years of exile should have run their course.

The incidents connected with Rama's exile to the forests, his life and rambles at Chitrakuta, Bharata's imposing march through the same wooded country which the exiles had traversed, affords the poet of the Ramayana rare opportunities of displaying his love for the picturesque and his strong natural leaning towards the serene, if uneventful, life of the hermit. Often in these early forest rovings, and indeed throughout the fourteen years of exile, does Rama, or some other one, linger to note and admire the beauties of woodland and landscape and to hold loving communion with the fair things of field and forest. Though he praises the cities, and pictures their grandeur of gold and gems, it is plain throughout that the poet's heart is in the woods, displaying on his part an appreciation of the charms of nature and scenery, very remarkable, indeed, when we consider how slowly the taste for the beauties of inanimate nature was developed in Europe. After Bharata's return to Ayodhya, Rama and his companions moved further southwards, in the direction of the great forest of Dandaka, which extended indeed as far as the Godavari. In their wanderings they came to the abode of a certain ascetic whose wife having performed severe austerities for ten thousand years was privileged, during ten years of drought, to create fruits and roots for the sustenance of the people and to divert the course of the river Jumna, so that its waters should flow by the thirsty asylum of the hermits. This ancient dame took a great fancy to Vaidehi and, woman-like, gave her fair disciple a worthy gift consisting of fine apparel, of beautiful ornaments, a precious cosmetic for the beautification of her person and a rare garland of flowers. Nor was the old lady contented until she had seen the effect of her present on Janaka's charming daughter, who had pleased her much by her good sense in affirming that "the asceticism of woman is ministering unto her husband."

Wheresoever the exiles turned their steps, in these almost trackless forests, they were told of the evil doings of the *Rakshasas*, who not only interrupted the sacrifices, but actually carried off and devoured the anchorites. Very curious too were the ways in which some of these *Rakshasas* compassed the destruction of the saints. One of them, the wily Ilwala, well acquainted with Sanskrit, would assume the form of a Brahman and invite the hermits to a *Sraddha* feast. His brother, in the assumed form of a sheep, would be slaughtered and cooked for his guests. When they had enjoyed their repast the cruel Ilwala would command his brother Vatapi to "come forth," which he would do unreluctantly, and with a vengeance, bleating loudly and rending the bodies of the unhappy guests, of whom thousands were disposed of in this truly Rakshasa-fashion. It is note-worthy that those ascetics who had, by long and severe austerities, acquired a goodly store of merit, might easily have made short work of the

Rakshasas ; but, on the other hand, if they allowed their angry passions to rise, even against such impious beings, they would, while punishing their tormentors, have inevitably lost the entire advantage of their long and painful labours. Hence many of the hermits made a direct appeal to Rama for protection.

Entering the forest of Dandaka the exiles encountered a huge, terrible and misshapen monster, besmeared with fat and covered with blood, who was roaring horribly with his widely distended mouth, while with his single spear he held transfixed before him quite a menagerie of lions, tigers, leopards and other wild animals. This awful being rushed towards the trio and, quick as thought, snatched up the gentle Vaidehi in his arms, bellowing out "I am a Rakshasa, Viradha by name. This forest is my fortress. Accoutred in arms I range (here), feeding on the flesh of ascetics. This transcendantly beauteous one shall be my wife. And in battle I shall drink your blood, wretches that ye are." At this juncture, Rama, as on some other trying occasions, gave way to unseasonable lamentations and tears ; but Lakshmana, always practical, bravely recalled him to the necessity of immediate action. The Rakshasa, having ascertained who his opponents were, vauntingly assured them that, having gratified Brahma by his asceticism, he had obtained this boon from him, that no one in the world could slay him with weapons; and he mockingly advised the princes to renounce Sita and go their way. But Rama's wrath was now kindled and he began a vigorous attack upon the monster piercing him with many arrows. A short though fierce combat ensued, the result being that the Rakshasa seized and carried off both Rama and Lakshmana on his ample shoulders. His victory now seemed complete, and Sita—who had apparently been dropped during the combat,—dreading to be left alone in the terrible wilderness, piteously implored the monster (whom she insinuatingly addressed as the "best of Rakshasas") to take her and to release the noble princes. The sound of her dear voice acted like a charm upon the brothers and, with a vigorous and simultaneous effort, they broke both the monster's arms at once and then attacked him with their *fists*. They brought him to the ground exhausted, and Rama, planting his foot upon the throat of his prostrate foe, directed Lakshmana to dig a deep pit for his reception and when it was ready, they flung him into it. The dying monster thus overcome, *though not with weapons*, explained that he had been imprisoned in that dreadful form of his by the curse of a famous ascetic and was destined to be freed from it only by the hand of Rama. With this explanation the spirit of the departed Viradha passed into the celestial regions.

Rama, with his wife and brother, now sought the hermitage of the sage Sarabhanga and on approaching it, a strange, unexpected and imposing sight presented itself to Rama's view:—Indra attended by his court in conversation with the forest sage! The God of Heaven, in clean apparel and adorned with celestial jewels, was seated in a wondrous car drawn by green horses up in the sky. Over him was expanded a spotless umbrella and two lovely damsels waved gold-handled *chowrees* above his head. About him were bands of resplendent celestials hymning his praises.

At Rama's approach the god withdrew and the sage advised the prince to seek the guidance of another ascetic named Sutikshna, adding "This is thy course thou best of men. Do thou now, my child, for a space look at me while I leave off my limbs, even as a serpent renounces its slough." Then kindling a sacrificial fire and making oblations to it with the appropriate *mantras*, Sarabhanga entered the flames himself. The fire consumed his old decrepit body and he was gradually transformed, in the midst of the flames, into a splendid youth of dazzling brightness, and, mounting upwards, ascended to the heaven of Brahma. After Sarabhanga had left the earth in this striking manner, bands of ascetics waited on Rama, reminded him of his duty as a king and solicited his protection against the Rakshasas. As Rama and his companions wandered on through the forests another wonder soon engaged their attention. Sweet music reached them from beneath the waters of a charming lake covered with lotuses and on enquiring about the strange phenomenon a hermit told them that a great ascetic had formed that lake. By his fierce austerities, extending over ten thousand years, he had acquired such a store of merit that the Gods, with Agni at their head, began to fear that he desired a position of equality with themselves. To lure him away from such ideas they sent five lovely *Apsaras* to try the power of their charms upon him. Sage though he was, he succumbed to their allurements and now, weaned from his old ambitions, he passed his time in youth and happiness—the reward of his austerities and Yoga practices—in the company of the seductive sirens whose sweet voices, blending with the tinklings of their instruments, came softly to the ears of the wandering princes.

Sita, who had confidently followed her husband, like his very shadow, through all these adventurous years in the forest, seems at length to have been somewhat shaken by the very risky encounter with Viradha of which she had been an unwilling and terrified eye-witness, in which her own person had been the object of contention and which had threatened, at one critical moment, to end very tragically for her and her loved ones. Under the influence of these recent and impressive experiences, Sita ventured, in her gentle, womanly way, to suggest to her husband the advisability of avoiding all semblance of hostility towards the Rakshasas. There were, she timidly assured her husband, three sins to which desire gave rise: untruthfulness, the coveting of other men's wives and the wish to indulge in unnecessary hostilities. Of untruthfulness and of allowing his thoughts to stray towards other women, Sita unhesitatingly exonerated her lord; but she artfully insinuated that, in his dealings with the Rakshasas, he was giving way to the sin of provoking hostilties without adequate cause and she advised his laying aside his arms, during his wanderings in the forest; since the mere carrying of bows and arrows was enough to kindle the wish to use them. To give point to this contention, Vaidehi related how, in the olden time, there lived in the woods a truthful ascetic whose incessant austerities Indra desired, for some reason or other, to frustrate. For the attainment of his end the king of Heaven visited the hermit in the guise of a warrior and left his sword with him as a trust. Scrupulously regardful of his obligation to his visitor, the ascetic carried the sword with him wherever duty or necessity directed his footsteps, till constant association with the weapon began to engender fierce sentiments, leading eventually to the spiritual downfall of the poor ascetic, whose ultimate portion was Hell. Rama received Sita's advice in the loving spirit in which it was offered and thanking her for it, explained that it was his *duty* to protect the saints from the oppression of the evil Rakshasas, and that *Kshatriyas* carried bows in order that the word "distressed" might not be known on this earth.

Several years of exile slipped away, not unpleasantly, in the shady forests through which the royal brothers roamed from hermitage to hermitage, always accompanied by the lovely and faithful Sita whose part throughout is one of affectionate, unfaltering and unselfish devotion to her husband. On the banks of the Godavari, Lakshmana, who has to do all the hard work for the party, built them a spacious hut of clay, leaves and bamboos, propped with pillars and furnished with a fine level floor, and there they lived happily near the rushing river. At length the brothers got involved in a contest with a brood of giants who roved about the woods of Dandaka, delighting, as usual, in the flesh of hermits and the interruption of sacred rites. This time it was a woman who was at the bottom of their troubles. Surpanakha, an ugly giantess and sister of Ravana, charmed with the beauty and grace of Rama, came to him and, madly in love, offered to be his wife. But Rama in flattering terms put her off, saying he was already married. In sport, apparently, he bid her try her luck with Lakshmana. She took his advice, but Lakshmana does not seem to have been tempted by the offer and, while artfully addressing her as "supremely charming and superbly beautiful lady", advised her to become the younger wife of Rama, to whom he referred her again. Enraged by this double rejection, the giantess attempted to kill Sita, as the hated obstacle to the fulfilment of her desires. The brothers, of course, interposed and Lakshmana, always impetuous, punished the monster by cutting off her nose. Surpanakha fled away to her brother Khara, and roused the gaint Rakshasas to avenge her wounds. These terrible giants possessed the power of changing their forms at will; but their numbers and their prowess were alike of little avail against the valour and skill of Rama, who alone and unaided,—for he sent Lakshmana away with Sita into an inaccessible cave—destroyed fourteen thousand of them in a single day. The combat which was witnessed by the Gods and Gandharvas, Siddhas and Charanas, is described at great length, and the narrative is copiously interlarded with the boastful speeches of the rival chiefs. In the bewildering conflict of that day his fourteen thousand assailants poured upon Rama showers of arrows, rocks and trees. Coming to close quarters they attacked him vigorously with clubs, darts, and nooses. Although hard pressed and sorely wounded, the hero maintained the conflict with undaunted courage, sending such thousands of wonderful arrows from his bow that the sun was darkened and the missiles of his enemies warded off by them. Finally Rama succeeded in laying dead upon that awful field of carnage, all but the entire number of his fierce assailants. Khara, the leader of the opposing host, a worthy adversary and possessed of wondrous weapons, still lived. Enraged at, but undaunted by, the wholesale destruction of his followers, Khara boldly continued the fight. In his war-chariot, bright as the sun, he seemed to be the destroyer himself as he fiercely assailed the victorious Rama. With one arrow he severed the hero's bow in his hand; with seven other shafts like thunder-bolts he severed his armour joints, so that the glittering mail fell from his body. He next wounded the Prince with a thousand darts. Not yet overcome, however, Rama strung another bow, the mighty bow of Vishnu, and discharging shafts with golden feathers brought Khara's standard to the ground. Transported with wrath at this ill-omened event Khara poured five arrows into Rama's bosom. The prince responded with six terrible bolts, some of them crescent-headed. One struck the chief in the head, two of the others entered his arms and the remaining three his chest. Following these up with thirteen of the same kind, Rama destroyed his enemy's chariot, killed his horses, decapitated his charioteer and shattered his bow in his grasp. Khara jumped to the ground armed with a mace, ready to renew the conflict. At this juncture Rama paused a moment to read the Rakshasa a homily on his evil doings; the latter replied with fierce boasts and hurled his mace at

Rama who cut it into two fragments with his arrows, as it sped through the air. Khara now uprooted a lofty tree and hurled it at his foe ; but, as before, Rama cut it into pieces with his arrows, ere it reached him, and with a shaft resembling fire put a period to the life of the gallant Rakshasa. At this conclusion of the conflict the celestials sounded their kettle drums, and showered down flowers upon the victorious son of Dasaratha. Thus perished the Rakshasa army and its mighty leader :

"But of the host of giants one,
"Akampan, from the field had run,
"And sped to Lanka to relate
"In Ravana's ear the demon's fate."

(GRIFFITHS).

This fugitive made his way to the court of Ravana, the king of the giants, and related to him the sad fate of his followers. Close on the heels of Akampan came Surpanakha herself, with her cruelly mutilated face. Transported with rage at the destruction of his armies and at sight of the disfigured countenance of his sister, the terrible Rakshasa chief vowed vengeance on Rama and Lakshmana. But the necessity for great caution in dealing with such valorous foes was apparent and Ravana did not seem over-anxious to leave his comfortable capital, Lanka, in order to seek out the formidable brothers in the woods of Dandaka. But Surpanakha, scorned and mutilated, was thirsting for an early and bitter revenge. Reproaching her brother for his unkingly supineness, she artfully gave him a description of Sita's beauty, far superior to that of any goddess, which served to kindle unlawful desires in his heart. She referred to Vaidehi's golden complexion, her moon-like face, her lotus eyes, her slender waist, her taper fingers, her swelling bosom, her ample hips and lovely thighs, till the giant was only too willing to assent to her suggestion, that the most effectual and agreeable revenge he could take for the destruction of his hosts, and the cruel insults to his sister, would be to carry off the fair Sita, by stratagem, from the arms of her devoted husband, and thus add the lovely daughter of Janaka, to the number, not very small, of the beauties who adorned his palace at Lanka. We shall presently see that the plot was ingeniously contrived and too successfully carried out.

How conveniently the race of Rakshasas could assume, at will, the forms in which they chose to appear, we know already. Taking advantage of this faculty of metamorphosis, a Rakshasha named Maricha, in obedience to Ravana's orders, showed himself near Rama's hermitage, in the shape of a wonderful golden deer, spotted with silver, having horns resembling jewels, a belly like a sapphire and sides like *madbuka* flowers. The strange creature captivated the fancy of Sita, and she was so eager to possess it, alive or dead, that Rama was induced to go in pursuit of it. Suspecting mischief from this unusual appearance, Rama left his brother with Sita, commanding him on no account to quit her side until he returned from his pursuit of the jewelled deer. The chase led him to a considerable distance from the hermitage. Weary of his endeavours to secure the deer, Rama grew angry and, with one of his flaming arrows, pierced it in the breast. It bounded off the ground to the height of a palm tree and, in the act of dying, began to cry, exactly in the voice of Rama, "Ah! Sita; Ah! Lakshmana." The words reached the hermitage as they were intended to do, and Sita, in an agony of terror, implored Lakshmana to go to the aid of his brother, who seemed to be in some dire trouble. Lakshmana, however, protested that it was all illusion and refused to believe that Rama could be in any real danger; for, as he assured the trembling wife, "even the Almighty Himself with the celestials and the three worlds, cannot defeat him" (Dutt, 609). But Vaidehi took another view of the matter and turning sharply upon her brother-in-law accused him roundly of desiring the destruction of Rama in order that he might gratify an improper wish to possess her himself. This, indeed, she said, must have been the reason that brought him all the way from Ayodhya. What, if any, grounds the charming lady may have had for this accusation does not appear. They could have been known only to herself and to Lakshmana who, with joined hands, humbly reproached her for her cruel words and bending low before her went off, with a heavy heart, in search of his brother.

In a garment (probably a *saree*) of yellow silk, Sita sat alone at the door of her thatched cottage, weeping bitterly, when Ravana presented himself before her, in the guise of a pious mendicant. Ravished by her beauty, this pious mendicant began, without ceremony, to praise the various charms of Sita's person with the most reprehensible license of detail. Nor did he stop there, but telling her that she had carried away his heart, as a stream carries away its banks, invited her to accompany him out of the gloomy forest, tenanted by Rakshasas and wild beasts, and quite unfit for the abode of a goddess like herself.

As her visitor was in appearance a Brahman, she dutifully attended to him, bringing him water to wash his feet with, and food to eat, while her eyes were straining through the forest for her absent lord. Dreading that her Brahman guest might curse her if she did not speak to him; Vaidehi began to relate the history of her exile, addressing the seeming mendicant in such flattering terms as "thou best of twice born ones." After listening to her story, Ravana revealed himself to her and, again declaring his love, invited her to become his wife in the great city of Lanka, where she should live in luxury, attended by five thousand maid-servants. Sita indignantly spurned the offer, threatening the Rakshasa with the consequences of her husband's anger. While indulging in boastful speeches regarding his own prowess, Ravana assumed his natural form, with ten heads and twenty arms. As he stood there before Vaidehi, "his eyes were bloody and he appeared beautiful like unto blue clouds being dressed in gold-hued apparel." (Dutt.) Approaching the adorable Sita, the enamoured giant caught her hair with one hand and her legs with another and carried her off, through the air, in his golden car drawn by asses. As she was being borne away, the fair lady cried aloud for help, invoking the sylvan deities to tell her husband whither, and by whom, she had been carried off. Her voice reached the virtuous Jatayus, the king of birds, who, though sixty thousand years old, immediately interposed to rescue her. A furious and picturesque battle ensued, in which the huge vulture-king, with his formidable beak, talons and wings, made a gallant stand against Ravana, in the cause of virtue and his friend Rama, but eventually lost his noble life in the struggle, and left his huge bones to mark, to this day, the scene of his terrible aërial conflict with the demon.* The victorious Ravana carried Sita away through the air in his arms. Some of her ornaments fell to the ground as the two sped along in their journey towards Lanka, and showers of blossoms, falling from her head, were scattered around. At this sorrowful event the sun hid his face and all nature was oppressed with grief. Not yet despairing of succour, the brave—hearted Sita observed, as she passed along in mid-air, five monkey-chiefs seated on the summit of a hill and, unnoticed by Ravana, dropped amongst them her gold coloured sheet and some glittering ornaments, in the hope that they might convey to Rama the intelligence of her abduction by the giant. But Fate had more sorrow in store for her. Over mountain peaks, over rivers, over the sea, Ravana conveyed his prize without meeting with further opposition, and lodged her safely in his magnificent palace in Lanka; where he treated her with the greatest consideration and wooed her like a youthful lover, placing her tender feet upon his *heads* and professing himself her obedient slave. On discover-

* Near Salem in Southern India are "some chalk hills supposed by the natives to be formed of the bones of the mythical bird Jatayus killed by Ravana when carrying off Sita." Professor Monier William's *Modern India*, page 165.

ing the loss he had suffered, Rama was in despair. Sometimes he would indulge in excessive lamentations, wildly calling upon the trees and streams, the deer of the forest and the birds of the air, to tell him where his love had gone. At other times, assuming a different tone, he would petulantly threaten to destroy "the three worlds," if the celestials did not restore Vaidehi to his arms. At such moments Lakshmana would address his brother in the most abject terms of flattery and gently remind him of the necessity of doing his duty and preserving his dignity.

Roaming about in search of the lost Sita, the brothers came across Jatayus laying, in mortal agony, amidst the fragments of Ravana's wonderful car and his shattered umbrella. All that Rama could learn from the dying king of the vultures was the name and rank of the Rakshasa who had carried off his wife and, in a frenzy of grief, he rolled upon the ground uttering vain lamentations. Presently the brothers piously erected a funeral pile for the dead bird and having cremated the body proceeded in their search for Sita, when they encountered a horrid deformed monster, named Kabandha ; thus described by the poet :

> " There stood before their wondering eyes
> " A fiend, broad-chested, huge of size,
> " A vast misshapen trunk they saw
> " In height surpassing nature's law.
> " It stood before them dire and dread,
> " Without a neck, without a head,
> " Tall as some hill aloft in air,
> " Its limbs were clothed with bristling hair,

"And deep below the monster's waist
"His vast misshapen mouth was placed.
"His form was huge, his voice was loud
"As some dark-tinted thunder-cloud.
"A brilliance as of gushing flame
"Beneath long lashes dark and keen
"The monster's single eye was seen."*

In the battle which ensued the terrible monster had his two arms cut off by Rama and Lakshmana respectively and, in this helpless condition, he explained that, though naturally endowed with a surpassingly beautiful form, he used to assume this monstrous one in order to frighten the ascetics in the forest; but one of these saints, in a moment of anger, invoked this curse upon him, that he should retain the disgusting form he had adopted at least till, in course of time, Rama should in person deliver him from its repulsive deformity. The brothers placed the giant's bulky body on a funeral pyre and from the ashes arose a beautiful being, clad in celestial raiment, at whose suggestion, Rama sought the friendship and aid of Sugriva, King of the Vanaras, by whose assistance he hoped to find out to what particular spot his beloved wife had been conveyed by Ravana. Rama, in due course, found Sugriva and made the acquaintance of his chief councillor the famous Hanuman, a son of the God of the winds. When Rama met Sugriva, the latter was, like himself, an exile from his native land, having been expelled from it by his elder brother, King Bali, who had also taken unto himself Ruma, Sugriva's wife. The deposed monarch was wandering, with a few faithful monkey companions, in

* Mr. Griffith's Ramayana Vol. III. page 324.

the forest, and it was amongst them, resting together on a mountain peak, that Sita had dropped her yellow robe and golden ornaments. A sort of offensive and defensive alliance was formed between the two banished princes who were, moreover, drawn towards one another by the fact that each had been forcibly deprived of his consort. Rama was to help Sugriva to overthrow Bali, secure the Vanar sceptre and recover his wife, Ruma; while Sugriva, on his part, was to assist Rama to discover Sita's whereabouts and to destroy her abductor. So great was the dread Sugriva entertained of the prowess of his warlike brother Bali, that, before committing himself to this alliance with Rama, he desired that prince to give him some practical illustration of what he could do as a wielder of warlike weapons; whereupon Rama shot, from his mighty bow, a wondrous arrow which, after passing through the stems of seven palm trees, traversed a hill which stood behind them, then flew through six subterranean realms and finally returned to the hands of the bowman. Before this feat all Sugriva's doubts vanished and he was ready for action.

At Rama's suggestion he proceeded to the great Vanar city Kishkindha, and, in a voice of thunder, dared Bali to single combat. The impetuous and passionate King of the Vanars accepted the challenge at once, and an exceedingly fierce encounter took place between the brothers, outside the walls of the city. At length Sugriva seemed to be failing, when Rama, who was standing by in ambush, pierced Bali in the breast with one of those fatal arrows of his. As might have been expected Bali, with the life-blood welling from his wounds, reproached Rama bitterly for his base, unfair, and cowardly interposition in the battle between himself and Sugriva; but Rama justified his action by saying that he was lord paramount of the whole country, that Kishkindha came within the realm of Dasaratha and that Bali had justly forfeited his life by his misconduct in appropriating his brother's wife. Rama further remarked, contemptuously, that the lives of mere Vanars or monkeys, as of other animals, were of little account in the eyes of men; a remark which seems strange, indeed, when we reflect that Bali was the King of a magnificent city decorated with gold, silver and ivory and that Bali's brother was Rama's much desired ally.*

As Bali lay prostrate on the ground his disconsolate queen, Tara, hastened to the fatal spot, with her little son Angad, and, in a passion of grief, threw herself upon the body of her husband. She gave way to the most touching sorrow and lamentation over the dying warrior and seemed inconsolable, both then and later on when performing the last rites for the deceased king. Had we seen no more of Tara she would have lived, as a tender and pleasant memory in our minds; but, unfortunately, she reappears a very short time after as Sugriva's much loved and ardent consort and actually appears grateful to Rama for the benefit his deed had conferred upon the new king and herself.

By the time Sugriva was formally installed in the

---

* As respects the Vanars it has to be noted that while implying that they were *monkeys* and nothing more, the poet has, for the most part, represented them—if we may judge by their sentiments and actions—as beings of a very superior order.

government of Kishkindha, the rainy season came round,—a time of the year when, in a roadless country, all military, or other, movements were impossible. Rama, faithful to the conditions of his exile, would not enter the city, and easily contented himself with a life in the woodland, which, with its glittering fountains and laughing streams, its stately trees, sweet-throated birds and odorous flowers, he was never tired of admiring.

In return for the service rendered him by Rama, his ally Sugriva, now king of the Vanars, assembled countless numbers (hundreds of hundreds of millions!) of Vanars (monkeys and bears of different colours—white, yellow and green—) and sent them forth to search for Sita. North, South, East and West these Vanars traversed every land and searched every possible retreat. From North, East and West were received reports of want of success; but from the South, came welcome tidings of the discovery of Sita by Hanuman, one of the chief captains of the Vanar host, a son of the wind-god by a nymph of Paradise. The discovery of Sita's place of captivity was made in this way. In their active search for traces of her whereabouts, some captains of the Vanar army of the South came across Sampati, the huge brother of Jatayus, the king of the vultures, lying upon the top of a high mountain. Bulky and powerful, the bird was yet quite disabled and helpless, having had his wings scorched and destroyed in a too adventurous flight towards the Sun, which he had once undertaken in a spirit of vanity and boastfulness. But even in this unhappy state, dependent for his daily food upon the filial devotion of his son, the old bird could, with his penetrating eye, see clearly to enormous distances. He had witnessed Ravana's hurried flight through the air, with his beautiful prize, and had noted also that she had been conveyed by the Rakshasa to Lanka beyond the sea. This information he now communicated to the enquiring Vanars and having thereby performed a signal service to the son of Dasharatha, his feathers sprouted again and he joyfully mounted once more into his native element on new and lusty pinions.

Sita's place of captivity was thus known to the Vanars; but how to reach Lanka—separated as it was from the mainland by an arm of the sea—became the urgent problem of the hour to the Vanar commanders of the army of the South. If Sita was to be restored to the arms of Rama, it was absolutely necessary that some one should get to Lanka as a spy, in order to ascertain the facts in regard to Sita's captivity there, and to discover the strength of Ravana's army and his means of resisting an attack from without. Ships or even boats were, in those primitive times, not to be thought of; but the monkey could *leap*, and so it was proposed that some leader of the race should essay the rather long jump across the strait which separated Lanka from the continent. Who was so fitted for this undertaking as the son of the Wind-God, the redoubtable Hanuman? Accordingly, after a good deal of boasting, Hanuman, assuming a gigantic size, took the flying leap. The gods were well disposed towards his brave venture, but there were also enemies on the path, who endeavoured to stop him on his way. One of these was Surasa, the mother of the Nagas, who, rushing upon him with wide-extended jaws, mockingly told him that he must pass through her mouth, before proceeding any further on his journey. Hanuman dilated his person till his stature attained many leagues, but the monster's mouth grew larger still. The cunning monkey now suddenly contracted his dimensions to the size of a man's thumb and jumped airily into and out of Surasa's gaping mouth. He had fulfilled his enemy's conditions and she, good naturedly, acknowledged her defeat. His next opponent, a terrific she-dragon, the fierce Sinhika, marvellously caught his shadow as it glided over the sea, and, in some mysterious way, retarded his progress thereby. With open mouth she made a furious onslaught upon the Windgod's son. Hanuman, equal to the occasion, craftily contracted his dimensions and jumping into Sinhika's cavern-like mouth inflicted so much injury upon her that she died. After this interruption he continued his aërial journey to Lanka, probably making Sinhika's carcass the base of a fresh leap towards the island, though this is not expressly mentioned by the poet.

When he had reached the island-kingdom of Ravana, the Vanar spy, contracting his dimensions to those of an ordinary cat, found his way, by moonlight, within the golden walls of the city, and, lost in admiration, wandered about the wonderful streets of Ravana's capital, where tonsured priests and mail-clad warriors mingled freely with bands of ascetics in deer skins and fiends both foul and fair. Eluding the guards, Hanuman crept into the Palace. Here every thing was on a scale to astonish even the Windgod's son, familiar with the glories of Kishkindha ; but most of all did he find food for admiration in Ravana's enchanted car, avowedly the most perfect work that had been produced by Visvakarma, the architect of the gods.

> There shone with gems that flashed afar,
> The marvel of the Flower-named car,
> Mid wondrous dwellings still confessed
> Supreme and nobler than the rest.
> Thereon with wondrous art designed
> Were *turkis* birds of varied kind,
> And many a sculptured serpent rolled
> His twisted coil in burnished gold.
> And steeds were there of noblest form,
> With flying feet as fleet as storm :
> And elephants with deftest skill
> Stood sculptured by a silver rill,
> Each bearing on his trunk a wreath
> Of lilies from the flood beneath.
> There Lakshmi, beauty's heavenly queen,
> Wrought by the artist's skill was seen.
> Beside a flower-clad pool to stand
> Holding a lotus in her hand.*
>
> (GRIFFITH : BK. V. CANTO VII.

The Zenana or women's apartment, guarded by she-demons, † which Hanuman next entered in the still hours of the night, when the feast was over, the music had ceased and all the inmates were hushed in slumber, affords the

* This car from the hand of Visvakarama recalls the famous embossed shield of Achilles, the master-piece of Vulcan's art, made of brass, tin, gold and silver and divided into twelve compartments each representing a distinct and complicated scene (for example a wedding procession or a battle) wrought with marvellous skill.

† There can be no doubt whatever that the seclusion of women was the common practice in ancient India. Wherever polygamy exists the seclusion of women is a necessity and that polygamy did exist in the India of the Ramayana is abundantly evident from what we are told concerning the courts of Dasharatha, Sugriva and Ravana. The Greeks kept their women a good deal in the background; but Helen's position in the court of her husband Menelaus, or Penelope's in ...nt of Ulysses was far more free than the position of any queen mentioned in the ...mayana.

poet the opportunity of painting a charming picture, which the reader will, I am sure, thank me for reproducing here in Mr. Griffith's agreeable version :

He stood within a spacious hall
With fretted roof and painted wall,
The giant Ravan's boast and pride,
Loved even as a lovely bride.
'Twere long to tell each marvel there,
The crystal floor, the jewelled stair,
The gold, the silver, and the shine
Of crysolite and almandine.
There breathed the fairest blooms of spring;
There flashed the proud swan's silver wing,
The splendour of whose feathers broke
Through fragrant wreaths of aloe smoke.
''Tis Indra's heaven, the Vanar cried,
Gazing in joy from side to side ;
The home of all the Gods is this,
The mansion of eternal bliss !'
There were the softest carpets spread,
Delightful to the sight and tread,
Where many a lovely woman lay
O'ercome by sleep, fatigued with play.
The wine no longer cheered the feast,
The sound of revelry had ceased.
The tinkling feet no longer stirred,
No chiming of a zone was heard.
So when each bird has sought her nest,
And swans are mute and wild bees rest,
Sleep the fair lilies on the lake
Till the sun's kiss shall bid them wake.
Like the calm field of winter's sky
Which stars unnumbered glorify,
So shone and glowed the sumptuous room
With living stars that chased the gloom.

'These are the stars,' the chieftain cried,
'In autumn nights that earth-ward glide,
'In brighter forms to re-appear
'And shine in matchless lustre here.'
With wondering eyes awhile he viewed
Each graceful form and attitude.
One lady's head was backward thrown,
Bare was her arm and loose her zone.
The garland that her brow had graced
Hung closely round another's waist.
Here gleamed two little feet all bare
Of anklets that had sparkled there.
Here lay a queenly dame at rest
In all her glorious garments dressed.
There slept another whose small hand
Had loosened every tie and band.
In careless grace another lay
With gems and jewels cast away,
Like a young creeper when the tread
Of the wild elephant has spread
Confusion and destruction round,
And cast it flowerless to the ground.
Here lay a slumberer still as death,
Save only that her balmy breath
Raised ever and anon the lace
That flouted o'er her sleeping face.
There, sunk in sleep, an amorous maid
Her sweet head on a mirror laid,
Like a fair lily bending till
Her petals rest upon the rill.
Another black-eyed damsel pressed
Her lute upon her heaving breast,
As though her loving arms were twined
Round him for whom her bosom pined.
Another pretty sleeper round

A silver vase her arms had wound,
That seemed, so fresh and fair and young,
A wreath of flowers that o'er it hung.
In sweet disorder lay a throng
Weary of dance and play and song,
Where heedless girls had sunk to rest
One pillowed on another's breast,
Her tender cheek half seen beneath
Red roses of the falling wreath,
The while her long soft hair concealed
The beauties that her friend revealed.
With limbs at random interlaced
Round arm and leg aud throat and waist,
That wreath of women lay asleep
Like blossoms in a careless heap.*

(GRIFFITH BK. V. CANTO IX.

Still in eager quest of Sita the Vanar roamed stealthily from place to place within the spacious bounds of the royal palace, and, as day was breaking, entered the enchanting *ashoka grove*, a sort of ideal retreat in fairy land. Here Rama's messenger discovered the weeping, but still peerless captive, guarded by fierce she-demons of monstrous shapes—a weird, frightful troupe—some earless, some with ears hanging down to their feet, some one-eyed, some long-necked and covered with hair, some huge, some dwarfish, some with the faces of buffaloes others with the heads of dogs and swine. Perched upon a bough, and concealed by its foliage, Hanuman watched his opportunity to open communication with the object of his search. Presently Ravana, in great state, heralded by music and attended by a crowd of ravishing beauties

* The lover of English poetry will recall to mind the similar description of sleeping Beauties in the VIth Canto of Don Juan, stanzas LXIV—LXIX.

with tinkling zones, entered the grove. Sita, in utter despair, fell upon the ground :

Like Hope when all her dreams are o'er.

Approaching her kindly, the king of Lanka, who was passionately enamoured of her beauty, endeavoured to re-assure her and wooed her softly with all the arts of flattery, with offers of boundless wealth and with protestations of deep affection.

> Methinks when thy sweet form was made
> His hand the wise Creator stayed ;
> For never more could he design
> A beauty meet to rival thine.
> Come let us love while yet we may,
> For youth will fly and charms decay.
>
> (GRIFFITH.)

Sita, ever faithful to her lord, treated his suit with scorn ; whereupon the demon-king waxing wrath, threatened to have her killed and served up at his table, if she persisted in rejecting his advances. Turning to leave the place in high dudgeon, he directed the demon guards to bend the fair captive to his will by threats and blandishments of every kind. Their persuasions being unsuccessful, these horrid monsters assailed the unfortunate princess with threatening weapons; but, even in this critical moment, the pure, chaste wife of Rama preferred death to dishonour.*

Amidst the persecutions of the luckless Sita an old Rakshasa matron, named Trajata, raised a warning voice ; for she had dreamed a dream which foreboded the destruction of Lanka by Rama, and she counselled the demons to

---

* The contrast between the fair Vaidehi and her ruthless persecutors in the enchanting Ashoka grove might make a striking subject for the canvas of an able artist. Indeed there is in the Ramayana no lack of suggestive and satisfactory *motifs* for the chisel and the brush. It is indeed a mine not yet wrought.

deal kindly by Sita, if they hoped for mercy from the conquerors.

It seems necessary to explain now, that it was not a sense of honour or a feeling of chivalry that had restrained the unscrupulous king of Lanka from the gratification of his passion. It was fear only that kept him back; for, as he confidentially explained to his assembled lords, having once, under the influence of ungovernable desire, dishonoured one of the nymphs of Indra's heaven, fair Punji—kashthala, Brahma had decreed that if Ravana commmitted the same offence again his head should be rent in pieces. Of course this fact and the protection thus enjoyed by Sita, through dread of Brahma's decree, were quite unknown to Rama, whose knowledge was merely human.

At length the Vanar found the long wished for opportunity of communicating with Sita and of consoling her with the hope of an early rescue. He even offered to carry her off, there and then, on his shoulders, but her modesty shrank from the mere thought of voluntarily touching the body of any male person beside Rama. The monkey-god then set about committing as much destruction as he could in the city of Lanka, which, built by Vishvakarma, the architect of the gods, is described as surpassingly beautiful and encircled by a golden wall. After a succession of fierce and successful battles with the giants—thousands at a time with their most famous captains—Hanuman, covered from head to foot with wounds, was *noosed* by means of a magic shaft from the bow of Ravana's son Indrajit, overpowered and taken prisoner. Exceedingly incensed, Ravana ordered the destructive and formidable Vanar to be put to death at once. One of his counsellors, however, suggesting that Hanuman might be regarded in the light of an envoy from Rama, it was decided to spare his life, but, at the same time, to treat him with the greatest indignity, before releasing him. In pursuance of this determination his tail was wrapped round with cloth dipped in oil, which was then set on fire ; but at the prayer of Sita, who came to know what was going on in the city, the flames abstained from harming her friend. By contracting his dimensions, Hanuman easily freed himself from his bonds, and now, by means of his blazing tail, carried fire and destruction through the beautiful city ; after which he once more performed his perilous journey through the air, back to the mainland of India, bearing tidings of his doings to his master and Rama.

When the place of Sita's captivity became known, the Vanar armies were rapidly advanced southward, and encamped on the border of the strait which separates Lanka from the mainland of India. Here they were joined by Vibhishana, Ravana's brother, who, with four attendants, had fled through the air from Lanka, in dread of the consequences of the offence he had given his king, by counselling conciliatory proceedings towards Rama, of whose formidable prowess he seems to have formed a just estimate.

Vibhishana on account of his local knowledge and great wisdom, was of much service to the Vanar host.

The sea, although it could be crossed by the Rakshasas and by the Wind-god's son, Hanuman, was a serious impediment to Rama and his Vanar allies. Standing on the margin of the trackless ocean which barred his march, the chief vented his impatience in a shower of his wonderful arrows, which he angrily shot into the wide bosom of the deep. His attack stirred the waters to their very depths and terrified its strange denizens out of their wits. As the hero laid against his bow a more formidable arrow than the rest (a fiery dart of mystic power), by means of which he threatened to dry up the waters of the sea and pass his legions over on dry land, all Nature was horrified, darkness fell upon land and sea, bright meteors flashed across the murky sky, red lightning struck the trembling earth and the firm mountains began to break and crumble away. At this critical moment of universal terror, the grand form of the king of the ocean, attended by glittering sea-serpents, rose majestically above the seething billows of his watery realm.* Addressing Rama with great reverence, the ocean-king protested that it was impossible to make a dry pathway through the sea.

> Air, ether, fire, earth, water, true
> To Nature's will, their course pursue;
> And I, as ancient laws ordain,
> Unfordable must still remain.
>
> (GRIFFITH.)

But he advised that Nala, a Vanar chief, who was the son of the architect of the gods (Visvakarma) should be requested to bridge the strait that intervened between Rama and the object of his expedition. Nala undertook

* Whoever has not forgotten his Virgil will probably be reminded of the famous storm in the Æneid and of Neptune's serene and majestic appearance above the troubled waters of the sea.

the work and, under his direction, the bridge was successfully completed. The construction of the bridge was not opposed, nor the passage disputed, so the countless hosts* of Vanars passed over to the island, with Rama mounted on Hanuman's back, Lakshmana on Angad's back, and camped† near Ravana's capital. Even at this stage of events Ravana, still under the spell of his passion for the lovely Sita, resorted to a stratagem to obtain her consent to his wishes. He got a magician of his court to prepare a head exactly resembling Rama's, and also a bow and arrows such as the hero usually carried, and had them brought into Sita's presence, with the tale that her lord had been killed while asleep in his camp. Sita, completely deceived by the wizard's art, was lamenting her bitter loss, when a messenger hurriedly summoned Ravana away to see to the defence of his capital, and a female attendant took advantage of the moment to relieve the fair captive's mind, by explaining the deception that had been practised upon her.

The attack that shortly followed and the defence made by the giants are described by Valmiki in considerable detail, and with much monotonous repetition. The Vanars had, for arms, uprooted trèes, rocks and mountain-peaks; while the Rakshasas fought with bows and arrows, swords and spears. Many single combats are described. Indrajit, the redoubtable son of Ravana, in a desperate

* Some hundred thousand billions (see note to Griffith's Ramayana Vol. V, page 88).

† *Camped*; but not like a modern army under canvas. The Vanars, I trow, needed no commissariat department, living as they did on fruits and roots. And the sons of Raghu were nearly as well used to woodland fare and lodging as their simian allies.

encounter, concealed himself in a magic mist. Under this protection he fired some wondrous serpent-arrows at Rama and Lakshmana, which bound the royal brothers in a noose. He then, with a storm of missiles, laid them prostrate and apparently dying. But it was not thus that the contest was to end. From their helpless condition Rama and Lakshmana were freed by the power of Garuda, the king of birds, who possessed a power over the serpent-arrows.

On another occasion the wounded and dying Rama with his brother Lakshmana, and ever so many of their Vanar allies, were restored to life and vigour, by the scent of some healing herbs brought by the swift-footed Hanuman from the distant Himalayas. In the combats around the walls of Lanka, as in other contests narrated in the Ramayana, the poet describes the power of the various archers to interrupt *with their arrows* the shafts of their adversaries, or even the most ponderous missiles hurled at them, such as trees and rocks.

With varying success the fierce contest raged round the walls of Lanka, when at length the giants, sorely pressed, called upon Kumbhakarna to assist them. This dreadful monster was Ravana's brother and a terror to men and gods. At his birth, or shortly after it, he devoured a thousand men: Indra interposed to save the human race from his ravages, but only to be himself discomfited and driven to seek the protection of Brahma, who decreed that Kumbhakarna should sleep for six months at a time, and then only wake for a single day. The mere appearance of the monstrous giant caused a panic in the Vanar army. Multitudes perished under Kumbhakarna's arm and were devoured by him; but such was his voracity that he captured and flung thousands of living Vanars into his mouth, out of which some fortunate ones managed to escape, through his nostrils and ears. But formidable as he was, Kumbhakarna at length fell by a crescent-headed arrow from Rama's bow.

> "Through skin and flesh and bone it smote
> "And rent asunder head and throat.
> "Down with the sound of thunder rolled
> "The head adorned with rings of gold,
> "And crushed to pieces in its fall
> "A gate, a tower, a massive wall.
> "Hurled to the sea the body fell,
> "Terrific was the ocean's swell
> "Nor could swift fin and nimble leap
> "Save the crushed creatures of the deep."

(GRIFFITH, BK. VI, CANTO LXVII).

One memorable episode in this siege of Lanka was a night attack, planned and successfully carried out by Sugriva. Overpowering the guards, the Vanars entered the city, and, amidst the most terrible carnage, gave beautiful and stately Lanka over to the flames:

> As earth with fervent head will glow
> When comes her final overthrow;
> From gate to gate, from court to spire
> Proud Lanka was one blaze of fire,
> And every headland, rock and bay
> Shone bright a hundred leagues away!

(GRIFFITH.)

Succeeding this night attack came the final struggle. Ravana sallied forth from Lanka with a marvellous array of chariots,* elephants, horses and men. He himself was the most formidable adversary yet encountered by Rama, having in his time subjugated the Nagas, defeated the gods of Heaven and even successfully invaded the land of departed spirits, ruled over by the dreaded Yama. During the battle that ensued, Indra, anxious, no doubt, to pay off old scores, sent his own chariot to Rama, who, mounted on it, encountered Ravana in single combat, and after a long contest killed his adversary with an arrow which had been made by Brahma himself. As the giant fell, celestial music filled the air, perfumed breezes wandered pleasantly over the field and heavenly blossoms were rained down upon the conquering hero, the champion of the gods.

With the death of Ravana the war was at an end and Vibhishana was installed king in his place. Sita, so long and so ardently sought, was now brought forth in state from Lanka, borne in a screened litter on the shoulders of sturdy Rakshasas, to meet her victorious lord. The inquisitive Vanars pressed round to see Vaidehi, on whose account they had so often risked their lives; but the attendants rudely drove them back. Rama, however, interposing, commanded that the lady should descend from the litter and proceed on foot, unveiled, so that his Vanar friends might have a good look at her; for, as he said:

> At holy rites, in war and woe
> Her face unveiled a dame may show;
> When at the maiden's choice they meet,

* "The chariots of Ravana's present army are said to have been one hundred and fifty million in number with three hundred million elephants and twelve hundred million horses and asses. The footmen are merely said to have been unnumbered." (Note to Griffith's Ramayana, Book VI., Canto XCVI.)

When marriage troops parade the street.
And she, my queen, who long has lain
In prison, racked with care and pain,
May cease awhile her face to hide
For is not Rama by her side?

The meeting between Rama and his long-lost queen is a highly dramatic and unexpected scene. Instead of Rama folding his darling in his arms, as one might have expected he would have done, after all his piteous laments about her loss and his often expressed desire to possess his peerless wife once more, we find him coldly repulsing her, on the ground of her long captivity in Ravana's power. More than that, he cruelly tells her that it was not love for her, but a desire to vindicate his outraged honour, that had brought him to Lanka. Quite unprepared for this undeserved and heartless reception, poor Vaidehi asks her husband most touchingly, if the past is all forgotton, if her love and unfaltering devotion have quite faded from his memory? And, waxing sadly indignant, she requests Lakshmana, in a voice broken with sobs, to prepare a funeral pile for her, the only refuge she had left to her in her dark despair. With Rama's tacit consent the pyre was erected and ignited. Boldly did the virtuous queen enter the flames and, as she fell overpowered by them, a cry of grief rose from the bystanders. At this important moment a band of celestial beings, headed by Brahma himself, appeared before the assembled multitude and revealed to Rama his true nature, that he was Vishnu and no mortal man, while the God of Fire raised Sita out of the flames and, publicly attesting her purity, restored her to Rama, who now joyfully received her back to his heart and home. Before the Gods departed to their celestial abodes, Indra, at Rama's considerate request, restored to life all the Vanars who had fallen in his cause. Thus was the great war brought to a conclusion.

Rama now proceeded to Ayodhya, carried aloft through the clouds, over sea and land, in the famous magic car *Pushpak*, already described. With the returning hero went Sita and Lakshmana, the Vanar chiefs and Vibhishana too. After a meeting with his brother Bharata, who came forth with joy to welcome him back, Rama assumed the government of Dasharatha's kingdom and reigned over it for ten thousand years.*

But his life and Sita's had still more trouble in them. The people of Ayodhya mocked at Rama for taking back his wife, after she had been so long in the giant's power. They even attributed a famine which desolated the land to the anger of the gods on account of Rama's conduct. About to become a mother, Sita expressed a great desire to visit the forest hermitages of the saints. Her husband accorded his consent to her wishes and directed Lakshmana to conduct her thither. Unable to endure the jibes of his people, Rama resolved to abandon his innocent, unsuspecting wife, alone and unprotected, in the immense forests of Dandaka, near the sources of the Godavery. The bitter duty was entrusted to Lakshmana, who, ever obedient, carried it out to the letter. Alas ! poor Vaidehi, such was the reward of her pure, unselfish love and devotion through many trying years of hardship and

* At this point the great epic of Valmiki properly ends ; but a supplementary work, also popularly attributed to Valmiki, exists which affords further details of the lives of the principal personages of the poem. Upon the particulars supplied in this work the succeeding paragraphs are based.

sorrow! Cast adrift, alone, in the pathless wilderness, Sita was found by the saint Valmiki himself and tenderly entertained by the holy women of the hermitage. Shortly after this she gave birth to twin-sons who were named Kusa and Lava. In his forest home, Valmiki, under divine inspiration, composed the Ramayana and taught the sons of Sita to recite the immortal epic. On the occasion of a grand ceremony at Ayodhya, Kusa and Lava had the honour of reciting the great poem in the presence of their father, who, after enquiry, acknowledged them as his sons and invited Sita to come forward and assert her innocence publicly.

"But Sita's heart was too full, this second ordeal was beyond even "her power to submit to and the poet rose above the ordinary Hindu "level of women when he ventured to paint her conscious purity as "rebelling. Beholding all the spectators and clothed in red garments "Sita clasping her hands and bending low her face spoke thus in a "voice choked with tears: as I, even in mind, have never thought of "any other person than Rama, so may Madhavi, the Goddess of Earth, "grant me a hiding place. As Sita made the oath, lo! a marvel appeared. "Suddenly cleaving the earth a divine throne of marvellous beauty rose "up borne by resplendent dragons on their heads, and seated on it the "goddess of Earth, raising Sita with her arm, said to her 'welcome to "thee' and placed her by her side. And as the queen seated on the "throne slowly descended to Hades a continuous shower of flowers fell "down from heaven on her head."*

Thus in sadness, and with the sting of injustice rankling in her heart, does the gentle Sita disappear for ever.

---

* Professor E. B. Cowell (Academy No. 43). In Bhavabhuti's drama entitle Uttara Rama Charitra the *denouement* is different. Sita's purity is attested by the goddess Gunga (the Ganges) and by Prithivi (the Earth.) The people bow in respectful homage to her. Rama welcomes her back and with her two sons Kusa and Lava they pass many happy years together.

In bidding farewell to Vaidehi we would notice that throughout this epic all the female characters are much more human than those of the opposite sex and, in their genuine womanhood, they naturally interest us in a far greater degree than the heroes of the story, be they lofty demi-gods, cruel Rakshasas, volatile Vanars, or Rishis endowed with superhuman powers.

We have yet to trace the further fortunes of the sons of Dasaratha. When Rama had reigned for a long period at Ayodhya, Time, as an ascetic, sought an interview with him, at which no one might intrude on pain of certain death. As messenger from Brahma, Time explained to Rama his real nature and position, leaving it to him to continue longer on Earth or to return to Heaven. During the interview an impatient Rishi desired immediate audience of Rama. Lakshmana, who knew the penalty of intruding upon him at this moment, raised some difficulties ; but the irate saint threatened to launch a curse against Rama and all his kinsfolk, if he were not admitted to his presence forthwith. Lakshmana, dreading, for Rama's sake, the Rishi's curse, interrupted his interview with Time and thereby incurred the penalty of death. Lakshmana accordingly went to the river Sarayu and was thence conveyed bodily to Heaven. Rama, accompained by his brothers Bharata and Satrughna and attended by the goddess of earth, also by *all his weapons in human shapes, the Vedas in the form of Brahmans* and his women and servants, proceeded to the Sarayu and entered its waters. As he did so the voice of Brahma was heard from the sky saying ; "approach Vishnu, Raghav, thou hast happily arrived with thy godlike brothers. Enter thine own body as Vishnu or the eternal ether." He and his followers were then all of them translated to Heaven.*

Such is the famous story of Rama and Sita. Ordinary men and women are of little account and scarcely figure at all amongst the poet's creations. Nearly everything in the Ramayana is superhuman. The dire conflicts which occupy so large a part of the epic are waged between demigods and fiends, or giants. The weapons employed are celestial, or perhaps only charmed. Mystic spells are of the greatest efficacy and the results are proportionally great.

In the war that raged around the walls of Ilium the gods did, certainly, interfere in the combats, and sometimes unfairly too; they even attacked each other occasionally; but, notwithstanding the supernatural element, the Trojan war was still a war of men and heroes. Not so that which ensanguined the hills and plains of Lanka.

The India of the Ramayana was covered with forests and it is noteworthy that Rama's progress is traced rather from forest to forest, than from city to city, which last were very few and far between.

The hero of the tale is a very different one from those who figure in the Homeric poems. As a son he is most dutiful, pushing the idea of filial respect and obedience to the extreme, bearing no enmity even towards his designing stepmother. As a layman he is religious and unfeignedly respectful to Brahmans and saints. As a prince he is patriotic and benign; as a warrior, skilful and fearless

* Muir, Sanskrit Texts, Part IV, Appendix.

in the fight. As an elder brother, however, he is often somewhat exacting and inconsiderate and as a husband his behaviour is, to say the least, disappointing. On the whole the prominent characteristic of this hero, limned by Brahman artists, is a spirit of mild self-sacrifice, as distinguished from bold self-assertion.

The reader who has glanced through even the brief epitome of Valmiki's poem now presented will not have omitted to note the wealth of imagination displayed by the author or authors, nor will he have failed to be charmed by many a beautiful picture and many an interesting situation.

CHAPTER III.—The Ram Lila or passion-play of Rama.

Let us now see how the stirring events of this Indian epic are brought dramatically before nineteenth century spectators.

Days before the time fixed for the Dasarah festival, men, done up like monkeys and attended by drummers, may be seen in the bazaars collecting money for the fair, at which the more striking leading incidents of the epic are annually performed, part by part, in a rude pantomimic fashion. Sometimes the opening scene is a great marriage procession. One such, on an unusually large scale, was got up in Lahore in 1884, at the expense of certain rich bankers. This motley and gigantic procession was made up of very heterogeneous elements. Several camels led the way; some bulky elephants put in an appearance, and a great number of mounted men, on good cavalry horses, gave dignity to the procession. Three or four well filled carriages, gaily decorated with tinsel, flowers and coloured cloths, had the honour of accommodating the friends of Rama. A few huge litters, each borne aloft on the shoulders of sixteen or twenty bearers, were conspicuous objects in the throng. On some of these sat men personating the gods and goddesses of India, in all their grotesqueness; on others squatted favourite female singers, with their attendant minstrels who delighted the audience with their grace and vocal performances. Imitation artillery armed with explosive bomb, dancers, mountebanks, musicians and an innumerable crowd of ordinary citizens on foot, raised noise and dust enough to gratify the most pleasure-seeking Indian mob. The hero, Rama, and his inseparable brother, were dragged along on wooden horses, placed on a wheeled platform. There they sat, side by side, holding tiny bows and arrows in their hands, in a most ridiculous way, while the less important mythological personages, divine or other, came along in carriages or litters. There was a painful want of organization about the procession and the usual mixture of the sumptuous and tawdry, the rich and squalid to which one is accustomed in India.

A feature of the Dasarah festival is the number of men, disfigured with paint and ashes, who go about with iron skewers or pieces of cane passed through the skin of their arms, legs, sides and throat, or even through the tongue. I once called up a party of these men and examined them. In answer to my remark, thrown out as a feeler, that the skewers had been passed through old perforations, the leader of the party indignantly pulled a young man before me, pinched up a good bit of the skin of his forearm and, there and then, passed a blunt iron needle through it, which could not have been much thinner than an ordinary lead pencil. No blood flowed and certainly the man operated upon did not wince in the slightest degree. After this the leader of the party having satisfied me that the skin of his own neck below the chin was perfectly sound passed a skewer through it with his own hand. In both cases a tolerable amount of force was necessary to pass the iron through the skin, but no blood flowed. These men, who are looked upon with a sort of awe by the vulgar, assured me that they were protected from pain or injury by a secret *muntra* of Guru Goruck-nath's known only to themselves. They have probably learned, by the experience of many generations, safe places for the insertion of their skewers; but I was told by a native medical man that serious consequences sometimes follow their senseless ill-treatment of their own persons. The present of a rupee sent these absurd fellows away apparently well satisfied.

Near the temple of Vishnu, by Rattan Singh's Serai, arrangements had been made for a dramatic representation of Rama's famous history. When I first came upon the spot there were five or six hundred people assembled. The women and children, arrayed in their holiday best, crowded the roofs of the surrounding buildings to witness the performance and, with the gay red and yellow of their dresses and their tinkling anklets, gave colour and animation to the scene. Men and boys were below. Three merry-go-rounds, of the kind patronised by the people, were in full operation, creaking hideously.

Of the Ram Lila itself the only signs were two wooden horses, like those to be seen in European nurseries, only nearly life-size, standing, side by side, on a single wooden platform placed on wheels. They were painted white, with gaudy patches of red all over them. A few boys with monkey-masks on, capered about with switches in their hands. The crowd gradually increased, and the arrival of the performers was eagerly expected. But even yet some money-making bunniahs, surrounded by their pots and pans, their jars and other vessels, were busily plying their trade in oil, right in the midst of the assembling crowd; while on one side several women kept diligently separating the chaff from the wheat and sending clouds of dust amongst the spectators. At length a great shout announced the arrival of Rama and Lakshmana who were carried in a gaudy litter on the shoulders of a number of men. This was the signal for the commencement of business. The crowd began to settle down. The central space was cleared. Rama and Lakshmana walked barefooted round the arena, showing themselves to the spectators. They were attired in yellow garments adorned with tinsel and had on their heads high and much decorated hats, which, I happened to learn subsequently, cost just *three rupees* each. Garlands of flowers encircled their necks, and their hats were literally covered with floral wreaths. Their faces were thickly painted with what looked like yellow turmeric, daubed over with some red powder, these pigments being, no doubt, considered most suitable for imparting beauty to an Indian complexion. The brothers carried small bows, like those usually placed in the hands of Cupids, and were attended by a man who vigorously waved a *chowree* over their heads. After this preliminary exhibition, during which several masked figures began to appear on the scene, a white-headed Brahman, book in hand, (it was the Hindi version of Tulsi Das*) began to instruct the

* The Ramayana of Tulsi Das, which differs in some respects from the original poem of Valmiki, has been translated into English by Mr. F. J. Growse of the Bengal Civil Service.

performers in their several parts. Seated all together—demigods, monkeys and Brahman—in the open space, before all the spectators, they learned the first act of the day's performance. In deference to their position, and probably also out of consideration for their fine clothes, Rama and his brother were made to sit on a white sheet, whilst the others squatted comfortably in the dust. When the actors had received their instructions, they proceeded to carry them out, in a style which rendered it very difficult to comprehend what they actually meant to represent; but the Hindu spectators, familiar with the old tale and its usual dramatic rendering, seemed to recognise at least the leading events which it was intended to bring before them. At the conclusion of the act, or scene, Rama and his brother, with the rest, came together again to receive their instructions from the old Brahman stage-manager, and, when duly instructed, again dispersed to perform their several parts in a more or less imperfect manner. One portion of the performance consisted in dragging the brothers round the arena on their wooden horses. The acting or pantomime was very rude and the whole seemed childish in the extreme. But the old story, thus brought before them, was evidently as much appreciated by the spectators as it had been by their ancestors for fifty generations. And rude and childish though the performance might be, it was probably not more so than the Miracle Plays, which delighted our forefathers in the Middle Ages.

The dramatic representation extended over several days, the most popular scenes being the amputation of Surpanakha's nose and the abduction of Sita. The former, a mere rough and tumble performance, without any thing striking or dramatic about it, was greeted with uproarious mirth by the spectators, and may, possibly, be the original suggestion and sanction of much of the female nose-cutting so commonly practised in India by jealous husbands. In the other scene Ravana appeared as a hermit. The supernatural doe was dragged about the arena. Rama and his brother were, of course, lured into pursuit of the deceiver and Sita, left alone, was carried off by Ravana. Jatayus, the vulture king,—represented by a huge paper bird carried about by a man hither and thither in a wild sort of way—rushed to the rescue of the fair dame; but after a brief, though fierce, struggle was hacked to pieces by the demon. After this lamentable encounter, Sita, to the great grief of the on-lookers, was carried away to Lanka.

The downfall of Lanka and final triumph of Rama are scenes of too great importance to be dealt with like the rest. For these special preparations and as large a theatre as possible—some wide open plain for example—are requisite, as thousands gather to see Lanka and the demons given over to the flames.

I select for description a favourable instance of the siege and destruction of Lanka, which I witnessed, at the military station of Meean Meer, a few years ago. It was got up by the sepoys of some of the native regiments stationed there.

Upon an open *maidan* or plain was assembled an eager crowd of spectators. A large space for the performance of the Ram Lila was kept clear by sepoys, placed as sentries at short intervals. About the centre of this space towered two huge effigies, without legs, probably forty feet high, representing Ravana and Kumbhakarna. Each figure stood with its arms extended right and left, level with the shoulders, in the most absurd of attitudes, resembling the pictures of men which young children are so fond of drawing. Ravana had ten faces* and two arms with twenty hands,† while Kumbhakarna had two hands only. There they stood, the terrible demon King of Lanka and his no less formidable brother, grotesqueness itself. At one side, opposite to and facing the figures, was a painted wooden car, lent by the king of the celestials to Rama on this memorable occasion—standing on small wheels, like a child's toy, with two wooden horses attached to it. On the car were seated two handsome bare-legged and bare-footed boys, dressed in yellow satin robes, with bows in their hands. Their hats somewhat resembled a bishop's mitre in shape and were made of red and silver materials. These boys, the reader does not need to be told, represented Rama and his brother Lakshmana. In attendance upon them were about thirty men, dressed in dusky red clothes and with masks on their faces, who personated the army of monkeys that assisted the heroes. To the right of the two huge figures was an enclosed space which stood for the city or citadel of Lanka. Various mythological figures were also to be seen moving about the plain in a more or less objectless manner. Two

* Ravana is described as having ten heads; but the effigy I saw had several faces, I do not think so many as ten, with the head of an ass surmounting all.

† Properly the figure should have had twenty *arms*.

tall men, got up as women, went springing about, brandishing naked swords. They represented female *Rakshasas.* A man dressed up to look very corpulent, clothed in yellow, with long flowing hair and serpents coiled round his throat was dragged about upon a wooden bull over the field. This corpulent personage was no other than Mahadeva (*Siva*) on his bull (*Nandi*). Thus far the show was, at least, mythological and *Hindu*. But, by a curious anachronism, the features of a modern fair mixed themselves up with the old-world representation. Perhaps Indian taste in this nineteenth century demanded something more than the undiluted ancient epic. Whatever may have been the cause, I observed, with surprise, that within the enclosure several natives with painted faces personated Europeans of both sexes, to the great amusement of the on-lookers. A man in shaggy furs, holding a torn umbrella over his head, and attended by a fellow disguised as a European policeman, was announced to the spectators as the "Nawab of Cabul." There were also imitation bears with their leaders and such like grotesque shows for the amusement of the populace. Although the vast majority of the spectators were natives, many Europeans were present, some in their carriages, some on elephants and one or two on camels. The scene, which was certainly strange and picturesque, became especially lively when, towards the close of the proceedings, the explosion of bombs and the discharge of rockets alarmed the horses and elephants. One huge beast carrying a European gentleman and three ladies in a big *howdah*, was an object of interest and a cause of some anxiety to me, for his restive and erratic movements seemed to threaten destruction to me or at least to my carriage.

The proceedings commenced by Ravana's car, wooden horses and all, being dragged by men round the enclosure attended by the monkeys. This was apparently a challenge to the enemy; for during the second circumambulation a party of men, dressed in dark blue or black, who had hitherto been kept out of sight, sprang forward to oppose Rama's progress. These sable warriors were terrible Rakshasas, before whom Rama and his allies had to beat a retreat pursued by the victors. Before long, however, the tide of battle seemed to turn. Victory changed sides! The Rakshasas retreated followed by Rama and his people. This alternate success of one party or the other was repeated several times, apparently to prolong the proceedings, and was a most uninteresting and childish exhibition. Whenever Rama was advancing he was carried along discharging feeble arrows that rarely fell beyond the line of men yoked to his car. But when the hero was retreating before the enemy he was generally on foot, probably to obviate the necessity of his turning his back to his foes. At length the demigods made a furious and altogether successful onslaught. The black warriors were supposed to have been completely exterminated. They lay stretched on the field dead and dying for a minute or two and then, in the most inconsistent manner, got up and squatted on the grass to watch the further proceedings. When Ravana's forces were thus destroyed, a number of fireworks were lighted all over the field. Then the fort of Lanka was given over to the flames and as it was well filled with fire-works it made a brilliant display. Next perished Kumbhakarna, similarly in a blaze of rockets, and amidst the thunder of exploding bombs. And last of all, the gigantic Ravana disappeared, by what to any bystander would seem a process of spontaneous combustion. All the time the drama lasted a regimental brass band played European music; so that Rama's forces may be said to have been animated to the assault of Lanka by the soul stirring music of European composers.

This was all! Sita the patient, faithful, loving wife was never brought forward. The woman's part was a quite subordinate one and was left to the imagination of the spectators. The conquering Rama was every thing; the long-suffering Sita was forgotten on this occasion. However, the gentle wife of Rama has a place of her own in the affectionate regard of the people of her native land and her history is well remembered. I have seen a picture of the car in which Sita was abducted, tattooed on the arm of an ignorant woman of the lower classes and found on enquiry that she knew the old old story well.

The Ram Lila I have just described was a particularly good example of the annual celebration. Ordinarily huge figures, stuffed with straw, represent the Demons. Rama and Lakshmana seated on a stage are carried about on the shoulders of men and, after traversing the ground, hither and thither, without any apparent object, at length set fire to the effigies whose combustion concludes the play, if such it can be called; whereupon the crowds assembled to see the sport depart in clouds of dust and smoke. Often several sets of Demons and Ramas may be seen on the same field, got up by rival parties, by different sections of a city, or by separate villages.

It appears that there is some difficulty in getting boys to personate Rama and his brother on the occasion of the Ram Lila festival, as it is the popular belief that they never live to attain manhood.* There is also another if less superstitions reason for the difficulty in question, and it is this : At the close of the festival Rama and Lakshmana have to feast the Brahmans and that involves no inconsiderable outlay of money. Hence, in the somewhat lawless border districts on the Indus, it is the usual thing for the sons of well-to-do persons to be actually kidnapped and carried off to play Rama and Lakshmana at the annual festival.

For ten days during the feast they are believed to be literally possessed by the god and are worshipped as Vishnu. But the worship of these boys creates, I was told, a curious and interesting difficulty about the selection of Rama and Lakshmana. The two heroes were men of the warrior caste, and so should their modern representatives be, but, as they have divine honours paid to them during the festival, it would not suit the Brahmans to bow down to and touch the feet of youths of inferior caste, while even personating demigods, and so, in defiance of history, Brahman youths are generally selected to repre-

* Bishop Heber was told that, in the *good old times*, the poor children were always "poisoned in the sweetmeats given to them the last day of the show, that it might be said their spirits were absorbed into the deities whom they had represented." Heber's Narrative of a Journey through the Upper Provinces of India (1824—25) page 191.

sent the heroes in the Ram Lila.

What the Indian artist's conception of the form and appearance of Rama is, may be partially understood from the statuettes in stone, made at the present day and frequently to be met with, at least in Northern India. They are usually sculptured in white marble, but painted (I may say enamelled) jet black, the only unblackened portion being the whites of the eyes. The eyebrows are gilded and so is the loin-cloth or *dhoty*, which is the only piece of clothing on the person of the god-man. Two big ornaments, shaped like stumpy reels, fill big holes in the lobes of the ears, and make them stick out on either side. On the forehead is the Vishnu caste-mark, the central line in red and the two side lines, diverging from the top of the nose, in gold. These figures chiselled by the Indian sculptor are always stiff and somewhat conventional.

The Dasarah festival of Northern India is replaced in Bengal by the Durga Puja and consequently the Bengalees do not perform the Ram Lila, but I remember to have seen, years ago, in Bengal, a large collection of colossal groups of figures representing favourite incidents in the Mahabharata and Ramayana, prepared at the expense of the Maharajah of Burdwan, to which show, an annual one I believe, the public were freely admitted. The grotesque forms of the monsters of the Indian epics were reproduced in huge clay statues, variously coloured and clothed. Some, armed with the strange weapons which the poets had imagined, were engaged in deadly combat. Gigantic arrows were conspicuous and some of them, with the aid of thread supports, were shown in the air on their way to some ill-fated warrior or other. More peaceful scenes were also represented, as where Ravana, in the disguise of a Brahman visits Sita in the forest. Various holy hermits were also there in all the repulsiveness of dirt and emaciation. The figures were coloured yellow, blue, green, brown or black, according to the text of the poet, the conventional notions of the people or the taste and fancy of the artists. Some of these clay statues were decidedly well modelled. They had real hair on their heads, faces and breasts; they were clothed in cotton fabrics, according to the not very elaborate fashions of the country, and, in some cases, were by no means inartistic representations of the men, demons and demigods of the sacred epics of India.

APPENDIX.

THE STORY OF THE DESCENT OF GANGA (THE GANGES) AS RELATED IN THE RAMAYANA.

In ancient times lived Sangara a virtuous king of Ayodhya. He had two wives but no children. As he and his consorts longed for offspring, the three of them went to the Himalayas and practised austerities there. When they had been thus engaged for a hundred years, a Brahman ascetic of great power granted this boon to Sangara; that one of his wives should give birth to a son who should perpetuate his race and the other should be the mother of sixty thousand manly and high-spirited sons. In due time the elder wife bore the promised son, who was named Asamanja, and the younger wife a *gourd*. From this *gourd*, when it burst open, came forth sixty thousand tiny sons, who were fostered, during their helpless infancy, by keeping them in jars filled with clarified butter. When his numerous sons had grown to man's estate the king, their father, determined to offer a *horse-sacrifice*. In accordance with this resolution a horse was, in the usual way, set free to wander where it listed, attended, for its protection, by mighty warriors of Sangara's army.

Now it came to pass that one day Vasava, assuming the form of a Rakshasi, stole the horse away. The sixty thousand sons of the king of Ayodhya thereupon commenced, at their father's command, a diligent search for the missing animal. They scoured the world in vain for the stolen horse and then set about making a rigorous search in the bowels of the Earth, digging downwards some sixty thousand *yojanas*. In these subterranean explorations they committed great havoc amongst the dwellers in the under-world; but they persevered in their quest and presently, in the Southern Quarter, came upon a huge elephant resembling a hill. This colossal elephant, named Verupaksha, supported the entire Earth upon his head and caused earthquakes whenever he happened to move his head from fatigue. Going round this mighty beast, the sons of Sangara continued their search in the interior of the earth. They at last found the stolen horse and observed, quite close to it, "the eternal Vasudeva in the guise of Kapila," upon whom they rushed with blind but impotent fury; for he, uttering a tremendous roar, instantly reduced them all to ashes.

As the princes did not return home Sangara became alarmed for their safety and sent his grandson—Asamanja's son—to look for tidings of them. This heroic prince, following the traces they had left of their eventful journey, at length reached the spot where the missing horse was detained and there discovered also the ashes of his sixty thousand uncles. Being piously desirous of making the usual oblations of water to the ashes of his deceased relatives, Asamanja's son looked about for water but could find none. However he met, in these nether regions, Suparna a maternal uncle of his, "resembling the wind," and from him he learned that the sixty thousand dead princes would be translated to heaven, if only the waters of Ganga could be brought down from the celestial regions to lave their dust.

Seeing there was nothing that he could do for the manes of his dead relatives the young prince took the horse and returning with it to Ayodhya helped to complete Sangara's sacrifice.

Sangara himself died after a reign of thirty thousand years. Ançumat, who succeeded him, practised rigid austerities, "on the romantic summit of Himavat," for thirty-two thousand years and left the kingdom to Dilipa whose constant thought was how he should bring Ganga down from Heaven for the benefit of his dead ancestors; but though he performed numerous sacrifices during his long reign of thirty thousand years he made no progress in this matter. Dilipa's son Bhagiratha earnestly devoted himself to the same object and practised severe austerities with the view of obtaining the wished-for boon. "Restraining his senses and eating once a month and surrounding himself with five fires and with arms uplifted he for a long lapse of time performed austerities at Gokara." Brahma pleased with the king's asceticism appeared before him and granted his wish, advising him, at the same time, to invoke the aid of Siva to accomplish it, as the earth would not be able to sustain the direct shock of the descent of Ganga from the celestial regions.

To obtain the assistance of Siva Bhagiratha spent a whole year in adoring that God, who at the end of that period was graciously pleased to say to the king: "O foremost of men, I am well-pleased with thee. I will do what will be for thy welfare—I will hold the Moun-

"tain's daughter on my head." Upon this Ganga precipitated herself from the Heavens upon Siva's head, arrogantly thinking to reach the earth without delay, but Siva, vexed by her proud thought, caused her to wander for many a year amongst the tangles of his long hair. It was only when Bhagiratha had recourse to fresh austerities that Siva "cast Ganga off in the direction of the Vindu lake," and she flowed in many channels over the joyful earth to the delight and admiration of the celestials who witnessed her wonderful descent from the sky.

Ganga following the royal ascetic Bhagaritha, flooded with her waters the "sacrificial ground of the high-souled "Jahna of wonderful deeds, as he was performing a sacri-"fice." The Saint drank up her waters in a rage. When this occurred the deities and *Gandharbas* began to worship the angry Jahna, who, being propitiated by their attentions, allowed the river to flow off through his ears. Proceeding again in the wake of Bhagiratha's chariot, Ganga, having reached the ocean, entered the under-world where the ashes of the sixty thousand sons of Sangara still lay. Her sanctifying waters flowed over their earthly remains and their spirits ascended to Heaven.

Such is the history of the most sacred river of the Hindus into whose heaven-descended waters millions upon millions of men and women crowd annually to have their sins washed away.

NOTES.

Antiquity of the Ramayana.—Older than the Ramayana ascribed to Valmiki is the Ramasaga itself, which exists as a Buddhist story known as the Dasarathajataka. This is substantially the history of Rama and Sita with the important omission of the rape of Sita and the expedition against Lanka which incidents the poet of the Ramayana is believed by Dr. Albrecht Weber to have borrowed from the Homeric legends.* If this conjecture be correct the treatment of the incidents in question by Valmiki is no slavish imitation of that of Homer. In the Mahabharata the story of Rama and Sita is narrated to Yudhisthira as an example, taken from the olden time, by way of consolation on a certain occasion, and agrees so closely with the work of Valmiki that it certainly looks very much like an epitome of that work. In regard to the age of this epic Sir Monier Williams says; "we cannot be far wrong in asserting that a great portion of the Ramayana if not the entire Ramayana before us, must have been current in India as early as the fifth century B.C.†"

II.—English versions of the Ramayana.—The English reader desirous of learning more of the details of the Ramayana than is contained in this epitome may consult the following works: (1) the excellent metrical version of Mr. Ralph Griffith, in five volumes, (2) the prose translation now in course of publication by Babu Manmatha Nath Dutt M. A, (3) Mr. Talboys Wheeler's History of India Vol. III, and (4) The Ramayana of Tulsi Das translated by Mr. F. T. Growse.

III.—The Ramayana only a nature myth.—While one scholar finds *history* in the pages of the Ramayana and discovers in its

---

* Vide "On the Ramayana" by Dr. Albrecht Weber (Trübner & Co., 1863.)

† Indian Epic Poetry, page 3 (Williams and Norgate; London, 1863.)

interesting details a poetical version of the conquest of southern India by the Aryans, another, with a turn for mythological interpretation, assures us that it is only a nature-myth. "The whole story" he writes, "is clearly an account of how the full moon wanes and finally disappears from sight during the last fourteen days of the lunar month which are the fourteen years of Rama and Sita's exile. Her final disappearance is represented by her rape by Ravana, and her rescue means the return of the new moon. In the course of the story the triumph of the dark night lightened by the moon and stars is further represented by the conquest of Vali, the god of tempests of the monkey race who had obscured the stars."*

* "Early History of Northern India," by J. F. Hewitt.— Journal of the Royal Asiatic Society, 1890 page 744.

PART II.

THE MAHABHARATA.

CHAPTER I.—Introductory Remarks

Standing on the beautiful fluted column of red sandstone, known as the Kutub Minar, which towers loftily above the lifeless quietude of ancient Delhi, the eye surveys a landscape which embraces one of the most classic regions in Hindustan.

Across the ruin-strewn plain, towards the lordly minarets and cupolas of modern Delhi, the spectator may note, just a little towards the east, the massive remains of the *Poorana killa*, or old fort, which still preserves, in its traditionary name of *Indrapat* or *Indraprasta*, a suggestion of the glory it enjoyed some fifteen centuries before Christ.

Not only in India and to the Hindus is *Indraprastra* a name of reverence; for, away in distant Cambodia, the people believe that they are descended from colonists who immigrated into the southern peninsula from the far off banks of the Jumna, and the stupendous remains of Angkor and Battambang near the great lake of Toulé-sap point unmistakably to Hindu and Buddhist origin and bear silent witness to the existence, in the remote past, of a powerful and flourishing kingdom of Indian origin.*

Delhi and the great plain north of it are associated

* Nouvelle Géographie Universelle par Elisée Reclus Tome VIII. page 873 et seq. Keane's Asia pages 678—680.

with the most stirring events in both the ancient and modern history of India and have witnessed the most decisive struggles for empire which have occurred south of the Himalayas.

Perhaps the Mahabharata was based on simple Aryan sagas like those of the Norsemen, historical traditions of deeds performed by gallant warriors to whose nervous hands the spear and axe were more familiar than the plough and the pen,* but, if so, the poets who have used the materials of the sagas of their ancestors to build up the great national epic have been not too careful to preserve the strict accuracy of the traditions and when the narrative of events is interrupted by long disquisitions and endless palavers, we discern unmistakably the hand of the Brahman compiler and *his* contribution to the record. We may, then, as well admit at once that little real history can be gleaned out of the one hundred thousand verses of the Mahabharata. Yet a very great deal of valuable matter, that does not fall under the usual denomination of history, may be readily found in this voluminous epic, giving it a high value for all time.

The authorship of the Mahabharata is ascribed to the sage Vyasa, or the *compiler*, and its production is at least as remarkable as that of the Ramayana already referred to. We are told in the introduction to the poem itself that; "The son of Satyavata (Vyasa) having by penance and meditation analysed the eternal Veda afterwards

* It is I think impossible, after reading the tedious genealogies of the kings in the Mahabharata, to avoid the conclusion that there is a substratum of history beneath it all, notwitstanding the clouds of mythological dust which obscure the view.

compiled this holy history." When he had completed the vast epic, without, however, committing any portion of it to writing, he began to consider how he could teach it to his disciples. Sympathising with his desire to extend to others the benefits of this most sacred and interesting poem, Brahma, the Supreme Being, appeared before the Saint. "And when Vyasa surrounded by all the tribes of Munis, saw him, he was surprised; and standing with joined palms, he bowed and he ordered a seat to be brought. And Vyasa having gone round him who is called Hiranyagarbha seated on that distinguished seat, stood near it, and being commanded by Brahma Parameshti he sat down near the seat full of affection and smiling in joy." (P. C. Roy)* After expressing his entire approval of the poem Vyasa had composed, the Supreme Being said: "Let Ganesa, be thought of, O Muni, for the purpose of writing the poem" and then "retired to his own abode." Ganesa the god of Wisdom, being invoked by Vyasa repaired at once to his hermitage and consented to commit the wondrous tale to writing, provided his pen were not allowed to cease its work for a single moment. This condition was agreed to and observed. Thus was the Mahabharata recorded, as undying and infallible scripture, from the lips of its inspired bard.

In respect to its importance and sanctity we need only cite the following passages from the poem itself. "There is not a story current in this world, but doth

*The Mahabharata of Krishna-Dwaipayana Vyasa translated in English prose; by Pratap Chundur Roy (Calcutta, Bharata Press).

If not otherwise stated all prose quotations from the Mahabarata included in the following pages are derived from this work.

depend upon this history even as the body upon the food that it taketh."

"The study of the Bharata is an act of piety. He that readeth even one foot believing hath his sins entirely purged away."

"The man who with reverence daily listeneth to this sacred work acquireth long life and renown and ascendeth to heaven."

"A Brahmana whatever sins he may commit during the day through his senses, is freed from them all by reading the Bharata in the evening. Whatever sins he may commit also in the night by deed, words, or mind, he is freed from them all by reading the Bharata in the first twilight (morning)"

What effects such beliefs were likely to have upon the morals of a people we do not stop to enquire.

"Chaque peuple," says Prévost-Paradol "a dans son histoire un grand fait, anquel it rattache tout son passé et tout son avenir, et dont la memoire est un mot de ralliement, une promesse de salut. La fuite d'Egpte disaient les Juifs; le renversement des Mèdes, disaient les Perses; les guerres mèdiques disent à leur tour les Grecs. On les rappellera à tout propos pour en tirer des arguments, des prétentions politiques, des mouvements oratoires, des encouragements patriotiques dans les grandes crises, et plus tard, les regrets éternels."*

For the Indian people it is the Mahabharata and the field of Kurukshetra which is the central event of their history. It closes for them their golden age. Before that

---

* Essai sur l'histoire universelle par M. Prévost-Paradol, Tome premier, page 166.

was a world of transcendent knowledge and heroic deeds; since then intellectual decay and physical degeneracy. Nor is this merely a sentiment, it is a deeply rooted belief, which the highly-educated Indian holds in common with his ignorant countryman. I have known an educated Hindu to maintain with much warmth that in the golden age, the *Rishis* and others were well acquainted with the art of aërial navigation and probably with other rapid modes of locomotion unknown to us moderns. I have heard him assert boldly that even the telephone, microphone, and phonograph had been known to the Hindu sages up to the time when the sciences and arts of the ancient world perished, wholesale and *for ever*, with the heroes of the Mahabharata on the fatal field of Kurukshetra. However little one might be disposed to import such romantic statements into a sober History of Science, they are at any rate true as regards the non-existence of anything like even the germs of progressive science amongst the people of India from a very remote date up to the present time.

Of the one hundred thousand verses of the Mahabharata not more than a fourth part is concerned with the main story of the epic—the rest consists of more or less irrelevant though often beautiful episodes, and of disquisitions on government, morals and theology. It is the main story that I have endeavoured to reproduce in brief outline in this volume, and I have also attempted to preserve, as far as possible, the important doctrinal features of the great epic.

THE MAHABHARATA.

CHAPTER II.—The Story of the Great War.

Amongst the long line of kings descended from Chandra, the Moon, who reigned in Northern India, was Shantanu with whom our narrative may conveniently commence. This king was, like most of the sovereigns of his house, a pious man and an able administrator, whose sway, we are told, was owned *by the whole world.* He had two wives in succession, first the goddess Ganga, afterwards Satyavati, and the story of his loves is worth recording.

Strange as it may seem, his marriage with the lovely Ganga, the divinity of the sacred river Ganges, resulted from a curse uttered by one of those terrible saints, so common in Indian poetry, whose irritability of temper seems to have been in direct proportion to the importance of their austerities. The saint in question, Vasishta by name, was once engaged in his devotions when a party of celestial beings known as Vasus unwittingly passed between him and the rising or setting sun. "Be born among men!" exclaimed the irate Rishi to the unwelcome intruders, and his malediction, once uttered was, of course, irrevocable.* Expelled from Heaven these unfortunate Vasus were met by the Goddess Ganga to whom they explained their sad destiny, imploring of her to

---

* Adi Parva of the Mahabharata, Section XCVI. A somewhat different story is told in Section XCIX.

become a woman, so that they might be born of her and not of a mere mortal. The Goddess, who, on account of a slight indiscretion on her part, was herself under the obligation of assuming the human form, agreed to their proposal and made choice of Shantanu to be their father. The goddess promised the Vasus that as each one of them was born of her, he should be thrown, a mere infant, into the water and destroyed, so that all might regain their celestial home as speedily as possible. But Ganga stipulated that each one of the Vasus should contribute an eighth part of his energy for the production of a son who should be allowed to live his life on earth, but should himself die childless. These preliminaries being settled amongst the gods, behind the scenes as it were, the play had to be played out on the terrestrial stage with men as the puppets. To this end Ganga took an opportunity of presenting herself before Shantanu for the purpose of captivating his heart,—no difficult task for the Goddess. So one day as he was wandering along the banks of the Ganges "he saw a lovely maiden of blazing beauty and "like unto another *Sree* herself. Of faultless and pearly "teeth and decked with celestial ornaments, she was "attired in garments of fine texture and resembled in "splendour the filaments of the lotus. And the monarch "beholding that damsel became surprised. With steadfast gaze he seemed to be drinking her charms, but "repeated draughts failed to quench his thirst. The "damsel also beholding the monarch of blazing splendour "moving about in great agitation, was moved herself and "experienced an affection for him. She gazed and gazed "and longed to gaze at him evermore. The monarch "then in soft words addressed her and said: O thou "slender-waisted one, beest thou a goddess or the daughter "of a Danava, beest thou of the race of the Gandharvas, or "Apsaras, beest thou of the Yakshas or of the Nagas or "beest thou of human origin, O thou of celestial beauty, I "solicit thee to be my wife."

This wooing, simple enough in form and very much to the point, was, we need not say, entirely successful, the goddess without revealing her identity, consenting at once to become the king's wife, on condition that she should be free to leave him the moment he interfered with her actions or addressed an unkind word to her. The enamoured prince readily agreed to these terms and Ganga became his wife. Seven beautiful children born of this union were, to the king's intense horror, thrown by their mother, each in its turn, into the waters of the Ganges with the words: "This is for thy good." Shantanu's dread of losing the companionship of his lovely wife of whom he was dotingly fond kept him tongue-tied even in presence of such enormities; but when the eighth child was about to be destroyed, like the others, his paternal feelings could not be controlled and he broke out in remonstrance and upbraidings which saved the son's life, but lost him his wife's society for ever. Ganga, with much dignity, revealed herself to the king, explained to him the real circumstances of the case and the motives which had influenced her actions and, reminding him of the stipulations of the contract between them, took a kind but final farewell of the husband of so many years. She thereupon disappeared carrying the child away with her.

Later on, the river-goddess appeared once more to king Shantanu and made over to him his half-celestial son, a youth of the most wonderful intellect, learning, strength and daring. This son named indifferently, Ganga-datta and Deva-bratta was eventually best known as *Bhishma* or the *terrible* for a reason to be explained immediately.

In the foregoing legend about the incarnations of the Vasus we have an instructive and interesting illustration of the ideas of the Hindus with respect to the soul in man, which, as in this case, might be a spirit from the celestial regions. We also learn how the poor mortal's destiny on earth is but the fulfilment of predestined events.

Shantanu deserted by his goddess-queen seems to have had a heart ready for the reception of another love, and, as his romantic fortune would have it, he was one day rambling on the banks of the Jumna when his attention was attracted by a delicious perfume. To trace this fragrance to its source the king roamed hither and thither through the woods, "and, in the course of his rambles, he beheld a black-eyed maiden of celestial beauty the daughter of a fisherman." In those primitive times when men carried their hearts on their sleeves and the forms of social life were simple and natural no tedious courtship was necessary; so, "the king addressing her said: 'who art "thou, and whose daughter? What dost thou do here, "O timid one?' She answered, 'Blest be thou, I am the "daughter of the chief of the fishermen. At his com-

"mand for religious merit I am engaged in rowing the "passengers across this river in my boat.' And Shantanu "beholding that maiden of celestial form endued with "beauty, amiableness and such fragrance, desired her for "wife. And repairing unto her father the king solicited "his consent to the proposed match."

The fisherman was willing to bestow his daughter on the king, but only on condition that the son born to her should occupy the throne to the exclusion of all others. This was a difficulty that staggered the king, for he could not find it in his heart to set aside Devabratta the glorious son of Ganga. The matter accordingly dropped, but his disappointment was very great and he could not conceal from the world that there was something preying upon his mind. Devabratta, much concerned about Shantanu's unhappiness, found out the cause of it and going to the father of the sweet-scented maiden, Satyavati, formally renounced his own right to the succession and recorded a vow of perpetual celibacy.

Upon this "the Apsaras and the gods with the tribes "of the Rishis began to rain down flowers from the "firmament upon the head of Devabratta and exclaimed "'This one is Bhisma' (the terrible.)"

Everything was now arranged to the satisfaction of the contracting parties and Satyavati, the ferry-girl, became the proud queen of Bharatvarsha. But this beauteous and odoriferous damsel had already a history, which though unknown to the king, her husband, may be unfolded here.

In the discharge of her pious office of ferrying across

the Jumna those who desired it, the maiden on one occasion had as her companion in the boat "the great and wise Rishi Parashara, foremost of all virtuous men." This illustrious Saint, who seems to have had an eye for a pretty wench, immediately made advances to the boat-girl. Dread of her father and a natural disinclination of being seen from the shore made Satyavati coy; but, on the other hand, she was also in terror of the Rishi's curse, in case she disobliged him. The sage Parashara was not to be denied. He enveloped the boat in a mist, and, promising the boat-girl that her virgnity should be restored and that a certain fishy smell which emanated from her person should be changed into a sweet perfume, had his way with her. The offspring of this union was no other than the renowned *Vyasa* who arranged the Vedas and wrote the Mahabbharata, and of whom we shall hear more very soon.

Satyavati by her union with king Shantanu became the mother of two sons Chitrangada and Vichitra-virya. The former was after a short reign killed, *in a three years combat*, by the king of the Gandharvas, and Vichitra-virya was placed on the throne; but being a minor the kingdom was ruled by Bhishma in subordination to queen Satyavati. When the king was old enough to be married Bhisma set about finding a wife for him. Learning that the three lovely daughters of the king of Kasi would elect husbands in a public *swyamvara*, or maiden's choice, he repaired thither and, acting in accordance with the lawless customs of the times, carried the fair princesses off in his chariot, challenging any one and every one to fight him for the coveted prize. A desperate battle ensued, of the kind familiar to the reader of the previous portion of this volume. Bhisma, alone and unaided, assailed by ten thousand arrows at the same time, was able to check these missiles in mid-air by showers of innumerable darts from his own bow and after prodigious slaughter effected the object he had in view.* Of the three captured princesses one was allowed to go back to her people, as she explained that she had fully made up her mind to elect the king of Sanva for her husband, that he had given her his heart and that her father was willing. In her case the Swyamvara was, *it would appear, only intended to be a formal ceremony.* The other two princesses became the wives of Vichitra-virya; but after a short reign he died leaving behind him no heirs of his body.

This failure of issue threatened the extinction of the Lunar dynasty. But according to the ideas of those primitive times the deficiency of heirs might still be supplied, for Vichitravirya's two widows, Amvika and Amvalika, still survived and some kinsman might raise up seed to the dead

* The battle, as described by the poet, is of little interest; but Bhishma's challenge to the assembled kings is worthy of reproduction as throwing light upon the marriage customs of the olden time in India. "In a voice like the roar of the "clouds he exclaimed: 'The wise have directed that after inviting an accomplished "person a maiden may be bestowed on him, decked in ornaments and along with "many valuable presents. Others again may bestow their daughters by accepting "of a couple of kine, some again bestow their daughters by taking a fixed sum and "some take away maidens by force. Some wed with the consent of the maidens, "some by drugging them into consent, and some by going unto the maidens "parents and obtaining their sanction. Some again obtain wives as presents, for "assisting at sacrifices. Of these the learned always applaud the eighth form of "marriage. Kings however, speak highly of the Swyamvara (the fifth form as "above) and themselves wed according to it. But the sages have said that that "wife is dearly to be prized who is taken away by force, after slaughter of "opponents, from amid the concourse of princes and kings invited to a Swyamvara. "Therefore, ye monarchs I bear away these maidens from hence by force. Strive "ye to the best of your might to vanquish me or be vanquished'"—P. C. Roy's translation of the Adi Parva of the Mahabharata, page 307.

man. Queen Satyavati pressed Bhishma to undertake the duty, but he, unwittingly fulfilling his destiny, held his vow of celibacy too sacred to be broken even in such a dynastic emergency. On his refusal Satyavati thought of her son Vyasa as perpetuator of the Lunar race, and the sage, nothing loth, undertook the family duty and visited the widows in turn. Now this celebrated sage had, by reason of his austerities, a terrible and repulsive appearance. The elder widow Amvika shut her eyes when she saw him, as he approached in the lamp-light, and the son born of her was, in consequence, blind. The other widow was so blanched with fear at the sight of the sage that the son she gave birth to was of quite a pale complexion. The blind son was named Dhritarashtra and the white one Pandu.*

Neither of these sons being perfect Satyavati desired Vyasa to beget yet another son. For this purpose he was to visit Amvika again; but she, poor soul, had had enough of the wild-looking anchorite whose grim visage and strong odour had made a deep and disagreeable impression upon her; so she sent a beautiful slave girl to him in her stead. The Sudra maiden made herself agreeable to the sage who was, of course, too wise to be taken in by the attempted deception. "And when he rose up to go away he addressed her and said 'Amiable one, thou shalt no longer be a slave. Thy child also shall be greatly fortunate and virtuous and the foremost of all intelligent men on earth.'" This third son of Vyasa was named Vidura, and, although the offspring of a Sudra

* The custom referred to in this paragraph and known as *niyoga* is considered briefly in the concluding chapter.

wench, was, it seems, no other than the god of Justice himself incarnate in human form, owing, as we might well guess, to the *potent curse of a holy ascetic.* This is how it came about. The ascetic was performing his penances under a vow of silence when there came to his asylum a band of robbers fleeing from the officers of justice. They hid their booty and themselves in the asylum. The police officers who were on their track came to the asylum and requested the hermit to point out where the thieves had hidden themselves. The ascetic vouchsafed no answer, but the officers themselves soon found both the thieves and the stolen property. As an accomplice in the crime that had been committed, the ascetic was apprehended and sentenced to death. He was in due course impaled, but, even on the cruel stake which was rending his body, he serenely devoted himself to contemplation. For days he lived quietly upon the stake, a fact which was brought to the king's knowledge and greatly alarmed him. He came in person to the ascetic, addressed him with great humility, begged his forgiveness and ordered his immediate removal from the stake. All attempts to extract the stake having failed, it was cut off at the surface of the body and the ascetic, apparently none the worse for this addition to his internal economy, went about as usual, but he was by no means content. Of the God of Justice he demanded what crime he had committed which entailed so heavy a punishment. The God explained that the ascetic had once in his childhood pierced a little insect with a blade of grass hence his unpalement. In the Rishi's opinion the punishment was out of all proportion to the offence, particularly as the Shastras exempted children from responsibility for their actions, and, waxing wroth, he uttered the following imprecation. "Thou shalt, therefore, O god of Justice, have to be born among men even in the Sudra order."*

Dhritarashtra was set aside on account of his blindness and Vidura on account of his servile birth, so the *raj* fell to Pandu, during whose minority the country was governed by his uncle *Bhishma*.†

Pandu became a great and celebrated rajah. He had two wives Kunti and Madri. The former although very beautiful had no suitors in her maidenhood; so the king, her father, invited to his court the princes and monarchs of the neighbouring countries and desired Kunti to choose her husband from amongst his guests. The princess attracted by the appearance of Pandu who was there approached him modestly, and "quivering with emotion," as the poet tells us, placed the nuptial garland round his neck. In this romantic fashion Pandu got his first wife. For the second, Madri, who was selected for him by Bhishma, he had to pay a very considerable price in gold and precious stones, elephants, horses and other things, for, it seems, it was the custom in her family for the daughters to be disposed of for such price as could be got for them.

After he had reigned a while Pandu retired with his

---

* P. C. Roy's Adi Parva p. 325. This story throws considerable light on the ideas of the Hindus with respect to their gods.

† Vyasa, as we have seen, was no blood relation of the house of Bharata. Similarly the widows of king Vichitra-virya and the Sudra slave girl were not connected to the family by ties of consanguinity; and *yet the children of Vyasa by these women* are, from the Hindu point of view, lineal descendants of king Shantanu.

two wives into the forests on the slopes of the Himalaya mountains to indulge his love of freedom and the chase.

One day while out hunting he discharged his arrows at two deer sporting together. Now these, as ill luck would have it, were in reality a Brahman sage and his wife. In the agonies of death the Brahman assumed his proper form and, as we might expect, *cursed* the unfortunate Pandu saying that he would assuredly die in the embrace of one of his wives.

Up to this time Pandu had had no children, and owing to his dread of the Brahman's curse was cut off from any further hope of offspring. Deeming it a most indispensable religious duty to have heirs, he consulted the ascetics in the woods on the subject, saying: "Ye ascetics I am not yet freed from the debt I owe to my (deceased) ancestors! The best of men are born in this world to beget children for discharging that debt. I would ask ye, should children be begotten in my soil (upon my wives) as I myself was begotten in the soil of my father by the eminent Rishi?"

The ascetics having given the king an answer in the affirmative he desired his wife Kunti "to raise up offspring from the seed of some Brahman of high ascetic merit." But Kunti had another resource to fall back upon. It seems that in her maiden days she had pleased a Rishi by her attentions and he had taught her, as a reward, a *Mantra* or spell by the repetition of which she could cause any celestial being she thought of to present himself to her and be obedient to her will, whether he liked it or not. Of the efficacy of this spell Kunti had already had practical experience, for in her early days she had, just to test the value of the spell, compelled the attendance of Surya the sun-god and had a son by him named *Karna* of whom we shall hear again. Prudently omitting any mention of Surya and *Karna*, Kunti told her husband of the mantra she possessed, and, with his consent, had three sons *for him* by three different gods *viz.*, Yudhisthira by Dharma,* Bhisma by Vayu and Arjuna by Indra.

But Pandu wanted more sons and persuaded Kunti to communicate the spell to Madri who, greedy of offspring, summoned the twin Aswins to her bed and gave birth, in due course, to two sons Nakula and Sahadeva. These five sons, known as the five Pandavas, are the real heroes of the great war which forms the main incident of the Mahabharata.

Pandu himself met with a tragic end, for one day, in lovely spring weather, when wandering with his younger wife, Madri, through the pleasant woodlands he, in a weak moment yielded to his passions and in fulfilment of the Brahman's curse died in the arms of his wife, who in testimony of her affection for her husband and on the ground that she was his favourite wife had herself burnt with his remains.†

The party opposed to the Pandavas known as the Kauravas, consisted primarily of the one hundred sons of Dhritarashtra by his wife Gandhari. Of course it was necessary that persons who had to play a leading part in

---

* This parentage is rather bewildering after what we have learned already about *Vidura* being no other than Dharma in human form.

† This is an instance of *suttee* in ancient India worth noting.

the poet's story should come into the world in some extraordinary manner, and equally necessary that a *Rishi* should have a prominent share in the event. Gandhari appears to have been lucky enough to please, by her hospitalities, the great ascetic Dwaipayana and he granted her the boon she asked, *viz.*, one hundred sons, each equal to her lord in strength and accomplishments. Instead of sons, however, the queen gave birth to a shapeless mass of flesh and, in despair, was about to throw it away when the sage who, in his hermitage, knew exactly what was transpiring at the palace, appeared unexpectedly on the scene and cutting the piece of flesh into one hundred and one pieces placed each separately in a pot full of clarified butter; whence, in due time, one hundred sons and one daughter were taken out. Of these hundred sons, four, Duryodhana, Dushashana, Vikarna and Chittrasena afterwards became prominent characters in the story of this epic.

During the practical abdication of the throne by Pandu, Dhritarastra seems to have ruled the country; but Pandu's *sons*, as the Pandavas were considered to be, had a claim to the throne and the surviving widow of the ill-fated king proceeded at once to Hastinapur with the five boys. A great number of ascetics accompanied them and having testified before Dhritarastra and his court to the celestial parentage of these sons of Kunti and Madri vanished into thin air before the eyes of all present. The young sons of Pandu were, after this, well received by the blind old king and took up their abode with his wife Gandhari and his sons. But the cousins, if such they can be called, could not live amicably together and many feuds arose between them. To such a pass did the bitterness of feeling between the kinsmen come that the eldest son of the blind king, jealous of the strength of Bhima, cunningly drugged him, bound him hand and foot and then flung him into the Ganges. But Bhima did not perish. As he sank through the water, snakes attacked him and the venom of their bites, counteracting the effects of the drug he had swallowed, restored him to consciousness. He immediately burst his bonds and found that he had descended to the city of the Serpent-king in the interior of the earth, where he was hospitably entertained and given a draught of nectar which endowed him with the strength of *ten thousand elephants*. After that he was carried by the Nagas from under the waters and restored to the place whence he had been thrown into the river. On his return to Hastinapur, Bhima related his adventures to his brothers, but was cautioned to say nothing about the matter in the presence of his cousins, so as not to awaken their suspicions.

In accordance with the warlike tastes of the times all the young princes, Dhritarastra's sons and nephews alike, were trained to arms and instructed in the science of warfare by a famous *Brahman* preceptor named Drona, on condition that they would fight for him against Draupada, Rajah of Panchala with whom he had a feud of long standing. This Drona, it is needless to say, was of extraordinary origin, otherwise he would not have been preceptor to the princes. He was the son of a Rishi named Bharadwaja, but was not born of woman. The Pandavas and their cousins had also another famous tutor named Kripa who had sprung into existence from a clump of heather.

When the scions of the royal house of Pandu had been sufficiently trained in the use of arms, their preceptor, Drona, arranged for an exhibition of their skill before the chiefs and people of the Raj. An auspicious day was fixed upon and the people informed by proclamation of the important function. It was a day of excitement and bustle in the land of the Kurus; spectators flocked from far and near to witness the royal assault-at-arms. The wealthier part of the visitors pitched their tents near the arena and others put up convenient stages from which to view the events of the day. For the king and his courtiers a theatre was erected "according to the rules laid down in the scriptures." It was constructed of gold and adorned with strings of pearls and lapis lazuli. The ladies had a separate gallery to themselves and came to the fête gorgeously attired.

Amidst the blare of trumpets and the sound of drums, Drona, all in white, his Brahmanical cord conspicuously displayed, entered the arena attended by his son. The young princes followed in the order of their ages. After some preliminary displays of dexterity in archery and fencing and of skill in horsemanship and the management of war-chariots, a contest with maces came off between Duryodhana and Bhima. They *roared* at each other "like two mad elephants contending for a female one" and what was meant to be a sham fight soon changed into a real combat. The princely competitors, actuated by mutual animosity, charged each other "like infuriated elephants" and battered each other most vindictively with their ponderous maces. This single combat caused great excitement amongst the spectators, who took sides, and applauded their favourites. Drona had to interpose between the heated combatants. He commanded the music to cease, and, to make a diversion, quickly brought forward Arjuna, clad in golden mail, to display his inimitable skill in bowmanship. In this art, the most important of the warlike arts in the India of those times, Arjuna hopelessly surpassed all his rivals and, indeed, besides the extraordinary skill he displayed, there was much to wonder at in his performances, for, "by the *Agneya* weapon he created fire and by the *Varuna* weapon he created water, and by the *Vayavya* weapon he created air and by the *Paryanya* weapon he created clouds and by the *Bhanma* weapon he created land and by the *Parvatya* weapon mountains came into being. And by the *Antardhyana* weapon these were all made to disappear."

When the exhibition was nearly over a formidable champion thundered at the gates of the arena. It was Karna, son of Kunti, already mentioned, and, as became the offspring of the Sun-god, an archer of most wonderful skill. On being admitted the tall and handsome Karna, proudly arrayed in the glittering coat of mail in which he was born and the ear-rings which had similarly come into the world with him, presented a dazzling and most striking appearance. He haughtily assured Arjuna that he would perform before the multitude there assembled, feats that would excel all that had been exhibited that day. He even expressed his eagerness for a single combat with the hero. The two glorious sons of Kunti, unconscious of their relationship, appeared in the lists; their respective fathers Indra and Surya anxiously watched events from their positions in the welkin and Kunti, as became a fond mother, fainted away. At this juncture Kripa interposed, enquiring the race and lineage of the new comer. This action on Kripa's part was, apparently, only a device to avert the threatened fight. Duryodhana was furious at this interruption and to remove any objection on the score of difference of rank between the contending parties raised Karna, on the spot, to the Rajahship of Anga not, however, without the indispensable aid of the Brahmans, their *mantras* and ceremonies. All this took time; and more time was wasted in altercations in which Bhima took a prominent part, insulting Karna in an outrageous fashion to the great indignation of Duryodhana. Presently the sun went down over the scene and the royal tournament with its exciting incidents was necessarily brought to an end.

The princes having thus publicly proved that they were capable of bearing arms, Drona called upon them to fulfil their part of the terms upon which he had educated them. Joint or common action amongst the cousins being out of the question the Kauravas and their friends went forth alone and attacked the Rajah of Panchala. They were defeated and compelled to retreat. Then the Pandavas marched out against their tutor's enemy and after a bloody conflict, of the usual kind,—in which arrows fly from each single bow like flights of locusts; in which thousands of elephants, horses and men are slain, in which the principal combatants although pierced with scores of shafts seem none the worse for them, the Pandavas met with complete success, bringing the defeated Rajah along with them as a prisoner. He was afterwards liberated at the expense of half his kingdom which was appropriated by the successful Drona.

Fresh causes of jealousy arose between the cousins. Yudhishthira's claim to the succession could not be set aside, as the people were all in favour of him ; so he was appointed by the blind king, very reluctantly we may presume, to the office of *Yuvarajah* or heir-apparent. The Pandavas elated by their success against the king of Panchala and confident in themselves commenced a series of unprovoked attacks upon the neighbouring princes. Of course the Pandavas performed prodigies of valour in these invasions. For example, two of them with a single chariot, "subjugated all the kings of the East backed by ten thousand chariots."

These great achievements inflamed the jealousy of even the blind king to such a pitch that he disclosed his feelings to Kanika his Brahman counsellor "well skilled in the science of politics." As became a sage politician Kanika advised his master to put the obnoxious Pandavas out of the way as soon as possible. He explained to Dhritarastra his obvions duty in such a case and impressed upon his sovereign such important maxims of state policy as the following : "when thy foe is in thy power destroy him by every means open or secret : Do not show him any mercy although he seeketh thy protection * * * * If thy son, friend, brother, father or even spiritual preceptor, becometh thy foe, thou shouldst, if desirous of prosperity, slay him without scruples. By curses and incantations, by gift of wealth, by poison, or by deception the foe should be slain. He should never be neglected from disdain"

His counsels fell on only too willing ears. Dhritarastra was ready to do his *duty* as thus explained to him ; but thought it best to act warily. Duryodhana suggested that the Pandavas should be induced to go to Varanavartha* and there disposed of.

Praises of this place were cunningly circulated in Dritharastra's court and the king suggested to the Pandavas that they might go there for a holiday. Suspicions naturally arose in the minds of the sons of Pandu; but there seemed to be no way of eluding the kings proposal. Their departure was a day of public mourning in Hastinapur and before they went Vidura found an opportunity to warn them of a plot which had been formed to burn them to death in a house made of combustible materials which would be erected for their reception at Varanavartha. To be forewarned was to be fore-armed, and the Pandavas determined to be even with their enemies. Purochana a confidential agent of Duryodhana's, preceded them on their journey and began, in all haste, to construct for their reception at Varanavartha and for their ultimate destruction by fire, the famous *house of lac*. What sort of a mansion this was we may judge from Yudhisthara's opinion of it expressed confidentially to Bhima, after a critical inspection of the edifice, on their

* The modern Allahabad and, at that time, probably a frontier town of the Aryan invaders.

arrival at their destination. "The enemy, it is evident by "the aid of trusted artists, well skilled in the construction "of houses have finely built this mansion, after procuring "hemp, resin, heath, straw and bamboos all soaked in "clarified butter."

To escape destruction should their house be set on fire the Pandavas secretly caused a subterranean passage to be made leading out of the dwelling. The work was executed by a trusty messenger, well skilled in mining, who had been sent to their assistance by Vidura. One evening Kunti fed a large number of Brahmans at this combustible house of hers. After the guests were gone the Pandavas, assuring themselves that their enemy Purochana was fast asleep, quietly fastened the doors of the house and themselves set fire to it in several places. As if impelled by *Fate*, a Nishada woman with her five sons had come uninvited guests to Kunti's feast and, becoming intoxicated with the wine of which they had partaken too freely, lay drunk upon the premises. These six drunk and incapable persons perished with Purochana, and their remains, found by the citizens after the conflagration had been extinguished, left no doubt in men's minds that Kunti and her sons had all been miserably burnt to death.

The five Pandava brothers *disguised as Brahmans*, accompanied by their mother Kunti, made their escape into the forests and commenced a long course of wanderings in which they experienced much hardship and many adventures. Often were they wearied out by their long marches, all except the giant Bhima, who on such occasions, would carry the whole family on his back and shoulders or under his arms. Of this episode Bhima is indisputably the hero. It is he who forces his way by giant strength through the almost impenetrable forests, treading down trees and creepers to make a passage for himself and his burden. It is he who kills the terrible Rakshasa bent upon devouring Kunti and her sons. It is Bhima with whom the cannibal's sister falls ardently in love and whom, after strange adventurous journeys through the air, she eventually makes the happy father of a son, Ghatotkacha, afterwards a famous champion in the final struggles between the rival parties. It is Bhima again who when they sojourned in Ekachakra (the inhabitants of which town had to pay a daily toll of a live human being for the table of a fierce Rakshasa) killed the monster single-handed and delivered the trembling citizens from the gloomy horror under which they had been living.*

During their residence at Ekachakra, where they lived disguised as Brahmans, the Pandavas were visited by the famous Rishi Vyasa, who, it will be remembered, was really their grandfather and also the compiler of the Mahabharata itself. By him they were informed that the lovely princess, Krishná or Draupadi, the daughter of the king of the Panchalas was about to hold a *swayamvara*, or "self-choice," at which she would select a husband. Vyasa also told them the wonderful history of this Draupadi and thereby greatly excited their interest and curiosity in the handsome maiden who was no ordinary girl, but had sprung into existence, mature and beautiful,

* I don't think it is at all unlikely that cannibalism prevailed in India at this early period, as it does in Africa to-day and these stories are only the Hindu bard's exaggerated way of recording the fact.

in the midst of a great sacrifice for offspring, offered by Draupada, king of the Panchalas.

When, as has already been narrated, Draupada was defeated by Drona and deprived by him of half his kingdom, a spirit of revenge took complete possession of the discomfited monarch and his one thought was to find a means of compassing the overthrow of his successful foe, the redoubtable son of Bharadwaja. How could this object be attained when there was not a single one amongst the heroes of Panchala to cope with Drona, that mightiest of bowmen and possessor of the terrible *Brahma-weapon?* In such a difficulty the Indian chieftain naturally built his hopes upon those great national resources—the assistance of potent Brahmans and the efficacy of properly conducted sacrifices. For the handsome fee of ten thousand kine the king succeeded in inducing a couple of learned Brahmans, who had long been engaged in austerities, to undertake a sacrifice for the express purpose of obtaining a son who should be invincible in war and capable of slaying Drona. The result of the ceremonies and sacrifices conducted by the learned and not too scrupulous Brahmans was completely successful, for out of the sacrificial flames which they had kindled emerged a stately youth encased in full armour, with a crown on his head and bearing a bow and arrows in his hands. He was wonderful to behold and appeared upon the scene uttering loud roars. This was Dhristadyumna. After him appeared a beautiful maiden. "Her "eyes were black, and large as lotus leaves, her complexion "was dark and her locks were blue and curly. Her "nails were beautifully convex and bright as burnished "copper, her eyebows were fair and her bosom was deep. "* * * * * Her body emitted a fragrance as that "of a blue lotus, perceivable from a distance of "full two miles" This damsel because she was so dark complexioned received the name of Krishni (the dark,) but is more commonly known as Draupadi. Being the most lovely woman in the world at that time, her *Swayamvara* would, naturally attract the chiefs and princes of all nations, and not chiefs and princes only, but also Brahmans in crowds ready to graciously accept the presents which the liberality or ostentation of the high-born suitors might prompt them to distribute on the occasion.

The young Pandavas were much excited about the coming event and set off without delay to witness and, if possible, to take part in the proceedings of lovely Draupadi's *Swayamvara*. When they arrived at Panchala they took up their abode in the house of a humble potter and, still disguised as Brahmans, supported themselves by begging alms of the people.

A great amphitheatre covered with a canopy was prepared for the important occasion. It was erected on a level plain surrounded by lofty seven-storeyed palaces covered with gold, set with diamonds and adorned with garlands of fragrant flowers. In these costly mansions "perfectly white and resembling the cloud-kissing peaks of Kailasa" were lodged the kings and princes who had been invited to the *Swayamvara* by the father of Draupadi. Commodious platforms were constructed all round the amphitheatre for the convenience of less august visitors, and on one of these platforms the Pandavas found places for themselves in the company of a number of Brahmans. Public rejoicings, music, dancing and performances of various kinds, extending over sixteen days, served as a prelude to the business of the great assembly. At one end of the plain a tall pole was erected and on the top of this pole was fixed a golden fish and below the golden fish a *chakra*, or wheel, kept whirling round and round. The condition of the *Swayamvara* was that each competitor should be provided with a particular bow and five selected arrows. If he succeeded with these in discharging an arrow through the *chakra* and in striking the eye of the golden fish behind it he should be the husband of the dark beauty of Panchala.

On the sixteenth day, when the meeting-place was quite full, Draupadi entered the amphitheatre richly attired and adorned with ornaments. In her hands she carried a golden dish with the usual offerings to Agni the god of fire and a garland of flowers for the neck of the happy man who should win her in the competition. After the offerings had been cast into the sacrificial fire and the appropriate *mantras* recited by the Brahmans appointed to perform the duty, Dhristadyumna led his sister before the assembly and, in a loud voice, proclaimed the conditions of the competition.

Amongst the innumerable suitors present there, we need only mention Duryodhana and Karna who are already known to the reader.

The sight of the beautiful Draupadi fired the ardour

of the assembled princes. One after the other they came forward to essay the feat, but, though they tugged and strained and sweated till their faces were distorted and their clothes disordered, they were not even able to string the mighty bow. Karna at length stepped up and stringing the bow with ease placed an arrow for the trial. But seeing Karna, Draupadi loudly exclaimed: "I will not elect a Suta for my lord."* "Then Karna, laughing in vexation and casting a glance on the sun, threw aside the bow already drawn to a circle." Other competitors, princes of great renown, still pressed forward to try what they could do, but met with no success. When all the Kshatriya lords had retired discomfited, Arjuna advanced from his place amongst the Brahmans and amidst a great deal of clamour strung the bow and, with unerring skill, shot the mark. A tumultuous shout arose from the assembled multitude, there was a great uproar in the firmament and the gods showered down flowers upon the happy hero. "And Krishná beholding the mark shot and beholding Partha (Arjuna) also like unto Indra himself, who had shot the mark, was filled with joy and approached the son of Kunti with a white robe and a garland of flowers." The Kshatriya Rajas and chiefs were wild at their defeat by a Brahman, and although they were prepared to admit that their kingdoms, and they themselves also, existed solely for the benefit of the Brahmans, they demurred to such a conclusion of the *Swayamvara* of a Kshatriya princess and made a fierce

* Karna had been brought up in the family of a Suta or charioteer and was reckoned as belonging to that caste.

attack upon king Draupada who was willing to hand Draupadi over to the victor. Arjuna rushed at once to the king's rescue, accompanied by the redoubtable Bhima armed with nothing less than an uprooted tree and, though a desperate fight ensued, the Pandava brothers succeeded, partly through the mediation of *Krishna*—whom we here meet for the first time—, in leaving the amphitheatre, closely followed by beautiful Draupadi.

Then those illustrious "sons of Pretha returning to "the potter's abode, approached their mother. And those "first of men represented Yájnaseni (Draupadi) unto their "mother as the *alms* they had obtained that day. And "Kunti who was there within the room and saw not her "sons, replied, saying, 'Enjoy ye all (what ye have obtain-"ed.)'" The moment after she beheld Krishná and then she said "Oh, what have I said?" However, Draupadi was fated to have five husbands, for, in a previous existence on the earth, she had, on five different occasions, asked the gods for a good husband as the reward of the austerities she practised. Yudhishthira knew this. It had been revealed to him by Vyasa. So when the matter was referred to him, as head of the family, he said simply: "The auspicious Draupadi shall be the common wife of us all;" a décision which pleased his brothers considerably for, as the poet tells us, "The sons of Pandu then hearing those words of their eldest brother, began to revolve them in their minds in great cheerfulness."

Their life in the potter's house was simplicity itself. Krishná prepared the food for the family and served it out to the several members, taking only a little for herself and eating it last of all. At night all seven slept on a bed of *kusa* grass covered with deer skins. The brothers lay side by side, their mother along the line of their heads, and Krishná "along the line of their feet as their nether pillow."

When Draupadi, nothing loth, had gone away with the handsome victor, the king of Panchala was naturally very anxious to find out who the successful suitor really was. By a little artful evesdropping on the part of Dhrishta-dyumna the secret became known to him and he rejoiced to find what a good match Krishá had made. Draupada caused great preparations to be undertaken for the wedding. He did not quite like the proposed five-fold arrangement; but was induced to consent to it, after Vyasa himself had explained to him how polyandry was not in itself sinful and how this particular marriage had been pre-arranged by *Destiny.* It only remained for Draupadi to be led round the sacred fire on five successive days by the five brothers in turn. After the five weddings the king of the Panchalas made valuable presents to Draupadi's husbands, including gold, chariots, horses and elephants, "and he also gave them a hundred female servants all in the prime of youth and decked in costly robes and ornaments and floral wreaths." Krishna also bestowed upon the happy Pandavas presents of various sorts,—costly robes, soft blankets, golden ornaments, and superb vessels set with gems and diamonds. And in addition to these, "many elephants and horses, crores of gold coins and thousands of young and beautiful female servants brought from various countries."*

The alliance thus formed with the Raja of Panchala made a great change in the fortunes of the Pandavas and induced their cousins at Hastinapur to make overtures of friendship to them. The negotiations led, at length, to an amicable arrangement by which the Kauravas continued to remain and rule at Hastinapur, while the Pandavas were assisted to settle themselves in Khandava-prastha on the banks of the Jumna. The portion of the country assigned to the sons of Pandu "was an unreclaimed desert" but they soon built a gorgeous and wonderful city there, Indra-prastha,† "surrounded by a trench as wide as the sea and by walls reaching high into the heavens * * * * * and the gateways that protected the town were high as the Mandara mountain and massy as the clouds."

At Indra-prastha the brothers lived happily with their wife, having, upon the advice of a Rishi, arranged "that when one of them would be sitting with Draupadi, if any other of the four would see that one thus, he (the intruder), must retire into the forest for twelve years passing his days as a Brahmachárin." One day a Brahman who had been robbed of his cattle came in great haste to the king's palace, and, lamenting bitterly, accused the Pandavas of allowing him to be deprived of his property by contempt-

* From this story of Draupadi it seems evident that polyandry was practised at least in parts of ancient India; as, indeed, it is, to this day, in portions of the Himalayan region. That it was not very uncommon in the old time we may gather from a remark attributed to Karna in reference to Draupadi herself,—"women always like to have many husbands." (Adi Parva of the Mahabharata Section CCIV.)

† "Again the site of Indra-prastha is far more distinctly indicated than the site of Hastinapur. The pilgrim who wends his way from the modern city of Delhi to pay a visit to the strange relics of the ancient world which surround the mys-

ible thieves. Arjuna, recognising his duty to afford the Brahman redress and protection, resolved to pursue the robbers; but his arms were in the room where Draupadi was sitting with Yudhisthira. Balancing against each other the sin of allowing the Brahman's wrongs to go unavenged and the breach of decorum involved in entering the chamber when his brother was engaged with Draupadi, he deliberately chose the latter, notwithstanding the consequences of their mutual agreement on that point. Once in possession of his arms he pursued the thieves, recovered the stolen property and restored it to the Brahman; but on returning to the palace be voluntarily determined to go into exile in fulfilment of the terms of the compact about Draupadi.

Arjuna's twelve years of exile were full of adventure. At the spot where the Ganges enters the plains (Hurdwar) he stepped into the sacred stream for a bath, was drawn down into the water by Ulupi the daughter of the king of the Nagas and taken by her to the beautiful mansion of her father. The love-sick Ulupi courted Arjuna so warmly that he could not find it in his heart to resist her solicitations. In return Ulupi bestowed upon Arjuna the gift of invisibility in water.

From one sacred stream to another, from one holy place to another, wandered the willing exile, giving away much wealth to the Brahmans. At length he travelled as far as Munipur. Now the king of Munipur had a beauti-

terious Kutub will find on either side of his road a number of desolate heaps of the débris of thousands of years, the remains of successive capitals which date back to the very dawn of history, and local tradition still points to these sepulchres of departed ages as the sole remains of the Raj of the sons of Pandu and their once famous city of Indra-prastha." Wheeler's History of India Vol. I. page 142.

ful daughter named Chitrángadá. Arjuna saw and fell desperately in love with the fair maiden. He asked her hand in marriage and obtained it on condition that the first son born of the union should be considered to belong to the king of Munipur, in order to succeed him on the throne of that country. Three years did Arjuna live at Munipur, but when a son was born to Chitrángdá he took an affectionate farewell of her and set out again upon his wanderings. Visiting many lands and experiencing strange adventures, he at length arrived at Dwarka on the shore of the Southern Sea, the capital of his kinsman, Krishna, King of the Yadhavas. A casual sight of Subhadrá, the handsome sister of Krishna, made a strong and visible impression upon the susceptible heart of Arjuna. Krishna perceived the effect produced by his sister's charms and was not indisposed to an alliance with the Pandava hero. Should Subhadrá, now of age, hold a *swayamvara* or maiden's choice? Krishna thought the result of such a plan might be disappointing; for who could say what choice a capricious girl might make! So, he artfully suggested to Arjuna to carry off the maiden by force, since "in the case of Kshatriyas that are brave, a forcible abduction for purposes of marriage is applauded, as the learned have said." Arjuna who was ready to achieve anything achievable by man to obtain "that girl of sweet smiles," soon put the suggestion into practice, to the great indignation of the Yadhava chiefs; but Krishna threw oil upon the troubled waters and everything was amicably settled in the end, the wedding being celebrated on a magnificent scale. After the prescribed twelve years of exile were completed, Arjuna returned to Khandavaprastha with Subhadrá and was loyally welcomed by all. But when he visited Draupadi she evinced very natural signs of jealousy and recommended Arjuna to go to the daughter of the Satwata race. However he coaxed her over and when Subhadrá, dressed in red silk, but in the simple fashion of a cow-keeper, approached and bowed down to Draupadi saying "I am thy maid," her resentful feelings were disarmed; she rose hastily and embraced her young rival with the significant greeting: "Let thy husband be without a foe."

Krishna the King of Dwarka now visited his brother-in-law in great state and brought with him a vast store of valuable gifts, amongst which we need only notice "a thousand damsels well skilled in assisting at the operations of bathing and at drinking." No light recommendations apparently, for it would seem, that in those good old times the practice of drinking wine was quite common; as we are told by the poet, in connection with a great picnic given by Arjuna and Krishna, that "the women of "the party, all of full rotund hips and fine deep bosoms "and handsome eyes and gait unsteady with wine, began "to sport there at the command of Krishna and Partha "(Arjuna). And some amongst the women sported as "they liked in the woods and some in the waters and "some within the mansions as directed by Partha and "Govinda (Krishna). And Draupadi and Subhadrá "exhilarated with wine began to give away unto the "women so sporting their costly robes and ornaments. "And some amongst those women began to dance in joy "and some began to sing, and some amongst them began "to laugh and jest and some to drink excellent wines."

The picnic referred to was succeeded by a terrible conflict in which Krishna and Arjuna, in the interests of Agni, opposed Indra and his celestial hosts. Agni, the god of fire, having drunk a continuous stream of clarified butter for twelve years, during the sacrifice of King Swetaki, was satiated with his greasy fare, had become pale and could not shine as before. To recover his health a change of diet was necessary for the god and he, therefore, wished to devour, with his flaming tongues, the forest of Khandava in that land; but whenever he attempted to do this, Indra opposed him, quenching the flames raised by the Fire-god with torrents of rain from above. However, Arjuna, in his wonderful way, "covered the forest "of Khandava with innumerable arrows, like the moon "covering the atmosphere with a thick fog," and in this, manner protected the burning forest from Indra's drenching showers. A fierce battle with Indra, backed by Asuras Gandharvas, Yakshas and a host of others, resulted in the complete victory of Arjuna and his kinsman, in the total consumption of the forest by fire, and the almost wholesale destruction of all its inhabitants, of every kind.

Only six of the dwellers in the forest of Khandava were allowed to escape with their lives, Aswa-Sena, Maya and four birds called *Sharugakos*. Now Maya was the chief architect of the Danavas and, in gratitude for his preservation, built a wonderful *Sabha*, or hall, for the Pandavas, the most beautiful structure of its kind in the whole world.

One day while the Pandavas were holding their court in this hall the celestial Rishi Narada visited them and the subject of conversation having turned upon the splendours of Maya's handiwork, the Rishi described the courts of Indra, Yama, Varuna and Kuvera, as also "the assembly-house of the Grandsire, that house which none can describe saying, it is such, for within a moment it assumes a different form that language fails to paint."

Within the narrow limits I have allowed myself, these highly interesting pictures of the different heavens of the Hindus cannot be reproduced; but their more salient features must not be passed over, since they are highly characteristic of the ideas of the people who conceived them. The hall of Brahma, the Supreme Being, the creator of everything, is an indescribable mansion, peopled by a most august, if somewhat shadowy, assembly. Here, in the presence of the Grand-sire of all, attend, in their personified forms, the various forces and phenomena of Nature, such as Time and Space, Heat and Air, Day and Night, the Months and Seasons the Years and *Yugas*. Here also are ever to be found Religion, Joy, Tranquility, Aversion and and Asceticism ; here Wisdom, Intelligence and Fame; here the four Vedas, Sacrifices and Mantras. Here also perpetually attend, Hymns, Dramas, Songs and Stories, together with all the Sciences, in the company of countless celestial Rishis and all the Dieties.

The courts of the other Gods which are less solemn and sedate, always resound with strains of delightful vocal and instrumental music and are enlivened with the graceful dancing of the charming Apsaras and Gandharvas.

But it is Yama's *Sabha* that most concerns the human race, for it is there that, for the most part, the disembodied spirits of men are to be found. "Bright as burnished "gold that assembly house, covers an area of much more "than an hundred *Yojanas*. Possessed of the splendour "of the sun it yieldeth everything that one may desire. "Neither very cool nor very hot, it delighteth the heart. "In that assembly-house there is neither grief nor weak-"ness of age, neither hunger nor thirst. Nothing disagree-"able findeth a place there, nor wretchedness or distress. "There can be no fatigue or any kind of evil feelings "there. Every object of desire, celestial or human, is to "be found in that mansion. And all kinds of enjoyable "articles, as also of sweet juicy, agreeable, and delicious "edibles in profusion that are licked, sucked and drunk, "are there. And the floral wreaths in that mansion are "of the most delicious fragrance, and the trees that stand "around it yield fruits that are desired of them. And there "are both cold and hot waters and these are sweet and agree-"able. And in that mansion many royal sages of great "sanctity and Brahmana sages also of great purity wait "upon and worship Yama, the son Vivaswat. * * * "* * * * * And Agastya and Mataiya and Kála and "Mrityu (Death), performers of sacrifices and Siddhas "and many Yogins; the *Pitris* * * * * the wheel "of time and the illustrious conveyer himself of the "sacrificial butter; all sinners among human beings as "also that have died during the winter solstice; those "officers of Yama who have been appointed to count the "allotted days of every body and every thing, the *Shing-*

"*shapa*, *Palasha*, *Kasha* and *Kusha* trees and plants, in "their embodied forms:—these all, wait upon and worship "the God of Justice in that assembly house of his * * "* * * * * * * * And many illustrious Gan-"dharvas and many Apsaras, fill every part of that man-"sion with music both instrumental and vocal and with "the sounds of laughter and dance. And excellent per-"fumes, and sweet sounds, and garlands of celestial flowers "always contribute to make that mansion supremely blest. "And hundreds of thousands of virtuous persons of celes-"tial beauty and great wisdom always wait upon and "worship the illustrious lord of created beings in that "assembly house."*

During the period in the history of the Pandavas which we have now reached Draupadi bore five sons† to her five husbands and Subhadrá also became the mother of the afterwards famous Abhimanyu.

In their new home the Pandavas had flourished greatly and having established an undisputed supremacy over all the chieftains in their immediate neighbourhood they thought of performing a *rajasuya* or sacrifice of triumph, a sort of formal declaration of imperial claims. But there was a serious difficulty in the way of the accomplishment of this proud function; for there reigned at Mathura the capital of Magadha a powerful king named Jarásandha who having himself already brought no less

* Such is the Hindu Poet's conception of the court of Yama, the god of departed spirits, a delightful place where there is no lack of sensuous pleasures. He places amongst the attendants in this court "all sinners amongst human beings;" but as, according to Brahmanical theology, there is punishment for the wicked, we may presume that the sinners referred to are only temporary sojourners in this pleasant abode, awaiting their trial and the judgment of Yama upon their deeds.

† Pratibhindhya, Sutasoma, Sutakarna, Shotanika and Srutasena.

than *eighty six* kings under his dominion was not, by any means, likely to acknowledge the superiority of Yudhisthira. Hence it followed that until Jarásandha were overcome the *rajasuya* could not be undertaken.

To conquer or otherwise dispose of Jarásandha was, therefore, the problem before the sons of Pandu. Their kinsman Krishna, "foremost of personages whose strength consists in wisdom and policy," was on a visit to Indraprastha and willingly accompanied Arjuna and Bhima (all three disguised as Brahmans) to Mathura. Once in the presence of their formidable rival they threw off the mask and made themselves known to him. Krishna upbraided Jarásandha with his cruel purpose of offering up the vanquished kings whom he held in captivity as sacrifices to the god Rudra and, without hesitation, intimated that he and his companions had come to Mathura expressly to slay him. In addressing the king of Magadha, Krishna gave expression to sentiments which remind one forcibly of the warlike ideas of the Norsemen. "Know," said he, "O bull among men that Kshatriyas engage in battle with heaven in view * * * * * * Study of Vedas, great fame, ascetic penances, and death in battle are all acts that lead to heaven. The attainment of heaven by the other three acts may be uncertain. But death in battle hath that for its certain consequence." The challenge thus given was accepted in the chivalrous spirit of the times. A single and public combat was arranged between Bhima and Jarásandha. Crowds of all classes of citizens, including women, were present to see the event. Both heroes fought without weapons. The encounter, which was carried on with great ferocity, lasted thirteen days without intermission for rest or food, and finally resulted in Jarásandha's back-bone being broken against Bhima's knee. "And the roar of the Pandava mingling with that of Jarásandha while he was being broken on Bhima's knee caused a loud uproar that stuck fear into the heart of every creature." After Jarásandha had been slain Krishna released his royal prisoners and engaged them to assist Yudhishthira in the celebration of the proposed *rajasuya* sacrifice.

After the occurrences at Muthura had been made known to Yudhisthira he dispatched his four brothers to the four points of the compass to collect tribute from all the Rajahs of the world.* These expeditions were fruitful of wonderful adventures, but we have not space to recount them here though we must not omit to note, in passing, that when those unprovoked aggressors, the sons of Pandu, vanquished any prince who offered resistance, he at once, and as a matter of course, joined the victors with his forces and helped to subjugate the unfortunate king upon whose territories the advancing tide of invasion next broke.†

As a sequel to the conquests of the Pandavas a crowd of Brahmans with scores of Rajahs flocked to Indraprastha, from all parts of the country and were right

* It would appear that only one of the armies—that which proceeded northward—went outside the limits of India to the countries immediately beyond the Himalayas. India, with the region just referred to, was, for the poets of the Mahabharata the *whole world*. On this point see Dr. Rajendra Lalla Mitra's Indo Aryans Vol. II pp. 9-12.

† This statement which is so consistent with what is known in respect to genuine historical events in India throws a strong side-light upon the utter inability of the Indian kings, from time immemorial, to unite for purposes of defence, their ready acceptance of defeat and their willing allegiance to the conqueror.

royally lodged and entertained by Yudhisthira's commands. The various duties demanded by the occasion were entrusted to the different members of the family and to intimate friends of the Pandavas. Dushasana was appointed to cater for the visitors. Kripa to look after the gold and gems. Duryodhana to receive the tributes. And Krishna, at his own desire, was engaged in washing the feet of the Brahmans.

Arrangements for the Rajasuya were pushed forward and all was hubbub and excitment in Indraprastha. The Brahman sages found the occasion a grand one for disputations with one another and they took full advantage of it; but a suppressed fire of discontent and jealously was smouldering in the hearts of the assembled Rajahs, which was set ablaze by a proposal to regard Krishna as the foremost chieftain present. Angry and contemptuous objections were made to his being given precedence in the assembly. The wise Bhishma, however, fully aware who and what his kinsman really was, solemnly, assured the malcontents that "Krishna is the "origin of the universe and that in which the universe is "to dissolve. Indeed this universe of mobile and immobile "creatures has sprung into existence for Krishna only. "He is the unmanifest primal matter, the creator, the "eternal and beyond (the ken of) all creatures." Notwithstanding this testimony the opposition did not cease. Indeed Shishupala, the mighty king of Chedi, ridiculed the old man's words, heaped contempt upon Krishna, and eventually, with many taunts and jeers, challenged him to fight. "And while Shishupala was speaking thus, the exalted slayer of Madhu thought in his mind of the discus that humbleth the pride of the Asuras. And as soon as the discus came into his hands the illustrious one skilled in speech loudly uttered these words! Listen, ye lords of earth, why this one had hitherto been pardoned by me. Asked by his mother an hundred offences (of his) were to be pardoned by me. Even this was the boon she had asked and even this I granted her. That number, ye kings, hath become full. I shall now slay him in your presence, ye monarchs. Having said this, the chief of the Yadus, that slayer of all foes, in anger instantly cut off the head of the ruler of Chedi by means of his discus. And the mighty-armed one fell down like a cliff struck with thunder. And the assembled kings then beheld a fierce energy, like unto the sun in the sky issue out of the body of the king of Chedi. And that energy then adored Krishna possessed of eyes like lotus leaves and worshipped of all the worlds and entered his body. And the kings beholding the energy which entered that mighty-armed chief of men regarded it as wonderful." And indeed they might well do so, yet the poet tells us that many of the chiefs were excited to fierce if suppressed anger by what they had witnessed.*

At length the great sacrifice for imperial sway was successfully accomplished and with the greatest imaginable splendour. After which the subject rajahs were courteously dismissed to their respective principalities.

---

* The whole story, though so bewilderingly strange, is yet so characteristically Hindu in its conception and motive that I could not exclude it even from this brief sketch. Nor could I venture to present it in words other than those of an orthodox Hindu translator.

But the grandeur and wealth displayed on this occasion served to re-awaken or enflame the old jealousy of the Kauravas, particularly of Duryodhana, who had been the unwilling collector of the vast tribute poured into Yudhisthira's treasury at Indraprastha. Despairing of injuring their rivals by open and fair means, the Kauravas determined to resort once more to artifice, having, as usual, discussed the pros and cons of the question from all points of view; for these old-time heroes of India were nothing if not argumentative.* They built a sumptuous reception hall, "a crystal-arched palace," full two miles square, decorated with gold and lapis lazuli, with a thousand columns and one hundred gates. Hither they invited a large number of royal friends, but the principal guests were the Pandavas, whom they challenged to a friendly gambling match. Yudhisthira well understood and clearly stated the objectionable features of gambling and was fully aware that the game of chance he was challenged to take part in would not be fairly conducted. However, as a Kshatriya, he could not decline the match and so sat down to play against Shakuni, queen Gandhari's brother, a skilful and unscrupulous dice-player, who was backed by Duryodhana.

In a succession of games Yudhisthira lost all his money and jewels, all his cattle, jewelled chariots, war-elephants, slaves and slave girls and then the whole of the Kingdom of the Pandavas. Driven to despair, the luckless gambler would persist in continuing to play while there remained

* Throughout these epics questions of right and wrong, policy and impolicy are discussed with rare acumen.

anything at all to stake. But his success was no better than before and he staked and lost his brothers, one by one, then himself and lastly the joint wife of the Pandavas, the famous Draupadi.

An exciting and most sensational scene followed. To complete the humiliation of their rivals the successful gamesters ordered Draupadi to be conducted into the gaming hall. She astutely objected that as Yudhisthira had first staked and lost himself, and thus entered a servile condition, before he played for her, he was not legally competent to dispose of her person; but her protest was unheeded. Being dressed, at the time, in a single robe of cloth, a simple *saree* apparently, she refused to appear in that attire before the assembled chiefs. But Dhusasana, with brutal unceremoniousness, dragged her into the great hall by the hair of her head, treating her, in the presence of her husbands, with the familiar licence which they were accustomed to indulge in when dealing with their female slaves. Dhusasana even went so far as to attempt to strip beautiful Draupadi in the presence of the assembly. In her trouble she prayed aloud to Krishna for help, invoking him as the lover of the *gopis* (milkmaids), the dweller in Dwarka, the soul of the Universe, the Creator of all things. And Krishna, hearing her prayer, miraculously multiplied her garments as fast as they were removed. Yet notwithstanding these manifestations of divine protection, Duryodhana, not to be behind in affronting his rivals, indecently bared his left thigh and showed it to the modest Draupadi, who, as she said, had never since the occasion of her

Swayamvara been beheld by an assembly like this. These gross indignities, it may be well imagined, must have driven the Pandavas frantic. Why then did they not dare to interpose? Because they were bound by the acts of their elder brother; and submission to authority seems ever to have been the highest virtue of these Hindu heroes! Only Bhima, with an impetuosity which was not to be restrained even by respect for his elder brother, took a solemn oath before the assembly, that for the deeds that they had done that day he would break the thigh of Duryodhana and drink the blood of Dhusasana, or forfeit his hopes of heaven. Both these vows he accomplished in the great war to be subsequently referred to.

While this sensational scene was being enacted a jackal howled in the *homa*-chamber of king Dhritarashtra. Terrified by this omen of dire evil the old king began to reprove Duryodhana for his conduct, and addressing Draupadi in respectful and affectionate terms desired her to ask of him any boon she pleased. Without hesitation she demanded at once that Yudhisthira should be freed from slavery. A second boon being offered her, she solicited the freedom of her other husbands; but when she was given the option of a third boon she declined to accept the favour saying: "O king, these my husbands, freed from the wretched state of bondage, will be able to achieve prosperity by their own virtuous acts." However, Dhritarashtra dismissed the Pandavas in honour to their own city, desiring them to think no more of the unpleasant episode of the gambling match.

The crest-fallen visitors hastened to take advantage

of the blind king's permission to depart, and they set out at once on their homeward journey, revolving in their minds many a scheme of future vengeance. The Kauravas, however, felt, and justly too, that after what had passed that day the matter could not be thus easily settled. They knew their outraged cousins would burn to wipe out the insults they had received, and so they entreated the blind old king, their father, to recall the Pandavas and induce them to play a final game upon the issue of which one party or the other should go into voluntary exile. The Pandavas were brought back to try the fortune of the dice once more, and it was arranged that the losing side should go into exile, spending twelve years in the forests and one additional year in any city they might find convenient; and that if the exiles were discovered, during the time of their concealment in the city, they would have to go through another exile of thirteen years. The game upon which so much hung was duly played, with the result that the Pandavas had to exchange the splendour and luxury of the palace for the simple life and scanty fare of the forest, with which they had already become acquainted in their earlier wanderings.

When Dushasana saw that Sakuni had won the game he danced about for joy and cried out: "Now is established the Raj of Duryodhana!" But Bhima said: "Be not elated with joy, but remember my words. The day will come when I shall drink your blood, or never attain to regions of blessedness!" The Pandavas seeing that they had lost the wager threw off their garments, put on deer-skins and prepared to depart into the forest with their joint-wife, their mother Kunti and their priest Dhanmya; but Vidura representing to Yudhisthira that Kunti was, by reason of her years, unfitted to bear the hardships of exile, proposed that she should be left to his care, and this kindly offer was readily accepted. From the assembly the sons of Pandu went out, hanging down their heads with shame, and covering their faces with their garments. Only Bhima, always more impulsive than his brothers, threw out his long, mighty arms and glared at the Kauravas furiously, while Draupadi spread her long black hair over her face and wept bitterly. The blind old king regarded the departure of his nephews with grave misgivings, for he felt that inevitable destruction awaited him and his at the hands of the Pandavas. All this, he well knew, was the work of his son Duryodhana constrained by Destiny, since "the whole Universe moveth at the will of the Creator under the controlling influence of Fate:" and, as Sanjaya said, in allusion to Duryodhana, "the gods first deprive that man of his reason unto whom they send defeat and disgrace."

Surely it is only a Hindu bard who could imagine such sudden and complete reverses of fortune and such tame, almost abject, acquiescence in the circumstances of the hour, on the part of such redoubtable heroes as the sons of Pandu! Nor is it comprehensible why exile to the forest should always entail the hermit garb and utter destitution.

That king Yudhisthira felt his altered position bitterly is evident from the words he addressed to the

Brahmans who accompanied him and his brothers out of the city. "Robbed," he says, "of our prosperity and "kingdom, robbed of everything, we are about to enter "the deep woods in sorrow: depending for our food on "fruits and roots and the produce of the chase. The "forest too is full of dangers and abounds with reptiles "and beasts of prey." However his anticipations were worse than the reality. By the advice of a Brahman the exiled monarch made an appeal to the Sun for help, addressing him in such terms as these. "Thou art, O Sun the eye of the universe! Thou art the soul of all corporeal existences! Thou art the origin of all things! * * * * Thou art called Indra, thou art Vishnu, thou art Brahma, thou art Prajapati! Thou art fire and thou art the subtle mind! and thou art the lord and the eternal Brahma."* In response to this appeal the Sun-god appeared to the king and presented him with a copper cooking-vessel which proved to be an inexhaustible source of fruits and roots, meat and vegetables to the exiles during their twelve years of enforced sojourn in the woods.†

Their forest wanderings were productive of many

---

* A little later Arjuna, addressing Krishna, says: "O slayer of all foes, having floated on the primordial waters, thou subsequently becamest Hari, and Brahma, and Surya and Dharma and Dhatri and Yama and Anala and Vayu and Vaisravana and Rudra and Kala and the firmament, the earth, and the ten directions! Thyself incarnate, thou art the lord of the mobile and immobile universe, the Creater of all, O thou foremost of all existences." It would appear that each Diety who is invoked is credited by his adorer with being the origin and support of the entire universe, the beginning and the end of all things.

† In a subsequent page, however, we find the following "Tell us now, O Brahman, what was the food of the sons of Pandu while they lived in the woods. Was it of the wilderness or was it the produce of cultivation? Vaisampayana said. "Those bulls among men collecting the produce of the wilderness and killing the deer with pure arrows first dedicated a portion of the food to the Brahmans and themselves ate the rest," (Section L.)

stirring adventures the narrative of which occupies a large portion of the original poem, but we can find space to notice only a few of these.

Following the advice of the sage Vyasa, Arjuna visited the Himalayas in order to gain the favour of Siva and to obtain from him certain most potent celestial weapons for the destruction of the Kauravas, of whom the Pandava heroes seem, notwithstanding their own wonderful fighting qualities, to have had a wholesome dread. Having arrived upon the sacred mountains, Arjuna went through a course of austerities "with arms upraised, leaning upon nothing and standing on the tips of his toes." For food he, at first, had withered leaves, but eventually he fed on air alone. Such was the fervour of his penances that the earth around him began to smoke and the alarmed Rishis came in a body to Siva and asked him to interfere. The chief of all the Gods sent them away with comforting assurances and having assumed the appearance of a *Kirata*, or low-class hunter, came upon Arjuna and provoked him to an encounter. The battle was fierce, culminating in a desperate personal struggle; but where one of the combatants was the Supreme Being the issue could not be doubtful and Arjuna fell smitten senseless by the God. He soon recovered consciousness and "mentally prostrating himself before the gracious god of gods and making a clay image of that deity he worshipped it with offerings of floral garlands."* To his surprise he found the garland he had offered to the clay image adorning the head of his victorious enemy the Kiráta, who thus revealed himself to

* This is an interesting and noteworthy instance of idolatry attributed to one of the ancient Aryan heroes by the Brahman authors of the Mahabharata.

the much relieved son of Pandu. Arjuna prostrated himself before the Deity who expressed his approval of his worshipper and presently bestowed upon him the gift of a terrible celestial weapon called the Pácupata, with instructions in regard to the appropriate *mantras* or spells to be used with it. At that moment the whole earth with its mountains, plains and rivers trembled with excitement, a terrible hurricane expressed the concern of Nature in the important event and the "terrible weapon in its embodied form" stood by the side of Arjuna ready to obey his behests. When Siva had vanished from sight the guardians of the four regions (*lokapalah*) Kuvera, Varuna, Yama and Indra appeared, in great splendour, upon the mountain top and presented Arjuna with other celestial weapons; after which he was carried in a wonderous car to the heaven of his real father the god Indra. It was a glorious and delightful region, lighted with its own inherent brilliancy, adorned with the flowers of every season, fanned by fragrant breezes and resounding with celestial music. Here there were bands of lovely Apsaras and Gandharvas, who gladdened all hearts with their ravishing songs and dances. It was a region for the virtuous alone, and not for those "who had turned their back on the field of battle."

In this delightful place Arjuna passed five years of his life, treated with the highest honour and consideration, learning the use of the various celestial weapons with which he was eventually to overthrow those redoubtable champions, Kripa and Drona, Bhisma and Karna. Nor were lighter studies neglected. Arjuna, under a competent instructor, became proficient in the arts of music and dancing.

That he might be made, "to taste the joys of heaven" properly, the lovely Apsara,* Urvasi, of wide hips, crisp soft hair, beautiful eyes and full bosom, was specially commanded to make herself agreeable to Arjuna. Her sensual beauty, described in some detail by the poet, failed, however, to subdue the hero, who met her amatory advances with a somewhat exaggerated respect, which so enraged the fair temptress that she cursed him saying: "Since thou disregardest a woman come to thy mansion at the command of thy father and of her own motion—a woman besides who is pierced by the shafts of Kama,—therefore, O Partha, thou shalt have to pass thy time among females unregarded and as a dancer and destitute of manhood."

While Arjuna was in the heaven of Indra, King Yudhisthira passed some time in the forest of Kamyaka, in company with his three younger brothers and Draupadi, attended by his family priest Dhaumya and a number of faithful Brahmans. Here he learned, from an illustrious Rishi, Vrihadaçwa, "the science of dice in its entirety," ignorance of which *science* had cost him so dear. After a while the party set out on a pilgrimage to visit and bathe in those *tirthas*, or sacred waters, which abound all over India to this day. Each *tirtha* is famous for some event

* "*Apsaras*—The Apsaras are the celebrated nymphs of Indra's heaven * * * It is said that when they came forth from the waters (at the churning of the ocean) neither the Gods nor the Asuras would have them for wives, so they became common to all * * * * The Apsaras then are fairy-like beings beautiful and voluptuous. Their amours on earth have been numerous and they are the rewards in Indra's paradise held out to heroes who fall in battle."—Professor Dawsons classical Dictionary of Hindu Mythology &c.

in the history of the gods or the saints of the lands, and the water of each one has a virtue of its own. A dip in one cleanses the bather from all his sins, a dip in another confers upon him the merit of having bestowed a thousand kine upon the Brahmans, or, perhaps, that of having performed a horse-sacrifice. By a plunge in a third *tirtha* the pilgrim acquires the power of disappearance at will, or some other coveted power; while ablution in the water of a fourth places the heaven of Indra, or of some other god, within his reach. It is evident that by making a round of these *tirthas* a man might acquire superhuman power and the highest felicity in this and a future life.

Journeying leisurely from *tirtha* to *tirtha*, from the Punjab to the Southern Sea, under the guidance of the sage Lomaça, King Yudhisthira with the others pleasantly acquired an enormous store of merits of various kinds. But anxious for reunion with Arjuna they wended their way back to the North, visiting the *tirthas* on their route, till they found themselves in the Himalayas. Pushing into the sacred solitude of these giant mountains they met with many adventures in which Bhima's son, Ghatotkacha, was very helpful to them. At last from a lofty summit these fortunate travellers got a glimpse of the abode of Kuvera, the God of wealth, "adorned with golden "and crystal palaces, surrounded on all sides by golden "walls having the splendour of all gems, furnished with "gardens all around, higher than a mountain peak, beauti-"ful with ramparts and towers and adorned with door-"ways and gates and rows of pennons. And the abode "was graced with dallying damsels dancing around, and "also with pennons wafted by the breeze. * * * And "gladdening all creatures, there was blowing a breeze, "carrying all perfumes, and of balmy feel. And there "were various beautiful and wonderful trees of diverse hues, "resounding with diverse dulcet notes."

Kuvera came out to meet the Pandavas and after some excellent advice to Yudhisthira, in which he pointed out to the king that success in human affairs depended upon "patience, ability, (appropriate) time and place and prowess," requested them to retire to a somewhat less elevated position on the mountains and there await the return of their brother. And it came to pass that one day while they were thinking of Arjuna a blazing chariot driven by Indra's charioteer, Matali, filled the sky with its brilliancy and stopping near them their long absent brother descended from it, in a resplendent form, adorned with a diadem and celestial garlands. He paid his respects, in due form, first to the family priest and then to Bhima; after that he received the salutations of his younger brothers; he next cheered his beloved Krishná by his presence, and finally stood, in an attitude of humility, before the king. The Pandavas worshipped Matali as if he were Indra himself, and then "duly enquired of him after the health of all the gods." At dawn next day Indra himself, attended by hosts of Gandharvas and Apsaras, visited the Pandavas and, having received their adoration, and having assured Yudhisthira that he would yet rule the earth, desired him to go back to Kamyaka, whereupon the Pandavas, of course, commenced their return journey.

Arjuna, restored to the companionship of his brothers, related to them some of his adventures during the five years of his absence, and dwelt, in some detail, upon the successful destruction of certain Danavas named Nivata-Kavachas which he had carried out single-handed. These were ancient and powerful enemies of Indra, dwellers in the womb of the ocean and numbering thirty millions.* Against these puissant demons Arjuna was sent in Indra's chariot, driven by Matali, and, after prodigies of valour and the most marvellous performances with the celestial weapons which he had received from the gods, he completely overthrew them and destroyed their wonderful aërial city, Hiranyapura. Shortly after these events Krishna came on a visit to his friends and they were also joined by the sage Markandeya who lightened the tedium of their wanderings with interesting narratives of past events and profitable discourses on important religious and philosophical subjects. How competent he was for such a task will be readily admitted when we learn from himself that he, and he alone of the race of men or created beings, was privileged to see the entire universe run its cycle of changes through the four appointed *Yugas* or ages, to watch it undergo gradual degeneracy and decay and finally to witness its total destruction by fire,—with all animated beings even gods and demons,—only to be recreated again in order to run its appointed course through the ages once more.†

Markandeya relates to the Pandavas the whole story

---

* This is only a single instance of the perpetual and undying hostility between the celestials on the one hand and the demons on the other.

† Markandeya's description of the dissolution and re-creation of the world has

of the Ramayana and many another legend of the olden time. Let me here reproduce his story of the *flood*, as it has an interest not confined to India or Hindus and also his explanation of the doctrine of *Karma*, of which we are beginning to hear so much in these days.

Markandeya's account of the Universal Deluge. There was once a powerful and great Rishi named Manu who "was equal unto Brahma in glory." For ten thousand years he practised the severest austerities in the forest, standing on one leg with uplifted hand and bowed head. One day, as he was undergoing his self-inflicted penance, with matted locks and dripping garments, a little fish, approaching the bank of the stream near which the Rishi stood, entreated his protection against the cruel voracity of the bigger fishes; for said the little suppliant "this fixed custom is well established amongst us, that the strong fish always prey upon the weak ones." The sage, touched with compassion, took the little fish out of the river and put it for safety into an earthen vessel of water and tended it carefully. In its new home it grew apace, and, at its own request, was removed to a tank. Here its dimensions increased so wonderfully that "although the tank was two *Yojanas* in length and one *Yojana* in width" there was not sufficient room in it for the fish, who again appealed to Manu asking him to place it in the Ganges, "the favourite spouse of the ocean." Gigantic as the fish was the wonderful Rishi put it into the river with his own hands; but the Ganges itself was too small

undoubtedly a certain grandiose character about it, but betrays the extremely limited geographical knowledge of these omniscient sages whose acquaintance with the Earth's surface is strictly bounded by the Himalayas and the Southern Sea.

for this monster of the waters and the Muni carried it to the sea-shore and consigned it to the bosom of the mighty ocean.

"And when it was thrown into the sea by Manu "it said these words to him with a smile:* O adorable "being thou hast protected me with special care; do "thou now listen to me as to what thou shouldst do in "the fulness of time! O fortunate and worshipful sir, the "dissolution of this mobile and immobile world is nigh "at hand. The time for the purging of this world is "now ripe. Therefore, do I now explain what is well "for thee. The mobile and the immobile divisions of the "creation, those that have the power of locomotion and "those that have it not, of all these the terrible doom "hath now approached. Thou shalt build a strong and "massive ark and have it furnished with a long rope. "On that must thou ascend, O great *Muni*, with the seven "Rishis and take with thee all the different seeds which "were enumerated by regenerate Brahmans in days of "yore, and separately and carefully must thou preserve "them therein. And whilst there, O beloved of the "Muni's, thou shalt wait for me, and I shall appear to "thee like a horned animal and thus, O ascetic, shalt thou "recognise me."

Manu, having carried out the instructions of the fish in all its details, entered his ark and embarked upon the surging ocean. He thought of the fish and it appeared

* *A smiling fish* is at least an original idea. In another place we find the following in regard to a very ancient tortoise. "And as he came there we asked him saying: Dost thou know this King Indradyumna. And the tortoise reflected for a moment. And his eyes filled with tears and his heart was much moved. And he trembled all over and was nearly deprived of his senses. And he said with joined hands, Alas, do I not know that one?" Vana Parva page 604—P. C. Roy.

with horns on its head to which Manu fastened his vessel. A terrific tempest arose in which the ark "reeled about like a drunken harlot." Water covered every thing, even the heavens and the firmament. For many years the fish towed the vessel through the flood and at length conveyed it towards the highest peak of the Himavat (Himalayas) and instructed the occupants to moor their vessel to it. "Then the fish, addressing the "associated *Rishis* told them these words. I am Brahma "the Lord of all creatures; there is none greater than "myself. Assuming the shape of a fish I have saved "ye from this cataclysm. Manu will create (again) all "being—gods, asuras and men, and all those divisions of "creation which have the power of locomotion and which "have it not. By practising severe austerities he will "acquire this power, and, with my blessing, illusion will "have no power over him." Manu, of course, underwent the necessary austerities and re-created "all beings in proper and exact order."

Such is the *Legend of the Fish* and whosoever listens to it every day is assured of heaven.*

From this easy mode of reaching heaven,† as taught by the sage Markandeya, we turn to his exposition of the *doctrine of Karma*, which, if less comforting in respect to

* This Hindu legend of the destruction of the world by water affords materials for a comparison with the Mosaic account of the same event and the Chaldean story of the deluge as recorded on the tablets which have been deciphered by the late George Smith.

† There are, according to the Mahabharata, so many easy modes of obtaining a complete release from the penalties of sin and of attaining heaven that it would seem that only the most culpable negligence and obstinacy could lead the Hindu to lose his chance of being purged from sin and of enjoying beatitude hereafter. It must be remembered, however, that there are also passages in which it is emphatically laid down that *purity of heart* is an essential and indispensable condition of salvation. Eg. Vana Parva section CC.

the means of attaining heavenly joys, has at least, something of philosophical plausibility to recommend it to our attention.

The divine sage, addressing Yudhisthira, explained to him that happiness is to be attained neither by learning, nor good morals, nor personal exertion. There is yet another and more important factor than all these to be reckoned with and that is *Karma*. "If the fruits of our exertion," says Markendeya, "were not dependent on "any thing else, people would attain the object of their "desire, by simply striving to attain it. It is sure that "able, intelligent and diligent persons are baffled in their "efforts and do not attain the fruits of their actions. On "the other hand persons who are always active in injur- "ing others and in practising deception on the world, "lead a happy life. There are some who attain prosperity "without any exertion. And there are others who with "the utmost exertion are unable to achieve their dues, "miserly persons with the object of having sons born to "them worship the gods and practise severe austerities, "and these sons * * * * at length turn out to be "very infamous scions of their race; and others begotten "under the same auspices, decently pass their lives in "luxury with hoards of riches and grain accumulated by "their ancestors. The diseases from which men suffer, "are undoubtedly the result of their own *Karma*," that is of their actions in previous and unremembered existences. "It is," pursues Markandeya, "the immemorial, "tradition* that the soul is eternal and everlasting, but

* This appeal to *tradition* from a sage who had actually witnessed the destruction and re-creation of the entire universe is rather strange.

"the corporeal frame of all creatures is subject to destruc- "tion here (below.) When, therefore, life is extinguished "the body only is destroyed, but the spirit wedded to its "actions travels elsewhere." It inhabits innumerable bodies in succession, it lives countless lives, it passes through the infernal regions, it attains to the heaven of the gods, and, after untold woes and infinite struggles, is eventually re-absorbed in the divine essence from which it sprang.*

Turning from these episodes and mystic speculations to the Pandavas themselves we find that the ever-fair Draupadi having, by her perennial and faultless beauty, aroused the passions of Jayadratha Raja of Sindhu, was artfully carried off by him during the temporary absence of her husbands; but the ravisher was overtaken and suffered punishment at the hands of the ardent Bhima, who, after inflicting severe bodily chastisement upon the defeated raja, cut off his hair, all except five locks, and made him confess himself the slave of the Pandavas. At the request of Yudhisthira, backed by generous Daraupadi, Jayadratha was released.

* With important differences and limitations the modern doctrine of *heredity* may be regarded as the scientific analogue of the Hindu doctrine of *Karma*. One, however, is based on indisputable facts, the other on pure fancy. But whatever their merits or short-comings, whatever the bases of truth or reasonableness on which they rest neither the one doctrine nor the other can, unfortunately, afford a rational mind any *consolation* for the ills and apparent injustice of the present life, and assuredly, neither the one nor the other can supply any stimulus towards the performance of good actions. A small class of persons in Europe seem to have become profoundly enamoured of the subtle ideas which underlie the doctrine of *Karma*; but he must be strangely constituted whose sense of justice can be satisfied or who can derive any *comfort* in his present struggle against the evils of life from the thought that he is suffering the consequences of deeds done by his soul in previous and *unremembered* existences, or can be induced to make for righteousness by the reflection that after his physical death the happiness of some other being, possibly a cat, into which his soul transmigrates will be influenced by his deeds in the present life. But at the same time it may be admitted that the doctrine of *Karma* may certainly, in the case of some races, conduce towards a helpless and hopeless resignation, conterfeiting contentment.

This abduction and rescue recalled to the mind of Markandeya the story of Rama and Sita which he proceeded to relate, at considerable length, for the edification of the Pandavas. The sage also recounted the story of Savitri, more charming than that of Orpheus and Eurydice. How the lovely Savitri set her affections upon young Satyaván, the only son of the blind Dyumatsena ex-king of the Salwas ; how she learned from the lips of the celestial sage Narada that the beautiful youth was fated to die within a year ; how notwithstanding this secret knowledge she willingly linked her lot with his and how, when the inevitable hour arrived and the doom of Fate was accomplished in the lonely forest, her austere piety and devoted love enabled her to follow Yama, on and on with fearless footsteps and touching entreaties, as he conveyed away her dear husband's spirit to the Land of Shades, and at last to prevail upon the dread Deity to restore to her the soul of her Satyaván.

"Adieu, great God!" She took the soul,
  No bigger than the human thumb,
And running swift, soon reached her goal,
  Where lay the body stark and dumb.
She lifted it with eager hands
  And as before, when he expired,
She placed the head upon the bands
  That bound her breast which hope new fired,
And which alternate rose and fell ;
  Then placed his soul upon his heart
Whence like a bee it found its cell,
  And lo, he woke with sudden start!
His breath came low at first, then deep,
  With an unquiet look he gazed

As one awaking from a sleep
Wholly bewildered and amazed.*

Of the doings of the Kauravas, during the twelve years that we have been following the fortunes of their cousins, little is recorded, and that little is not to their credit. Knowing full well where the Pandavas were passing their term of exile in the forests, Duryodhana, upon the advice of Karna, went thither in great state, with a view of meanly feasting his eyes upon the wretchedness of his hated kinsmen and of intensifying their misery by the cruel contrast between his own grandeur and their destitution. This was the real, if unworthy motive of the journey to the forest of Kamyaka; the alleged reason was to inspect the royal cattle-stations in order to count the stock and mark the calves.† Attended by his courtiers, by thousands of ladies belonging to the royal household and by a great army of followers and soldiers, Duryodhana proceeded towards the sylvan abode of the Pandavas; but his advanced guard was refused admission into the forests by the Gandharvas, whose king had come with his celestial hosts and several tribes of Apsaras to have a merry time in those woods. As neither party would abate a jot of its pretensions, a terrible battle ensued, resulting in the complete defeat of the Kauravas, the ignominious flight of the redoubtable Karna, and the capture, by the victorious enemy, of Duryodhana himself, his court and all his harem.

In this extremity the beaten followers of the captive

* From "Ballads and Legends of Hindustan" by Miss Toru Dutt, the gifted Bengali girl whose premature death in 1877 at the early age of twenty one years caused a sad loss to India.

† Here we have a glimpse of the simple life of those primitive times.

king fled for help to the Pandavas. For the sake of the honor of the family, and particularly for the protection of the ladies of their house, Arjuna and Bhima, with the twins, came, by the magnanimous command of Yudhisthira, to the rescue of their kinsmen, and after performing feats of war which none but an Indian poet could imagine, obtained the release of the crest-fallen Duryodhana, whose bitterness against his cousins was only increased by this humiliating and never-to-be-forgotten incident.

Stung to the quick by the intolerable mortification of his position, Duryodhana, in despair, resolved to give up his Kingdom and his life. To the remonstrances of his friends he answered: "I have nothing more to do with "virtue, wealth, friendship, affluence, sovereignty and "enjoyment. Do not obstruct my purpose, but leave me "all of you. I am firmly resolved to cast away my life "by foregoing food. Return to the city and treat my "superiors there respectfully." He might have fallen upon his own sword; but the Hindu here elects to die otherwise. "And the son of Dhritarashtra, in accordance "with his purpose, spread kuça grass on the earth, and "purifying himself by touching water sat down upon "that spot. And clad in rags and kuça grass, he set "himself to observe the highest vow. And stopping all "speech, that tiger among kings, moved by the desire of "going to heaven, began to pray and worship internally, "suspending all external intercourse."

However, this meditated suicide was not fated to be accomplished. The Daityas and Danavas interfered, "knowing that if the king died, their party would be weakened." By means of certain rites and sacrifices they called into being "a strange goddess with mouth wide open," who carried Duryodhana into their presence at night. The Daityas and Danavas explained to the dejected king that he was of more than human origin and their especial ally. They undertook to help him in his struggles with the Pandavas and promised him a complete triumph over his rivals. Cheered by these assurances the would-be-suicide abandoned his purpose, resumed his royal position and, emulating the Pandavas, performed a great and costly sacrifice known as the *Vaishnava*. To this important rite Duryodhana insultingly invited his cousins, who prudently declined the invitation on the plea that the period of their exile was not yet completed.

Notwithstanding the recent defeat of Karna by the Gandharvas, and his precipitate flight from the field of battle, there seems to have been a lurking dread of his prowess amongst the friends of the Pandavas. Indra, the god of Heaven, determined, therefore, to render him less formidable, by depriving him of his native coat of golden mail and the celestial earrings with which he was born. For this purpose he presented himself before Karna in the guise of a Brahman and asked him for his armour and earrings. Now Karna had made a vow never to refuse anything to a Brahman and was thus placed on the horns of a cruel dilemma. However, he had been forewarned by his own father, the Sun-god, of Indra's intentions and had been advised to ask for an infallible weapon in exchange for his armour and earrings. Recognising the god of Heaven under his Brahmanical disguise,

Karna preferred his request, which was granted with conditions which made it almost nugatory. Karna peeled off his natural armour, which act, by Indra's favour, left no scar upon his person. "And Sakra (Indra)," says the poet, "having thus beguiled Karna, but made him famous in the world, thought, with a smile, that the business of the sons of Pandu had already been completed." The Pandavas were naturally elated and the Kauravas depressed when the news of these events reached them. Though the sons of Pandu had received repeated assurances that they would ultimately triumph over their enemies, they were, it seems, subject to frequent fits of somewhat unreasonable depression; so Vyasa, ever devoted to the interests of the heroes, visited them in their forest-home and consoled Yudhisthira, once more, by the prediction that, after the thirteenth year of exile had expired, he would regain his kingdom and his influence in the world.

The twelth year of exile was now drawing to a close, the thirteenth year, it will be remembered, was to be passed by the Pandavas in disguise in some city or other. Their last experience in the woods was as wonderful as any they had previously gone through. A wild stag carried away on its branching antlers the sticks with which a Brahman ascetic was wont to kindle his fire. The five brothers were appealed to by the hermit in his trouble and pursued the animal, but could neither kill it nor run it down. Overcome with fatigue and thirst they sat down to take rest. One climbed a tree to look out for signs of water, and having discovered them, Nakula was sent to fetch water for the party. Not far away he found a pleasant pond, but was warned by the commanding voice of some unseen being not to touch the water. He was too thirsty to give heed to the injunction, and proceeding to drink of the crystal spring fell down dead. Wondering at Nakula's prolonged absence Sahdeva set out to look for him and, coming upon the pond, heard the warning voice. He too disregarded it and suffered the same penalty as his brother had done. Arjuna and Bhima in turn went through the same experiences with the same sad result. At last the wise Yudhisthira came upon the scene. He prudently refrained from touching the water when warned against doing so, and entered into conversation with the aërial voice which now took an embodied form,—that of a mighty *Yaksha*. This being of terrible aspect interrogated the king upon a number of important points, and receiving satisfactory answers,* revealed himself to

---

* A few of the questions put and answers given on this occasion may afford some insight into Indian modes of thought.

Q. What is it that maketh the Sun rise? Who keep him company? Who causeth him to set? In whom is he established?

A. Brahmá maketh the sun rise: the Gods keep him company: Dharma causeth him to set: and he is established in truth.

Q. What is that which doth not close its eyes while asleep? What is that which doth not move after birth? What is that without a heart? And what is that which swells with its own impetus?

A. A fish doth not close its eyes while asleep: an egg doth not move after birth: a stone is without a heart: a river swelleth with its own impetus.

Q. What constitutes *the* way? What hath been spoken of as water? What as food? And what as poison?

A. They that are good constitute *the* way. Space hath been spoken of as water. The cow is food. A request is poison.

[To this answer the translator Babu P. C. Roy appends the following notes among other. "The çrutis speak of the cow as the only food, in the following sense. The cow gives milk. The milk gives butter. The butter is used in *Homa*. The Homa is the cause of the clouds. The clouds give rain. The rain makes the seeds to sprout forth and produce food. Nilakantha endeavours to explain this in a spiritual sense. There is however no need of such explanation here."]

Yudhisthira as his father, Dharma, god of Justice. He then restored the dead Pandavas to life and bestowed this boon upon them, that during the thirteenth year of their exile, if they even travelled over the entire earth in their proper forms, no one *in the three worlds* would be able to recognise them.

The twelfth year was now nearly completed and the brothers left the woods, resolved to spend the next twelve months in the city of Virata, which seems to have been close at hand. Before entering the city they had to conceal their weapons in order to avoid detection (for they do not seem to have placed implicit confidence in the boon granted by *Dharma*). Just outside the city they came upon a cemetery with a gigantic *Sami* tree. To the topmost boughs of this tree they fastened their weapons. They also hung a corpse on the tree that people might avoid it. This action of theirs was evidently noticed, for the poet tells us that on being asked by the shepherds and "cowherds regarding the corpse, those repressors of foes "said unto them. This is our mother, aged one hundred "and eighty years. We have hung up her dead body, "in accordance with the custom observed by our fore-"fathers."

On the way Yudhisthira, ever anxious for divine help, invoked the goddess Durga in terms which reveal at once the attributes of the goddess and the Hindu poet's idea of the most suitable expressions to be employed in addressing a female divinity. "Salutations to thee "O giver of boons * * * Salutations to thee, O thou "of four hands and four faces, O thou of fair round hips "and deep bosom, O thou that wearest bangles made of "emeralds and sapphires, O thou that bearest excellent "bracelets on thy upper arm * * * Thou art the only "female in the universe that possessest the attribute of "purity. Thou art decked with a pair of well-made "ears graced with excellent rings. O goddess thou "shinest with a face that challengeth the moon in "beauty! With an excellent diadem and beautiful "braid, with robes made of the bodies of snakes, "and with also the brilliant girdle round thy hips thou "shinest like the Mandara mountain encircled with snakes! "Thou shinest also with peacock-plumes standing erect "on thy head, and thou hast sanctified the celestial "regions by adopting the vow of perpetual maidenhood. "It is for this, O thou that hast slain the *Buffalo-Asura*, "that thou art praised and worshipped by the gods "for the protection of the three worlds! O thou foremost "of all deities, extend to me thy grace, show me thy "mercy and be thou the source of blessings to me! "Thou art Jaya and Vijaya and it is thou that givest "victory in battle! Grant me victory, O Goddess, and "give me boons also at this hour of distress. Thy "eternal abode is on Vindhya—that foremost of moun-"tains! O Kali; O Kali that art the great Kali ever "fond of wine and meat and animal sacrifice. Capable "of going everywhere at will and bestowing boons on "thy devotees, thou art ever followed in thy journeys "by Brahma and the other gods,* &c &c."

* This sudden and rather inartistic introduction of the Goddess Kali, unmentioned before, looks very much like a clumsy addition to the epic made at a comparatively modern date in the interests of the later developments of Hinduism.

"Thus praised by the son of Pandu, the goddess showed herself unto him" and promised the exiles that, through her grace, they would remain unrecognised either by the Kurava spies or the inhabitants of the city, as long as they resided in Virata.

Under such favourable auspices and protection the Pandavas and their joint-wife entered Virata. Yudhisthira presented himself before the Rajah and was engaged as a companion and teacher of dice-playing, in which art, as the reader will remember, he received special instruction from a Rishi in the woods of Kamyaka. Bhima was taken on as superintendent of the cooks, being it seems especially clever in preparing *curries.* Arjuna who personated a eunuch, was appointed music and dancing master to the ladies, having learned those accomplishments in Indra's heaven. Nakula was taken on as master of the horse and Sahadeva, who was skilled in milking and managing kine, as superintendent of the cattle. Draupadi professed to be a *Sairindhri* or maid-servant ready to serve anybody who would maintain her. The queen chanced to see Draupadi and took her into her service, although she felt and expressed some reluctance to have about her person a woman of such an attractive appearance. The Rani apparently had her suspicions about Draupadi to whom she candidly expressed her opinion that she was too beautiful to be a servant, for, said she "your heels are not prominent "and your "thighs touch one another. And your intelligence is "great and your navel deep and your words solemn. "And your great toes and bust and hips and toenails and "palms are all well developed." The Rani also naively added: "What man will be able to resist thy attractions? "Surely, O thou of well-rounded hips, O damsel of exquisite charms, beholding thy form of superhuman "beauty, king Virata is sure to forsake me and will "turn to thee with his whole heart." But the fair wife of the five Pandavas seems to have allayed the Rani's natural jealousy and fear, by assuring her that she was watched over by Gandharvas, and that if any one attempted to make improper advances to her the Gandharvas would put an end to him. However, the Rani's anxiety was fully justified by after events. Her brother, Kechaka, smitten with the charms of the new maid-servant, prevailed upon his sister, by his importunities, to send Draupadi to his house on the pretext of fetching some wine from his stock. Draupadi went as directed to the house of the Rani's brother; but on his making insulting proposals to her she made her escape from him and fled direct to the king's council-chamber, followed by the baffled and enraged Kechaka, who seized her by the hair of her head before the assembled courtiers and shamefully kicked the beautiful lady in the presence of the king and his attendants. The Raja would not interfere and Bhima, who was present* and boiling with suppressed indignation, was restrained by the command of his elder brother from taking notice of the affair. But Draupadi was not to be pacified. Bent on having revenge she went at dead of night to Bhima and heaped reproaches upon him and his brothers, and well she might, for all

* The cook in the council-chamber! This is a sample of the primitive ideas which underlie the epic.

the degrading insults she had had to endure while they looked tamely on. Between them they planned that Draupadi should pretend to yield to Kechaka's desires, and should appoint a secret meeting with him, when Bhima should be her substitute and kill the man who had insulted and ill-used her. The plan was successfully carried out. A terrible fight took place between Kechaka and Bhima. The latter at length slew his antagonist by whirling him swiftly round his head and dashing him against the ground. He then broke all his bones into small pieces, formed his body into a great ball of flesh, and brought Draupadi to behold the complete *vengeance* he had taken upon her hated persecutor. To wreak their malice on the person they believed to be the cause of Kechaka's death, his kinsmen seized Draupadi, "of faultless limbs," who was found leaning against a pillar hard by the scene of the grim revenge, and carried her off outside the city-walls with the intention of burning her with the dead man's body. In her distress she cried aloud for help, and Bhima, in disguise, came to her rescue. Panic-stricken at the sight of this supposed Gandharva, the men who had assembled at the cremation ground fled for their lives, but were pursued by Bhima who killed a great number of them.

Of course this event created an immence sensation and even the king feared to speak to Draupadi, while the Rani only ventured to ask her to leave Virata. But Draupadi begged permission to stay just a few days longer, assuring the Rani that her Gandharva husbands would yet be of great service to the king. Shortly after the occurrences just related, and as a consequence of the death of Kechaka, who was a man of great note and generalissimo of Raja Virata's forces, Suçarman king of the Trigartas, an old enemy of Virata's, thinking it a favourable opportunity, proposed a raid into his territory for the purpose of plunder. The Kauravas willingly agreed to make a separate but simultaneous attack upon their neighbour. When intelligence of the inroad into his territory reached Virata he hastened to repel the invasion, taking in his train his servants Yudhisthira, Bhima, Nakula and Sahadeva who volunteered to fight for him. The Tregartas and Matsyas soon came into conflict, and Virata was, after a bloody fight, taken captive by Suçarman but was rescued by the Pandavas who, as usual, performed prodigies of valour.

Meanwhile the Kauravas made an unexpected attack in another direction and began carrying off the royal herds. There was no one at the capital who could go out to oppose them, the troops being all away with the king—but the King's son Uttara ventured out against the invaders with only Arjuna as his charioteer. At sight of the forces arrayed against him and the mighty heroes who led them, Uttara's courage failed him; and leaping off his chariot he fled from the field, but was brought back by Arjuna who directing him to take the reins, boldly resolved to give battle to the enemy. After providing himself with the famous and deadly weapons he had concealed a year previously in the *Sami* tree near the cemetery, he went out alone, with Uttara as his charioteer, to attack the Kaurava host. All the redoubtable heroes of the party were present that day. Old Bhishma the terrible, and well-skilled Drona with his mighty son Açwatháman and Kripa and Karna the famous offspring of Kunti and the Day-god. There too, arrayed in all the glittering panoply of war, were the formidable Duryodhana and his brother Dusçasana with the other proud princes of Dhritarashtra's race. But Arjuna alone, armed with his wonderful bow Gándiva, complelety defeated them all in one of those incomprehensible battles which delight the Hindu bard, but bewilder the European reader. In the unfortunate rank and file of the Kaurava host the slaughter caused by Arjuna was prodigious ; but not a single one of the leading heroes engaged in conflict that day was killed, or even seriously incommoded—although each of them, including Arjuna himself, was pierced by scores of deadly arrows.

The defeated Kauravas, of course, recognised their conqueror ; but the stipulated period of exile was now fully completed and the enforced truce was at an end.

Raja Virata, now enlightened as to the names and proper rank of the Pandavas, engaged to assist them in regaining their Raj, though, after recent events, it is hard to comprehend what assistance such heroes could want from Virata, or any one else. To cement the alliance between his royal house and that of the Pandavas, Virata offered his lovely daughter Uttará in marriage to Arjuna. That hero, however, had been the fair damsel's dancing-master and on intimate terms with her in the harem. He, therefore, with fine delicacy of sentiment declined the offer, lest suspicions injurious to the lady's reputation might be whispered about; but, to attest her fair fame in the most conclusive and impressive way, he accepted her hand for his son Abhimanyu to whom she was duly married, in the presence of an assembly of kings invited for the occasion, including Krishna who came attended by a "hundred millions of horse and a hundred billions of foot-soldiers."

A resort to the final arbitrament of battle seemed inevitable, and warlike preparations were vigourously pushed on by both parties, who despatched their envoys in all directions, requesting the assistance of their friends and allies. Krishna had returned to Dwarka after the marriage festivities at Panchala. Both sides anxiously sought his alliance. Duryodhana and Arjuna posted in hot haste to Dwarka to secure the aid of the mighty monarch of the Vreshnis, and both of them arrived simultaneously at Krishna's abode, while he was asleep. As privileged kinsmen they entered his bed-chamber and placed themselves near his bed, Duryodhana at the head and Arjuna at the foot, but did not dare to disturb him. As soon as Krishna awoke from his slumber the two chieftains eagerly claimed his help. As he was equally related to both he desired to divide his favours between them. He placed himself, but strictly as a non-combatant, on one side, and on the other his army of a hundred million soldiers and offered Arjuna, as he had seen him first upon awakening, the choice between the two. Without any hesitation Arjuna chose Krishna himself, leaving the mighty army of one hundred millions to swell the ranks of Duryodhana's host.

But before having recourse to arms one party at least deemed it expedient to endeavour to effect a reconciliation by negotiations; and it takes one's breath away with astonishment to find the mighty Pandava heroes—after all the gross indignities they had suffered, after the outrageous insults to which their joint-wife had been exposed and after their terrible vows of vengeance publicly uttered—tamely proposing to make peace with their arrogant cousins on condition of having nothing more than *five villages* assigned to them. All this too in the face of Draupadi's bitter and indignant taunts. However, even this humble offer of theirs was scornfully rejected by Duryodhana. But the Pandavas, even Bhima and Arjuna, being still anxious to avoid shedding the blood of their kinsfolk, Krishna, undertook to act as their ambassador, and in this capacity presented himself at the capital of Dhritarashtra. His reception was of the most magnificent kind and his mission was attended by many supernatural events. When the princes and great Officers of State were assembled in solemn conclave, to consider Krishna's proposals, a number of Brahman sages appeared in the sky and were respectfully invited, to come down and take part in the deliberations of the assembly, an invitation they readily accepted. A prolonged sitting of the council took place, during which many speeches, embellished with instructive stories of olden times, were made, in order to induce Duryodhana to come to terms with the Pandavas. Advice was, however, thrown away upon the haughty and obstinate prince, who left the chamber in great indignation.

Krishna, seeing that Duryodhana was bent on pushing matters to extremities, expressed an opinion that the best course for the old Maharajah to pursue would be to seize the young prince and his abettors and make them over to the Pandavas. He argued that: "For the sake "of a family an individual may be sacrificed; for the "sake of a village, a family may be sacrificed; for the "sake of a province a village may be sacrificed and lastly "for the sake of one's self the whole earth may be "sacrificed," and concluded with this exhortation: "O "monarch, binding Duryodhana fast make peace with the "Pandavas. O bull among Kshtriyas let not the whole "Kshatriya race be slaughtered on thy account." This proposal being secretly communicated to Duryodhana, he in turn plotted to seize and confine Krishna, but his plan was discovered by that monarch. Now, as the reader is aware, Krishna was no mere mortal, but an incarnation of the Supreme Being. Addressing the Prince the next time they met he said:

"From delusion O Duryodhana thou regardest me to "be alone and it is for this, O thou of little understand- "ing, that thou seekest to make me a captive after "vanquishing me with violence. Here, however, are all "Pandavas and all the Vrishnis and Andhakas. Here "are all the *Adityas*, the *Rudras* and the *Vasus* with all "the great *Rishis*. Saying this Keçava (Krishna), that "slayer of hostile heroes, burst out into loud laughter. "And as the high-souled Cawri laughed, from his body, "that resembled a blazing fire, issued myriads of gods, "each of lighting effulgence and not bigger than the "thumb! And on his forehead appeared Brahman and "on his breast Rudra. And on his arms appeared the "regents of the world and from his mouth issued Agni, "the Adityas, the Sáddhyas, the Vasus, the Açwins, the "Maruts with Indra and the Viçwedevas. And myriads "of Yakshas and Gandharvas, and Rakshasas also, of the "same measure and form, issued thence. And from his "two arms issued Sankarshana and Dhananjaya. And "Arjuna stood on his right, bow in hand, and Rama stood "on his left armed with the plough. And behind him "stood Bhima and Yudhisthira, and the two sons of "Madri and before him were all the Andhakas and the "Vrishnis with Praddyumna and other chiefs bearing "mighty weapons upraised. And on his diverse arms "were seen the conch, the discus, the mace, the bow called "Cáruga, the plough, the javelin, the Nandaka and every "other weapon all shining with effulgence and upraised "for striking. And from his eyes and nose and ears and "every part of his body, issued fierce sparks of fire mixed "with smoke." All except a few privileged ones closed their eyes unable to bear the splendour of this divine manifestation, which was attended with an earthquake, celestial music and a shower of heavenly flowers.

After this amazing display of his personality as the very embodiment of all the gods, Krishna, resuming his human form, left the hall leaning on the arms of two of his kinsmen. The perverse Duryodhana, however, regarded this exhibition of Krishna's godhood as a mere illusion—a clever conjuror's trick*—and, doomed to des-

* Mahabharata Udyoga Parva section CLX.

truction as he was, treated it with contemptuous disregard.

The envoy's mission having thus failed he prepared for an immediate return to his friends. Before setting out he paid a friendly visit to his aunt Kunti, the mother of the Pandavas, and, as a last piece of diplomacy, artfully endeavoured to detach Karna from Duryodhana's party. He disclosed to the famous bowman that he was Kunti's son, and *therefore*, morally, a son of Pandu; since, according to the scriptures, sons "born of a maiden have him for their father who weddeth the maiden." According to this system of paternity, Karna was not only Pandu's son, but the elder brother of Yudhisthira, and, as such, entitled to the headship of the Pandava family, to the sovereignty of Hastinapur and to supremacy over the kings of the whole earth. Krishna represented this aspect of the matter to Karna in the most tempting manner possible, not failing to mention that if he joined his brothers the fair Draupadi would be *his* wife too. But he, who had thus far gone through life known as the humble Suta's son, had the manliness to treat these offers and suggestions of the divine king of Dwarka with proud indifference, adhering with unshaken loyalty to his friend Duryodhana and the party with which he had been so long associated. The crafty Krishna then urged the absolute certainty of the complete success of the Pandavas in the contest which was approaching; but no cowardly fears disturbed the settled resolution of the hero, who, as he said, was pledged to meet Arjuna in the field of battle and would not, even if sure destruction awaited himself, withdraw from his obligations, or shirk his obvious duty to the

Kauravas.

Kunti herself next made an effort to win over Karna to the side of the Pandavas. For this purpose she stealthily followed him to the banks of the Ganges and stood silently behind him while he piously performed his devotions. When he discovered her, and respectfully enquired the object of her presence there, she disclosed to him the secret of his parentage and with well-chosen arguments urged him to join his brothers. An affectionate voice issuing from the Sun, the voice of Surya himself, confirmed the statements and supported the advice of Kunti. But Karna, "firmly devoted to truth," even though thus solicited by both his parents, protested his determination to remain firmly faithful to the cause of his friends. He gently reproached his mother for her abandonment of him in his infancy and her subsequent neglect of her maternal duties, but, with noble generosity, he made an important concession in favour of the Pandavas. "I will not speak deceitfully unto thee:" said the hero, "For the sake of Dhritarashtra's son I shall "fight with thy sons to the best of my strength and "might! I must not, however, abandon kindness and "the conduct that becometh the good. Thy words, "therefore, however beneficial cannot be obeyed by me "now. This thy solicitation to me will not yet be fruit- "less. Except Arjuna, thy other sons—Yudhisthira, "Bhima and the twins though capable of being withstood "by me in fight and capable also of being slain—shall not "yet be slain by me." Thus did the magnanimous Karna worthily close one of the most interesting incidents in the great epic.

War was now inevitable, Krishna returned to Yudhisthira and both parties prepared to join issue on the famous field of Kurukshetra.*

The Pandavas gave the supreme command of their forces to Dhrishtadyumna, who, as the reader will remember, was the destined slayer of Drona. The Kauravas, marshalled their cohorts under the leadership of the terrible Bhishma. This ancient chief had performed mighty deeds in his day, and proudly recounted, in the camp at Kurukshetra, his terrible and successful dual with Rama the son of Jamadagni, a hero who had single-handed vanquished all the Kshatriyas of the earth.

The old man's end was, however, approaching, and he himself was well aware that he must fall by the hand of one Cikhandin, an ally of the Pandavas, since that prince in a previous existence (being then a woman and subjected to great humiliations though Bhisma's conduct) had undergone the most dreadful austerities for the express purpose of compassing his destruction.

Both parties with their armies and their allies

---

* "The plain of Kurukshetra," says Mr. Talboys Wheeler, "is generally identified with the field of Panipat which lies to the north-west of the modern city of Delhi. This plain is famous in modern history as being the site of two of the greatest and most decisive battles that have been fought in modern times. It was here that Baber in A. D. 1525 overthrew the Afghan rulers at Delhi and established the dynasty of the Mogals and it was here in 1761 that Ahmad Shah Abdali the sovereign of Cabul inflicted such a crushing blow upon the Marhattas as indirectly cleared the way for the establishment of British supremacy."—Note to Wheeler's History of India, Vol. I. page 272.

The identification of Panipat with Kurukshetra in the above passage is incorrect and probably led to the disappointment experienced by Sir Edwin Arnold when he visited Panipat and found that the inhabitants of the place were ignorant of the history of Kurukshetra and its precise position (see his "India Revisited" page 193). It is near *Thanesar* and not Panipat that the Brahmans find *Kurukshetra* and the various incidents of the old story are associated with many spots in that locality. In Chapter III, entitled The Sacred Land, I have given some account of the modern aspects of Kurukshetra.

marched to and encamped upon the famous battle-field. The Pandavas had seven and the Kauravas eleven *akshauhinis* of soldiers on the ground, making a total of eighteen akshauhinis in all. Now an *akshauhini* consisted of 21,870 chariots, 21,870 elephants, 109,350 foot-soldiers and 65,610 cavalry; so that there were at *Kurukshetra* altogether 393,660 chariots with their fighting men, drivers, and horses; 393,660 elephants with their drivers and riders; 1,968,300 foot-soldiers and 1,180,980. cavalry.* All this, of course, exclusive of camp followers—a mighty hosts in themselves; for we learn that there were crowds of artizans of all sorts, also bards, singers, panigyrists, vendors, traders and prostitutes; besides surgeons, physicians, spies and spectators—all housed and provided for by the chiefs.

The commissariat arrangements were necessarily on a gigantic scale and the arsenals in proportion to the mighty hosts assembled for mutual destruction on that famous battle-field. The leading heroes had their own peculiar weapons, often of celestial origin, or possessed of magic properties, and their own inexhaustible quivers of wondrous arrows. For the rank and file there were heaps, as high as little hills, of bows and bow-strings, coats of mail and weapons of every kind; such as battle-axes, lances, poisoned darts, scimitars, nooses and lassoes.

* These are large numbers indeed; but the poet does not limit himself to them and in one of his flights of imagination speaks of a hundred millions of warriors having been slain in ten days by a single hero. (Bhishma Parva, section XIV.) In another moment of inspiration he places "a hundred millions and twenty thousand" cars in a certain strategical position on the field. (Bhishma Parva, section L.) There is in the Mahabharata generally an affectation of precison in regard to numbers, as when the narrator informs us that such a one was hit with *three* arrows another with *four* and a third with *seven*, but there is no attempt to preserve consisency and whenever the Bard is so disposed he revels without scruple in the biggest figures imaginable.

There was also an ample supply of hot oil, treacle and sand to be thrown upon the enemy, and a store of inflammable materials such as pulverised lac. And lastly there was a collection of earthen pots filled with deadly serpents, designed to cause confusion in the ranks amidst which they might be cast.

Before hostilities actually commenced Duryodhana sent a message to the camp of the Pandavas challenging them to the fight, and scornfully reminding them of the many gross insults and humiliating indignities they had had to endure at his hands. He sent an especially insulting message and challenge to Krishna, making light of his prowess and former achievements. Vaunting and blood-thirsty rejoinders of a suitable kind were, of course, carried back from the insulted Pandavas to Duryodhana and the leaders of his armies.

Before joining issue it was arranged between the hostile parties that only "persons equally circumstanced should encounter each other, fighting fairly;" that car-warriors should engage car-warriors; those on elephants should fight those similarly mounted; that horsemen should encounter horsemen and foot-soldiers foot-soldiers. It was agreed that no one should strike a disarmed, a panic striken or retreating foeman; that no blow should be given without due notice, and that stragglers, charioteers and chariot-horses, and drummers with a host of others were not to be assailed on any account. It is almost needless to say that in the succession of battles which took place at Kurukshetra these generous covenants were never observed. They seem, indeed, to have been only a formal and somewhat farcical preliminary drawn up in accordance, possibly, with some ideal but inoperative code of Kshatriya honour.

While the hosts were assembling Vyasa presented himself before king Dhritarashtra and offered to restore the blind old king's eyesight, but Dhritarashtra, unwilling to behold the bloodshed of his kinsfolk, declined the proffered boon, preferring that his charioteer, Sanjaya, should be enabled by the *Rishi's* favour to survey any portion, however remote, of the field of battle and relate all the events to him in the minutest and most circumstantial detail.

As preparations for the approaching contest were pushed on many strange portents occurred. A shower of flesh and blood fell from the skies. Unusual solar and lunar eclipses took place. Earthquakes shook both land and ocean, and rivers were turned into blood. Revolting acts of immorality were being commonly committed. Some women were giving birth to five daughters at a time, who, as soon as they were born, began to dance and sing. Other women, as well as lower animals, were bringing forth strange monsters, and, as Vyasa assured the blind king: "The images of gods and goddesses sometimes laughed and sometimes trembled, sometimes vomited blood and sometimes fell down."*

After Vyasa had gone away the blind king remarked to Sanjaya that, since "many hundreds of millions of heroic men" had assembled at Kurukshetra, he desired

* Here is a reference to the images of gods and goddesses existing at the period of the great war which is both important and suggestive. They are also referred to again in section CXIII. of the Bhisma Parva.

to know all about the countries from which they had come, for there were many nationalities represented in the two armies. Sanjaya, having been endowed with superhuman perception by the Rishi Vyasa, gave his master, the king, a long lesson in geography, which it is rather disappointing to find so largely mythical as to be of little value, except perhaps as an indication of the very imperfect geographical knowledge possessed by the authors of the Mahabharata. Sanjaya's inspired description of the countries of the world abounds in mountains of gold and gems; it embraces oceans of butter, milk, curds and wine; and dwells upon such objects in nature as trees yielding fruits which measure 2,500 cubits in circumference. While revelling in these glories of sea and land Sanjaya's descriptive narrative does not quite overlook the causes of natural phenomena, for he, no less than the modorn scientist, has his own theory of the winds. It is we learn from him all due to "four princely elephants adored by all." These magnificent beasts, whose enormous proportions Sanjaya does not venture to calculate, seize with their lithe trunks the wandering winds and then breathe them over the Earth. "The winds thus let out by those respiring elephants, come over the Earth, and in consequence thereof creatures draw breath and live."

In the wonderful lands pictured by the inspired geographer the men were necessarily long-lived. Some races, indeed, were exempt from death and there were others whose lives extended to many thousands of years. In respect to their own land of *Bharatvarsha*, where the great battle was about to be fought, Sanjaya makes some statements which seem worthy of note. He says, for example, after naming certain mountain-ranges, that there are many "smaller mountains inhabited by barbarous tribes" and he adds that "Aryas and *mlecchas*, and many "races mixed of the two elements, drink the waters of "the following rivers *viz.*, magnificent Ganga, Sindhu and "Saraswati; of Godavari and Narmuda * * * and "that large river called Yamuna &c."

At length the day of real battle arrived. The chiefs on both sides made their final preparations. With tall and handsome standards, borne conspicuously aloft,* drums beating and conchs sounding, they took up their positions on the great plain. Karna alone, held aloof from the contest, resolved to take no part in it while Bhishma lived, for he was smarting under some unbearable insults received from the aged leader of the Kauravas

As both armies, drawn up for battle, awaited the dawn, a dust storm arose which wrapped everything in darkness. When the air cleared and each party could see the other, as well as hear the blare of its trumpets, a sort of mutual dread seems to have afflicted them, for the warriors on either side trembled at the sight of the mighty heroes of the opposing hosts.

At this critical juncture in the fate of the world, Arjuna, by the advice of Krishna, offered a special prayer for victory to Durga. The goddess in answer to this invocation appeared in the sky and assured her votary

* Bhisma's standard was a gold palmyra palm, Drona's a golden altar, Duryodhana's an elephant wrought in gems. Arjuna carried on his car a banner whereon was seated a gigantic ape. Each chief of note had his own distinguishing standard or banner.

of complete success.

As the virtuous Yudhisthira, his white umbrella borne above his head, moved about marshalling his forces he was attended by a crowd of Brahmans and Rishis hymning his praises and praying for the destruction of his enemies. Of course the pious king could do no less, even at such a busy and anxious moment, than bestow upon these saintly allies of his what, indeed, they with their habitual proud condescension were there to receive,—rich presents of kine, ornaments, clothes and gold.

When the armed millions were finally ranged for immediate hostilities, in all the pomp and glitter of approaching battle, Arjuna desired Krishna to place his chariot in the open space between the two armies. Surveying the embattled hosts from this position, Arjuna appears to have been dismayed at the thought of the unparalleled slaughter of kinsmen which a struggle between such colossal armies would inevitably lead to, and, in view of this deplorable issue, hesitated to join battle with his foes, doubtful whether any personal consideration whatever could justify an appeal to arms under such circumstances.

Krishna undertook to remove his doubts and succeeded in doing so, the dialogue between them, known as the *Bhagavatgita*, or divine song, which is introduced into the great epic at this stage of the narrative, forming, from a religious point of view, one of its most important parts.*

When Arjuna, convinced of the lawfulness of enter-

* This famous dialogue is too long to be dealt with in this place and too important to be passed over altogether; so I have appended a Note on the subject, to which the reader's attention is invited.

ing into the contest, had taken up his bow *Gandiva*, in readiness for the fray, his followers raised a joyful shout, and the gods with the Gandharvas, the Rishis and the rest, crowded to the spot eager to witness the impending battle.

But there was still another interruption. Yudhisthera, suddenly laying down his arms and divesting himself of his armour, advanced eastward towards the opposing forces. Although filled with astonishment at this proceeding, his dutiful brothers immediately followed him, themselves unarmed and unprotected by armour. What was the mission the king had undertaken? Was he bent on making a final effort to effect a reconciliation, or was he, terror-striken by the superior numbers of his adversaries, going to offer an unconditional surrender? No, it was neither the one object nor the other which stirred the heart of the virtuous king to this strange performance in presence of the two armies drawn up for deadly strife. He, pious soul, was only going to crave the permission of his elders and preceptors in Dhritarastra's army to engage in battle with them; to solicit, with childlike trustfulness, their *blessing* in the coming contest with themselves and, if possible, to induce them to tell him how their own destruction might be compassed by him! The leaders he went to propitiate, though resolved to fight to their utmost for the king whose cause they had espoused, were very affable to the pious son of Dharma; received him with affection and dismissed him with honour. The conduct of the Pandavas on this occasion excited universal admiration and met with the hearty approval of all, and we learn that, "in consequence of this, the minds and hearts of every one there were attracted towards them, and the *mlecchas* and the *Aryas** there, who witnessed or heard of that behaviour of the sons of Pandu, all wept with choked voices."

The battle of Kurukshetra which closed the golden age of India lasted for eighteen consecutive days.

During the first ten days Bhishma commanded Dhritarashtra's forces; while Karna held aloof in sullen indignation. A goodly volume is devoted to the incidents of these ten days, each of which seems to have had its own special heroes, who, under the influence of a sort of divine fury, like that attributed by the Norsemen to their *Berserkers*, carried everything before them. In picturing the events of these battles the Hindu bards have allowed their imaginations to run riot in a most incomprehensible way. Not only the demigods, but the merely human leaders (very little inferior to the demigods in martial qualities) in both armies, perform the most astonishing feats of arms, and display the most wonderful indifference to wounds. Sometimes a hero will shoot at his adversary arrows enough to envelop him completely and shroud him from view, or to darken the whole sky; but his antagonist, well skilled in the art of self-defence, will, with the greatest composure, stop those myriads of arrows† in mid-air with an equal or superior number of shafts from his own bow;‡ or, as

---

* This allusion to the *Mlecchas* and *Aryas* fighting side by side is interesting and noteworthy. Later on we shall have occasion to note the presence of *Rakshasas* also in either army.

† Millions upon millions. Vide section CXV of the Bhisma Parva.

‡ "Then with a thousand arrows well shot Pandu's son Arjuna, famed for his skill in battleshrowded Bhishma on all sides. That arrowy net, however, of Partha Bhisma the son of Cantanu baffled with an arrowy net (of his own). * * * And

Cikhandin did, cut in pieces with his dexterous sword the shower of arrows poured upon him. Sometimes a heavy mace, hurled by a powerful arm with well directed aim, will whiz through the air towards some leader of men ; but as it is hurtling along it will be cut into many fragments by crescent-headed arrows discharged at it, with unerring skill, by the hero for whose destruction it was intended. Sometimes standards are brought down by sharp arrows, sometimes the bow is severed in a warrior's hand by the shaft of an opponent, while horses and elephants, though cased in mail, fall easy victims to the archer's skill. Occasionally, in pressing emergencies, superhuman weapons are called into requisition, and *mantras* or spells are employed to give them more destructive force. Nor are the powers of producing strange illusions to terrify or baffle the foe neglected by those who possess them, namely the Rakshasas in either army.* These terrible beings, capable of assuming any shape at will, and able to deceive their foes by strange illusions, would at one time raise up a spectral host of demons to terrify their opponents and at another time, perhaps, paralyse them by producing before their startled eyes a false picture of their friends and allies lying cruelly slaughtered around them, or in head-long flight before the enemy.

Notwithstanding their inimitable skill in the arts of attack and defence the heroes do not get off unscathed. In a single fight one of them might be pierced with any

---

the successive flights of arrows shot from Bhishma's bow were seen to be dispersed by the shafts of Arjuna. And so the flights of arrows shot by Arjuna cut off by the arrows of Ganga's son all fell down on the ground." Bhishma Parva, section LII.

* It is worthy of note that *Rakshasas* are present in both the Kaurava and Pandava armies.

number of arrows, from one or two to five hundred or a thousand* as the case might be, yet, usually, the chiefs seem hardly the worse for the punishment. Indeed the poets love to depict their dauntless favourites bristling with arrows and streaming with blood, when they resemble in beauty blossoming *kincukas* in spring time, or "clouds tinged with the rays of the sun." One warrior with three arrows fixed in his forehead is likened to Mount Meru with its triple summits of gold; another, with a circle of sharp arrows lodged in his ample breast, resembles "the sun with his rays at midday." Odds are of no account when the heroes are once carried away with ungovernable fury, roaring tremendously, and "licking the corners of their mouths like lions in the forest." Bhima on foot with his club in his hand, is, under such conditions, a match for whole armies, through which he rages, with leonine roars, crushing chariots and horses under his blows and smashing luckless elephants and their riders by thousands, himself bespattered with the blood, fat and marrow of his slaughtered foes, resembling, as the poet tells us, the Destroyer himself, with wide open mouth, as he appears at the end of the *yuga*. Similarly Arjuna, when attacked simultaneously by forty thousand charioteers and hemmed in by them, kills the entire number of his rash assailants with arrows from Gandiva. When

* Mahabharata, Bhishma Parva, section LXIX. That the numbers are intended to be precise will be apparent from the following passage which is quoted merely as a sample.

"Then Bhishma the grandsire of the Kauravas struck Arjuna with seventy seven arrows, and Drona (struck him) with five and twenty, and Kripa with fifty; and Duryodhana with four and sixty and Cala with nine arrows, and Drona's son, that tiger among men, with sixty and Vikarna with three arrows; and Saindhava with nine and Cakuni with five. And Artayani pierced Pandu's son with three broad-headed arrows. And though pierced on all sides by them with sharp arrows, that great bowman, that mighty armed (warrior) wavered not, like a mountain that is pierced with arrows"—Ditto, section LII.

Yudhisthira, ordinarily cold-blooded, blazed up with wrath on the battle field, "the thought that arose in the minds of all creatures was that this king excited with rage will to-day consume the three worlds." Bhishma too and Drona and many another hero semi-divine or only mortal, seems in his turn quite irresistible and carries everything before him when excited to mad (*Berserk*) fury.

The dire confusion caused by the vast multitudes of resolute combatants, the blind rage and terror of thousands of wounded elephants and horses trampling wildly through the midst of friends and foes, the deafening uproar of the strife, where the tumultuous shouts and cries of contending warriors, mingled with the clash of arms, the twang of bow-strings, the blare of trumpets, and the bellowing of elephants, are all vividly pictured by the poet of Kurukshetra.

It would be too tedious to recount the innumerable combats which the author describes, or to follow the varying fortunes of the field, as victory inclines now to one side, now to the other. It would be cruel work, to dwell upon the prodigious slaughter of the rank and file which occurred each day, or to picture the vast plain covered with the mangled corpses of men, horses and elephants. Nor would it be either profitable or pleasant to wander over the ground encumbered with shattered chariots, broken standards and abandoned weapons of every kind, amidst which pitiful wreck flowed great sluggish streams of crimson blood. Somehow the sickening horror of the terrible scenes of carnage which the epic bards have conjured up does not seem to have struck them, for when they remark upon the appearance of the field—strewn with mangled corpses and broken armour, with banners and weapons all reeking with blood—it is usually with admiration of its *beauty*, unmingled with any feeling of aversion or regret. In their eyes the scene of death and ruin, with its gory trophies, "shines as if with floral wreaths," or "looks beautiful like the firmament in autumn," or "like a damsel adorned with different kinds of ornaments." In the gloom of night, however, the Hindu poets realize, with superstitious awe, the abhorrent nature of the dreadful battle-field, "abounding as it did with spirits and with jackals howling pitiously."

How the multitudinous dead and the wreckage which littered the field were desposed of we do not learn, but the opposing parties retired each day at sunset to their respective camps and renewed the battle with the dawn of next day. However, occasional allusions to hungry dogs and vultures, howling jackals, stealthy hyænas and fierce cannibals give a dark, if not very intelligible, hint of the fate of the unburied dead.

The death of Bhishma is the prominent and crowning event of the battles which raged with unabated fury for the first ten days of the war. The old hero performed prodigies of valour and many a time proved himself more than a match for his brave opponents, slaughtering no less than "a hundred million of warriors in ten days."* Such huge work, it must be admitted, required great celerity of action and we learn, accordingly, that in one battle Bhishma "felled the heads of car-warriors like a

* Mahabharta, Bhisma Parva, Section XIV.

"skilful man felling (with stones) ripe (palmyra) fruits "from trees that bear them. And the heads of warriors "falling upon the surface of the earth produced a loud "noise resembling that of a stony shower."† His success against the Pandavas aroused the anger of Krishna, who had not escaped unwounded in these hotly contested fights, and, jumping off the car he was driving, he rushed impetuously forward to slay the son of Ganga, "and the end of his yellow garments waving in the air looked like a cloud charged with lightning in the sky."

Bhishma cheerfully awaited his doom from such hands and Arjuna with difficulty restrained the fury of his divine ally and kinsman by promising to slay the chief himself. Later on Krishna was again roused to fury against the aged champion of the Kauravas and this time could only be dissuaded from taking his life by being reminded, that he had engaged *not to enter personally into the contest.* So despondent did Bhishma's remarkable success make king Yudhisthira that the latter, accompanied by his brothers and Krishna, actually sought an interview with the ancient chief, for the express purpose of ascertaining from himself in what manner his death might be compassed and victory secured for the Pandavas. In consequence of what Bhishma said on this occasion, Cikhandin was, on the tenth day of the war, placed prominently in the forefront of the battle, supported by Arjuna and the best men of his party. A well directed and persistent attack was made upon Bhishma. A fierce battle ensued, but the chivalrous Bhishma refused to assail Cikhandin, *because he had once*

† Mahabhara, Bhishma—Parva Section LXXXVII.

been a woman and he was eventually overpowered, mostly, however, by the arrows of Arjuna. There was nowhere about the person of the hero a space two fingers wide free from the shafts of his enemies, and when he fell from his chariot he did not touch the ground, being literally supported on a couch of arrows. Although so sorely afflicted by the darts of his enemies, Bhishma did not die immediately. The time was inauspicious and he postponed his death, as he possessed the privilege of doing, till a more propitious moment. "Meanwhile the valiant and intelligent Bhishma, the son of Cantanu, having recourse to that *Yoga* which is taught in the great Upanishads, and engaged in mental prayers, remained quiet, expectant of his hour."

The fall of the aged leader was the signal for a cessation of the battle, the chiefs of both sides pressing forward to pay their respects to the dying general. While conversing with those around him he complained that his head was unsupported. Luxurious pillows were quickly brought for his use, but he rejected them all. Upon this Arjuna made a rest for his head with three arrows, and the grim warrior was satisfied. To allay Bhisma's burning thirst Arjuna shot an arrow into the ground, whence a fountain of pure water came springing up to the great comfort of the wounded veteran. Guards were placed round the old man, as he lay on his arrowy couch and both sides retired to rest.

In the dead of night Karna came to pay his homage to the dying general and to ask forgiveness for any faults he may have committed. Bhishma freely forgave him, and advised him to transfer his allegiance to the Pandavas, but Karna, nobly faithful to the path of honour, rejected the suggestion as on so many previous occasions.

After the fall of Bhishma the command of the army was given to Drona, and the contest was carried on with unabated vigour, resulting more than once in the defeat of the Pandavas. The record of Drona's command abounds in numerous descriptions of single combats, in which, besides the more prominent leaders, many another chief fought with marvellous skill and daring. As was inevitable, many heroic warriors were killed—such as Abhimanyu the son of Arjuna and the mighty Rakshasa Ghatotkacha, Bhima's son, who in his fall crushed to death a whole *aukshauhani* of Dhritarastra's troops.

In one of the battles Jayadartha, king of the Sindhus, performed, single-handed, deeds of matchless daring; for he alone held in check all the sons of Pandu. Arjuna, enraged at Jayadartha's success and attributing Abhimanyu's death to him, vowed, in the prsence all men, either to slay the victorious chief before the day was done, or to lay down his own life on the funeral pyre. But the Raja of Sindhu was so well supported by his friends that there appeared every likelihood that he would survive the day. Rather than this should occur and Arjuna fall by his own hand, Krishna obscured the sun by his *Yoga* power. The unsuspecting Jayadartha and his friends, believing that the sun had set and night come on, were filled with joy at the prospect of Arjuna's doom, and were carelessly looking up towards the darkened sky, when Arjuna, at Krishna's suggestion, taking advantage of their being off their guard, renewed the battle with redoubled vigour. He eventually struck off Jayadartha's head with one of his wonderful weapons, and sped it along through the air with his arrows till it fell into the lap of Vriddhakshatra, the father of Jayadartha, whence it rolled on to the ground. It appears that when Jayadartha was born, a voice, proceeding from some unseen being, predicted that he would meet his death by having his head cut off. His pious father thereupon prophesied that the man who should cause his son's head to fall to the *earth*, would have his own cracked into a hundred pieces. For his own protection, therefore, Arjuna, at Krishna's suggestion, had hurled the dead man's head into Vriddhakshatra's lap, and, as it fell to the earth, lo! the old man's head cracked into a hundred fragments in grim fulfilment of his own prophecy.

Other marvellous events are not wanting in the narrative; as when, in the thick of battle, Arjuna, piercing the earth with one of his arrows, creates in a moment a lake of water for his thirsty horses to drink from—a lake inhabited by swarms of aquatic birds and covered with lotuses—or when Açwatthaman employs the irresistible *Narayana* weapon and the Pandavas on their part *pacify* and *propitiate* this destructive missile by laying down their arms before it.

Drona himself, although advanced in years, defeated the Pandavas many times, and it was only by a cruel stratagem that his destruction was ultimately effected. When he was carrying every thing before him in the battle the Pandavas informed him, falsely, that his son had been killed. He did not credit the report at first, but when assured of its truth by the virtuous Yudhisthira himself, who stooped to this mean falsehood upon the advice of Krishna, the old hero threw away his arms and, devoting *himself to Yoga contemplation*, passed away immediately. After his spirit had ascended to heaven in great glory, Dhrishtadyumna beheaded his lifeless corpse,* upon which Dhritarastra's troops fled precipitately from the field.

Karna succeeded Drona as generalissimo of the forces, but his command was of short duration; for although he performed wonders of gallantry against his adversaries, *Fate* was too strong for him and on the second day he was overthrown by Arjuna. There was something unfortunate, if not unfair, in the circumstances attending his death; for just when he had obtained an advantage over Arjuna who seemed likely to get the worst of the contest, a wheel of Karna's chariot came off. He was obliged to leap to the ground and, in this unfavourable position, was despatched by Arjuna.

In the battles which took place under Karna's direction an eventful combat occurred between Bhima and Duhsasana, ending in the defeat and death of the latter, whose warm blood Bhima drank in fulfilment of his vow on the occasion of Draupadi's humiliation in the gaming hall. Another incident of some interest is the vigorous, but unsuccessful, attack made by an army of

---

* Drona being a Brahman it would never have done form him to have actually died by the sword of Dhrishtadyumna. Yet this prince was borne expressly to destroy Drona—hence this very clumsy attempt to reconcile Brahman sensitiveness and pretensions with the details of the old legend.

Mlechchas on Arjuna, as the narrative shows the poet's high opinion of the martial qualities of the non-Aryan races in the Kaurava army.

For the fourth time Dhritarastra's forces were without a commander. This time the choice fell upon Salya king of Madra who gallantly emulated the deeds of his heroic predecessors. But though he fought with vigour and determination, though he was ably supported by chiefs like Sakuni who still survived, though his *Mlechcha* allies, under their leader Salva, did great execution amongst the enemy, victory eventually declared for his opponents. A terrific battle was followed by a complete rout and the utter annihilation of the Kaurava forces, of whose eleven *aukshauhinis*, there remained, at the end of the eighteenth day of the war but *four* men,—*four men only* out of all the countless hosts who had joined the blind king's party!

These four were Duryodhana himself, Kripa, Aswathaman and Kritavarman. Now Duryodhana possessed a charm by which he could remain under water as long as he pleased; and, taking advantage of this, he hid himself in the lake carrying his mace in his hand. But he was traced to his hiding place. Yudhisthira approaching the lake taunted Duryodhana with cowardice and challenged him to come out and fight as a Kshatriya should. Stung by his taunts Duryodhana emerged from his hiding place, dripping with blood and water, having agreed to engage in a single combat with the giant Bhima, both being armed with clubs only. So equal were the combatants that a prolonged fight ensued. Tremendous blows were freely given and received. The very earth trembled under the dreadful contest and the Pandavas began to entertain grave fears that if Bhima were vanquished, the rest of them would be easily defeated and slain in detail by Duryodhana who was a proficient in the use of the mace. At this critical moment Krishna artfully suggested by a gesture to Bhima that he should strike Duryodhana on the thigh and thus fulfil his vow and vanquish his enemy at the same time. A successful blow delivered upon this suggestion, which was contrary to the recognised rules of club fighting, laid Duryodhana low, and left the Pandavas undisputed masters of the day. But, even though countless millions of human beings had already perished on the fatal field of Kurukshetra, and Duryodhana the cause of all this havoc lay there mortally wounded, more blood was yet to flow. Of the Kaurava hosts there still remained three men and of these one, Açwatthaman, lived only in the hope of avenging to some extent, the blood of his father Drona. Brooding schemes of vengeance through the dark hours of the night, the young man observed, in a forest where he had taken refuge, an owl approach noiselessly some sleeping crows and destroy them one after another. Accepting this event as a suggestion for his guidance he persuaded his two companions to join him in an attempt to steal into the camp of the Pandavas—whose followers were sleeping in fancied security—with the object of wreaking their vengeance on their unarmed and unsuspecting enemies. They justified this nocturnal attack by calling to mind the many unfair advantages which the Pandavas had taken of their more honourable foes, during the course of this fratricidal war—as in the cases of

Bhishma, Drona and Karna.

At the entrance to the camp the three desperate warriors were met by an awful figure who barred their progress. With him Açwatthaman fought a fierce battle during the course of which be recognised in his redoutable adversary the great god Siva, before whom he humbly prostrated himself. Presently there appeared a golden altar attended by hideous monsters, and Açwatthaman, to obtain the favour of Siva, offered himself as a sacrifice in the fire which blazed upon the altar. Siva was propitiated by this pious act and himself graciously entered the body of Açwatthaman, after explaining to him that he had up to that time protected the family of Draupada in order to please Krishna, but that he would do so no longer as their hour was at hand.

Açwatthaman thus inspired by Siva, and now glorious to behold, boldly penetrated the hostile camp, while Kripa and Kritavarman stood at the gate to intercept and destroy all fugitives. The five Pandavas themselves were away in the now vacant camp of the Kauravas, whither they had gone to take possession of the spoils of the vanquished.

The revenge taken by Açwatthaman and his associates was complete and bloody. The first to perish in the nocturnal attack was the generalissimo of the Pandava, army Dhristadyumna himself whom Açwatthaman found sleeping in his tent and whom be literally trampled to death under his feet. An indescribable panic was caused by the massacre which followed the murder of the commander-in-chief, and, in the dire confusion of darkness, friends fell upon each other, fathers killed their own sons and sons their fathers. In this terrible "night of slaughter" Açwatthaman killed the five sons of Draupadi, one after the other, and carried away their bleeding heads with him to gratify the heart of the chieftian, his master, who lay in the agony of death upon that field of carnage.

Açwatthaman approaching the prince told him that he had slain the Pandavas and had their heads in his possession. Even with his life ebbing fast away the feelings of gratified revenge put a transient vigour into Duryodhana and he leaped from the ground in a transport of fierce joy. The morning was not far distant, and in the uncertain twilight preceding the dawn he examined the heads and was deceived by the resemblance the sons of Draupadi bore to their respective fathers. Gloating over the complete vengeance which had been wreaked by Açwatthaman he took into his hands what he believed to be the head of Bhima and squeezed it with all his might. The skull burst in his hands under the violent pressure and Duryodhana at once perceived that some deception had been practised on him; for he felt that Bhima's skull would not have thus yielded in his grasp. He desired to see the other heads and on close inspection understood what had really occurred. With reproaches on his lips and bitterness in his heart the dying man expired, while his three followers made haste to quit the spot and flee from the pursuit of their enemies.*

The war was over. The five Pandavas, now undisput-

* This description of Duryodhana's death scene is based upon the version in Mr. Talboys Wheeler's History of India, Vol. I, page, 351—352 which is derived from a translation of the epic in the library of the Asiatic Society of Bengal supposed to have been prepared by Prof. H. H. Wilson.

ed masters of the situation, sought a reconciliation with the blind king. Helpless though he was, Dhritarastra's feelings of bitterness against Bhima, for the unfair defeat of his son Duryodhana, were so intense, that he meditated crushing the hero to death in his mighty arms, under the pretence of a friendly welcome; but Krishna, divining his intention, placed an iron image in his embrace, which the blind king, who possessed gigantic strength, crushed to pieces against his breast. Eventually, however, a reconciliation was effected between the Pandavas and the heart-broken old monarch.

The scene of the terrible carnage during eighteen consecutive days was now covered with mourners seeking, with breaking hearts, to recognize their beloved dead amongst the reeking corpses. At length arrangements were made for the cremation of the bodies that lay upon the battle-field, and they were duly disposed of, according to their rank.

A triumphal procession was next arranged from the plain of Kurukshetra to the city of Hastinapur, where Yudhisthira was installed, with great pomp and ceremony, as Raja, under the nominal sovereignty of his blind uncle. At the inauguration, a friend of Duryodhana's began to revile the new king for the slaughter of his kinsfolk; but the Brahmans looked upon the reviler with angry eyes and he fell upon the ground like a tree struck by lightning and was burnt to ashes upon the spot.

Yudhisthira, though now enthroned at Hastinapur, seems to have found his new office so beset with anxieties that he desired to have the advice of Bhishma for his guidance. He accordingly proceeded to the battle-field, at Kurukshetra, where the old hero was still alive upon his couch of arrows. The dying sage gave the king excellent advice on many important subjects relating to the duties of kings and the conduct of life, which we cannot, unfortunately, find space for. When he had passed fifty-eight days on his uncomfortable bed Bhishma resolved to die. At once the cruel arrows left his body; his head split open and his released spirit ascended to heaven like a bright star.

As soon as Yudhisthira was firmly established on the throne of Bharata he determind to perform an *Aswamedha*, or horse sacrifice. The performance of this sacrifice was an assertion of sovereignty over the whole earth, and had such peculiar virtue that the successful performance of one hundred *Aswamedhas* gave the sacrificer power even over Indra, the god of Heaven. In Yudhisthira's case, it is true, the *Aswamedha* was suggested by the sage Vyasa, as atonement for all the monarch's sins. A horse of a particular colour had to be obtained, and, as a preliminary to the sacrifice, the animal was set free to wander, at its pleasure, for one year. The Rajah who proposed performing the Aswamedha or the Deputy of such Rajah, followed with an army in the track of the horse. If the animal found its way into the territories of any foreign State, the ruler of that state was bound either to seize the horse and fight the invader, or else to acknowledge his own inferiority, and, in proof of submission, to swell with his own forces those of his superior lord.

In order to be present at the ceremony of loosing the horse Krishna journeyed to Hastinapur. A detailed account of his march is given in the Mahabharata, and is of special interest when it is remembered that this Raja is regarded as an incarnation of the Supreme Being. Krishna's trip to Yudhisthira's capital was a joyous progress. He was accompanied by Rukmini and Satyabháma and his other favourite wives, as well as various members of the family. The crowd that attended him was a motley one, and included no small number of loose characters, dancing girls and performers of all sorts, with whom Krishna seems to have been on the most familiar footing. And they are represented as having been aware of his divine nature, for a harlot having met with an accident which excited the mirth of the by-standers, remarked: "There is no occasion for laughing, for every day I behold the divine Krishna and therefore all my sins are forgiven me."*

The horse destined for the sacrifice was at length set free and was followed by Arjuna at the head of a mighty army. It led him and his followers into many strange adventures, but we shall here only allude to a few of them. The horse, in his wanderings, entered the country of the Amazons, young and lovely warriors—"perfect in the arts of love, and in the various ways of fascinating men."†—whose charms were as dangerous as their weapons; but who were prevailed upon to allow the horse free-pas-

* The Mahabharata quoted in History of India by J. Talboys Wheeler, Vol. I, pages 386—390.

† Ditto Ditto page 401.

sage through their country. Then the host was conducted into a region where the trees bore men and women, and where the men had ears with one of which they covered their heads and with the other their bodies. In this land of marvels the terrible prime minister wore, as ear-rings, a dead elephant and a dead camel.

The horse next passed into the country of Manipura, which Arjuna had visited in one of his earlier wanderings, and over which a son of his was now ruling. This king's magnificence was such that his palace was surrounded by a golden wall, and his capital by a silver one. His reception-hall was supported on golden pillars, and illuminated at night by torches made of sandal wood, wound round with cloth steeped in perfumed oils. The greatness and power of the ruler of this country was commensurate with his wealth and splendour; but his filial respect was so great that he tendered his submission to the invader, his father Arjuna, in the most abject manner. Arjuna disdainfully repudiated a son who exhibited, as he thought, so much cowardice. The result was a terrible battle in which Arjuna's head was severed from his body by a crescent-shaped arrow from his son's bow. However, Arjuna was not to perish thus; and his son procured, from the King of the Serpents, who lived in the bowels of the earth, a certain jewel which possessed the power of restoring life. This when applied to the body of the dead Pandava caused the head and trunk to reunite. Arjuna, restored to life, was easily reconciled to his brave son, the mighty Raja of Manipur.

The year appointed for the wandering expedition at

length came to an end, and the horse with its escort returned to Hastinapur. The sacrifice was then performed with the usual magnificence. Gold, jewels, elephants, horses and cows were, as on all such occasions, freely given away, particularly to the Brahmans. With great ceremony the head of the horse was struck off by Bhima, and, immediately mounting towards the sky, soared out of sight. The body was cast into the sacrificial fire. To crown the great ceremony Indra with attendant gods presented himself to partake of the sacrifice, and, amidst general rejoicings feastings and further extravagent largesses, the *Aswamedha* was brougut to a successful conclusion.

Years passed; the blind old Maharaja, weighed down with the sorrowful recollections of his sons and followers who had fallen in the great war, retired with his wife Gandhari, into a jungle on the banks of the Ganges. Kunti also accompanied them. To this hermitage the Pandavas paid a visit. The conversation, as was natural, turned upon the friends and kinsfolk who had perished on the plain of Kurukshetra. While this sad subject was being discussed the sage Vyasa made his appearance, and promised the mourners that he would, that very night, show them the relatives for whom they had been sorrowing. After bathing in the Ganges the company stood together on the bank of the sacred river. Vyasa standing by the king summoned the dead to appear. A scene of inexpressible grandeur followed immediately. The river began to foam and boil. A great noise was heard, and, out of the troubled water, arose the men who had died at Kurukshetra. They came as when alive, but more beautiful and in all the pomp of martial glory, in full armour, upon their chariots and with music. The foes who had cruelly slaughtered each other now appeared as friends, and were attended by troops of singers and of dancing-girls. Dead and living communed freely with each other, and, in the joy of reunion, the sorrows of so many years were forgotten. But with the morning the ghostly visitants disappeared. And now Vyasa gave the widows who wished to rejoin their dead husbands permission to do so; upon which all the widows drowned themselves in the Ganges and were reunited to their lords.

The Pandavas with their followers returned to Hastinapur and, about two years afterwards, the old king, his wife and Kunti with their attendants perished in a jungle-fire.

Krishna, the friend of the Pandavas, also met with an untimely end, after another fratricidal civil war in his own country, and his capital city of Dwarka—from which the remaining inhabitants had been removed by Arjuna, to Hastinapur—was overwhelmed by a wave of the sea.

After the many trials and sorrows they had gone through, a weariness of life, such as would seem only too natural under the circumstances, took possession of the Pandavas, and they were minded to be done with earthly things.

> Let us go forth to die! Time slayeth all.
> We will find Death who seeketh other men.
>
> (SIR EDWIN ARNOLD.)

With this resolve the five brothers adopted the hermit's garb. Accompanied by the still peerless Draupadi, and attended by one faithful dog, they turned their steps towards Mount Meru—the abode of the gods. A long, circuitous and weary journey was theirs; performed on foot, and in decorous Indian file. The brothers walked one behind the other according to their respective ages. Draupadi, "with soft dark face and lustrous eyes,"* dutifully followed her husbands with unwavering devotion. The dog brought up the rear. Through hoary forests, by running streams, along the shores of the sounding ocean, over parched and burning plains lay their toilsome way to the sacred mountain. But alas! the king alone was destined to reach it alive. One by one the tired pilgrims succumbed to inevitable death. First Draupadi fainted and perished on the way, because—her only fault—her woman's heart had loved Arjuna too much. After her Sahadeva paid the penalty of pride, and Nakula of self-love. The three who still survived hastened on without looking back, for they knew that their loved companions were beyond the reach of any help. The king with Bhima and Arjuna pressed on for Meru. But the great archer's turn to die soon arrived, and the giant Bhima perished also. Of all the pilgrims who, weary of the world, had set out from Hastinapur king Yudhisthira alone, with the hound closely following him, reached the Celestial Mountain and was warmly welcomed by the gods.

With the gates of *Swarga* wide open for his reception the magnanimous king paused upon the very threshold of Paradise and, more mindful of others than of himself, asked that his brothers and Draupadi should accompany him into Heaven. Being assured that he would meet them there, his next solicitude was for his canine companion. At the gate he was informed that the hound must be left outside to the fate that might await him, for such could certainly not enter the abode of the gods. The large-hearted king, however, would not consent to abandon even this humble comrade of his weary pilgrimage, and lo!

> "Straight as he spake, brightly great Indra smiled,
> Vanished the hound, and in its stead stood there,
> The Lord of Death and Justice, Dharma's self." (ARNOLD.)

In Swarga Yudhisthira did not find his noble brothers, nor the tender Draupadi, and learned that they were still in Purgatory, expiating the sins of their earthy lives. Without them Heaven had no charms for the king. He preferred to share the unhappy fate of his kinsfolk, and was conducted to the nether regions by a celestial messenger, along a dismal road reeking with loathsome corruption, and through hideous scenes of terrible suffering, such as have filled the morbid imaginations of men in every nation.

Yudhisthira's presence in those abodes of anguish brought some mitigation to the punishments of the many who were there undergoing a fierce purgation from the dross of their mundane existence. Wailing voices entreated the great king to stay awhile, for their comfort, amongst them, and he magnanimously consented to do so. But the gods, at length interposing, conducted him back to Swarga. With him were his brothers and Draupadi—all purified by punishment from such sins or frailties as had marred their perfection during their terrestrial life.

Thus, grandly, closes the wonderful story of the great war!

Chapter III.—The Sacred Land.

Round about the town of *Thanesar* lies *Bhramavarta*, the sacred land of the Hindus, and within a short walk of the town is *Kurukshetra*.

Thanesar itself is in ruins, and the lake near which the Pandavas and Kauravas fought their great battle is now a dismal swamp, yet adorned on one side by a beautiful fringe of really magnificent banian trees, under whose leafy covering are sheltered a few of those unimposing brick-and-plaster temples so common in upper India.

Unsparing Time has strewn the whole world with the ruins of man's handiwork. The crumbling remains of cities, temples and palaces may be found in every country under the sun, and, according to circumstances, appeal to widely different feelings and evoke widely different sentiments in the heart of the spectator. Thus, it is with a profound sense of the reality and greatness of Roman power that we muse amidst the columns of the Forum, or recall to mind, in the mighty Colloseum, the tragic pastimes of the imperial people. It is with a respectful admiration, not unmingled with pity, that we see in old Delhi the considerable ruins of the lordly mosque constructed out of the spoils of more ancient Hindu temples. But it is only with a feeling of simple depression, unrelieved by any other sentiment, that we wander amongst the extensive brick ruins of Thanesar, unredeemed by a trace of either beauty or grandeur and largely tenanted by monkeys, in whom a pious Punjabi graduate recognises "defunct "Brahmans * * watching as it were over their old "habitations."*

I visited the town in December 1892, and never have I seen a place which looked more utterly forlorn. Whole streets of brick-built houses, quite modern in appearance, falling into ruins, which are too mean to be interesting, too recent to be picturesque, and, for the most part, entirely uninhabited, except by the "defunct Brahmans" already referred to. Where shops and dwellings still exist they partake of the general tumble-down character of the town; but the wares for sale are by no means ancient and show that the remnant who burrow in Thanesar still indulge in the rich confectionary of the country and still take pleasure in the gay coloured *saree* and the glittering *chooree* of glass.

Amidst the general decay a few Hindu temples with tall, tapering spires still show a brave front, and the tomb of the Mussulman Saint, Shaikh Chilli, built on a slight elevation, rears its marble dome into the air with something of pride; but the rest, as I have said, is meanness and squalor itself.

Within the precincts of Shaikh Chilli's tomb is a school where I saw the boys at their tasks, as I passed in to see the place. "What unlucky boys," thought I, "to be brought up amidst the unwholesome moral atmosphere of a decaying city!"

---

* A pilgrimage to the field of the Mahabharata, by Madho Ram, B.A., *Punjab Magazine* June 1890.

Although there is no present glory or grandeur about Kurukshetra, a visit to it will repay the thoughtful student of Indian history and religion.

In an expanse of flat country, from which, however, the blue outlines of the Himalayas may be traced in the distance, the traveller finds, a short way outside Thanesar, a shallow swamp about three miles in circumference and overgrown with weeds. This is the historic lake which, according to General Cunningham, was a sacred place long anterior to the great war; indeed, as far back as the time of the Rig Veda itself. "Can it be possible," I mused, as I stood beside this weed-covered pool, "that for a hundred generations the affectionate devotion of the Hindu race has consistently and persistently clung to this unattractive bit of water in an open plain?" "And how is it," I asked myself, "that their piety never adorned its banks with temples (for there are here no ruins worth speaking of) and why is it now so neglected?"

Will the reader accompany me round the lake and survey it from all points of view? On the east side are* the only important buildings, the largest being a temple of very modern date and no architectural pretensions. It is an ordinary *Mandir*; but has just a slight local character in the fact that it contains five coloured clay statues of the Pandavas, railed off from the too curious or too pious spectator by a strong, rudely constructed railing of bamboos. It rejoices in the possession of a huge iron frying-pan—not less than 8 feet in diameter and about 9 inches deep—to which my attention was specially

* It is worth noting that it was on the Western side of the lake that the Pandavas encamped and the Kauravas on the Eastern side.

directed. This gigantic frying-pan is much in demand on festival days, when the multitude pays to be fed by the Brahmans.

A flight of steps leads from the temple into the water, and runs nearly along one-half of the eastern and northern sides of the lake. A causeway on arches extends into the lake and ends in a small temple picturesquely shadowed with trees. Another bridge, now but little above the level of the water, parallel to the causeway just mentioned, leads right across the lake, joining to both east and west banks a small island in the middle, on which that famous bigot, the Mughal Emperor Aurangzeb, erected a diminutive fort to accommodate a small garrison, entrusted with the duty of preventing the Hindus from bathing in their sacred pool.

Proceeding along the east bank we pass a number of small tumble-down shrines, overshadowed by majestic *banians*, extending their mighty arms in graceful curves over the tranquil green water. We still follow the steps and arrive at the north end which has quite a recent look about it. Our guide tells us that this modern addition was the work of one "Larkeen Sahib," an official in these parts, who was very fond of the Hindus and had built this *ghat* for them out of a feeling of gratitude; because his wife had owed her recovery from a mysterious illness to the intercession of the Brahmans. Oh! "Larkeen Sahib" I wonder if the pious local legend which is told about you has ever reached your ears!

On the western side we find a little brick cenotaph which commemorates the *suttee* of the five wives of a

Brahman whose name is now forgotten.

Somewhat in advance of this cenotaph, and a little away from the lake side, we are conducted to a "*bythuck*" of Guru Nanak, the original founder of the Sikh sect, and we take shelter within its walls from a pelting shower of rain which makes the landscape more cheerless than ever. Here our guide informs us Guru Nanak used to sit beside the sacred pool, to practise contemplation. But the admiring crowds who came to visit him would give him no peace, so one day, to avoid their unwelcome attentions, he just sank into the ground, and following a subterranean tunnel, emerged at Hurdwar on the Ganges. There could be no doubt about this miraculous underground journey, for there was the very tunnel itself to support the truth of the story, with a substantial flight of steps leading down into it. Yes, true enough, there were three or four steps leading down into a small hole within the walls of the shrine. But how about the tunnel? My son descended into the hole to explore it. A look of chagrin passed over the face of our Brahman guide. Why this unnecessary and irreverent curiosity? The story *must* be true, for *every one* believed it, and, certainly, the position of this *bythuck* of Guru Nanak is interesting, for it shows how persistently the Sikhs attach themselves to the old Hindu faith, to which the vast majority of professing Sikhs now practically belong.

If there is anything that strikes one at Kurukshetra—and similar places in India—it is that the Brahmans have clung with wonderful tenacity, through the vicissitudes of ages, to their sacred *spots* and that though they have, according to universal belief, enjoyed considerable revenues, they have, through all these ages, done nothing to adorn their sacred places, which owe what temporary embellishment they have to the not too magnificent and not too frequent liberality of individuals. It strikes one also that, with each changing fashion of belief, each rise of a new sect, the Brahmans have willingly accommodated it with a convenient local habitation and have hastened to associate its glories with those of its predecessors. Hence the shrine of Guru Nanak at Kurukshetra, alongside which we shall, no doubt, some day have one in honour of Swami Dayanand, when the Arya sect is sufficiently grown to impress the Brahmans with its importance; the mere matter of orthodoxy or unorthodoxy being somewhat unimportant.

The reason for the wonderful persistence with which the affectionate regard of the Hindus has hovered round their old shrines and holy places for thousands of years, though at first sight rather strange, is not difficult of explanation. *They have a hereditary priesthood*, a priesthood that lives by the proceeds of the shrines and to whom the shrines are what land is to the cultivator. In this simple fact lies the explanation of the matter, and of other points in Hindu religious history, and probably in the history of other nations with hereditary priesthoods. Successive generations of priests have, for their own subsistence, to attract to the shrine they have inherited, successive generations of pilgrims, by keeping alive the old traditions, or inventing new legends to suit the altered tastes of the times. As the weeds that flourish in the lake are lineal descendants of the weeds that grew in the same place time-out-of-mind, so are the Brahmans on the banks of the lake the lineal descendants of the Brahmans who flourished there in times immemorial. As the weeds live on the rank soil and stagnant water of the pond, so live the Brahmans on their wild legends and stale pretensions.

Guru Nanak's *bythuck*—whose presence on the lake side led to the above digression—is but a few hundred yards from the west end of Aurangzeb's bridge, and, as there appeared to be nothing of interest on the south side, we crossed over to the island, inspected the Mughal fort and, following the bridge, returned to the principal temple; but before doing so we managed to secure a few photographs of the pretty scene on the east bank as viewed from the bridge.

In the region round Kurukshetra, within a "circuit of 160 miles," says General Cunningham, "there are popularly said to be three hundred and sixty holy sites most of which are connected with the names of the heroes of the Mahabharata. Many of these are no doubt genuine ancient places, as attested by their high mounds and brick ruins. But the greater number appear to me to be the inventions of modern days. According to the Mahatmyas, of which only one is said to be old, the holy places had lain desolate for several centuries after the Muhammadan conquest, when a *Dandi* or mendicant, named Ram Chandra Swâmi, came from Kâsi to Kurukshetra. He was grieved to see the desolation, and determined to stop there and try to restore the holy places. But as even the sites of many were unknown he professed to have obtained a knowledge of them in his dreams and accordingly he wrote a book describing them, which is called the Mahatmya of 6000 slokas and also the 'Dandi Mahatmya.' Long afterwards a Pandit of Thanesar named Banmáli, traced all the holy sites from the positions given by the Dandi, whose account is now accepted as genuine by all Brahmans, although his only authority for the identification was a dream."*

With the foregoing in mind I was not very eager to visit the sacred places, which have neither scenic nor architectural attractions. However, I could not leave Brahmavarta without seeing the holy Saraswati. The only form of conveyance available at Thanesar was *the Ekka* and, though I knew, from sad experience, what Ekkas could do in the way of producing discomfort to every limb, I was fain to call them into requisition, as the time at my disposal was short. Two ekkas were engaged, one for my son and myself, the other for the indispensable *Babu* and the Brahman guide. What a sight we two *un-hindu* pilgrims did present as we contorted ourselves into the springless vehicles and set off for the Saraswati! In a drenching downpour of rain our *Ekka-wallah* drove us, almost jotted to bits, over the worst roads ever made, to a spot where the *Samadh* of a deceased Raja of Feridekote now stands. Here we had to dismount and proceed on foot to the river, famous since the time when the Aryans settled in India. Dripping-wet, and aching all over, I proceeded with the rest through the grass and slush a hundred yards or so

* Archeological Survey of India Reports, Vol. XIV (Punjab) by General Cunningham, page 90.

to find myself on the banks of a tiny stream not twenty yards wide which was sluggishly flowing at my feet. I had now seen the historic Saraswati and my visit to the sacred land was practically over.

It is at the time of a lunar eclipse, when the waters of all other sacred tanks mingle mysteriously with those of the ponds near Thanesar, that the Brahmans of Kurukshetra reap their harvest of gains; for then tens of thousands of pilgrims crowd to bathe in the sacred pool and, of course, fee the priests according to the measure of their means and their piety.* The Punjab University graduate already quoted gives us some curious particulars in regard to the largesses destributed on such occasions by the wealthy. He tells us, with reference to solar eclipses, that "The Rajahs and Maharajahs of the land, too, are not absent on such occasions. They untie their purse strings, and hundreds and thousands of rupees are considered as nothing when compared with the importance of the moment. The Brahmins with loads of sweetmeats on their backs and with money in their unknown (*sic*) pockets, go home cheerfully and thankfully. They do not fail to get many cows in addition and some fortunate few even receive at the hands of the Rajahs and other big men presents

* With the decay of Thanesar there has been a marked falling off in the number of pilgrims to the sacred places. "The sanitary arrangements introduced by the British authorities to prevent the spread of disease are said to be most unpopular and to deter large numbers of pilgrims from attending. * * * * It is said that whereas in former days great men used to march to Thanesar with small armies of followers and attendants they now come by rail with a few servants to the nearest station and return in the same way." Gazetteer of the Ambala District pp. 73—74.

On the other hand the Railways must bring to the shrines many who could not have spared the time or the money to visit them under the old conditions of travel.

of villages or of elephants, which are returned for a paltry sum on the following day. Maharajah Narendra Singh of Patiala is said to have gone the length of parting with one of his wives on a similar occasion, and when on being asked to name her price, the *parohit* seemed willing to accept a lakh of rupees, the Rani was very angry with him for demanding such a low sum in return for the wife of such a wealthy Raja."*

The writer of the above curious passage seems strangely unconscious of the real significance of the facts he records, and apparently finds nothing to condemn in the vain display of ostentatious liberality, masking actual meanness, to which he refers, and which is especially noteworthy as supplying a probable standard by which to measure the overpowering munificence of many personages who figure in the Indian epics. This, too, is not mere conjecture. We have a similar instance in the case of King Dhasaratha referred to at page. 20.

Although the attractions of Kurukshetra are greatest on the occasion of eclipses, a tiny stream of visitors to the shrines trickles through Thanesar all the year round. Of their visits particular note is taken by the Brahmans who keep a record of the names and family connections of the several visitors. On the arrival of a pilgrim the Brahmans enquire his name, caste and *gotra*, his native place, his place of residence and the objects of his visit. With these facts in their possession some one amongst them is almost sure to be able to

* "A pilgrimage to the field of the Mahabharata," by Madho Ram B. A. Punjab Magazine for June 1890.

produce the record of the visit to Thanesar, at some previous time, of some relative of the pilgrim. When the Brahman has established this, from one of his books, he thereby becomes the family priest, *pro tempore*, and the privileged guide of the new arrival out of whom he makes as much money as he can. I shall not readily forget how the Babu who kindly accompanied me was pounced upon by the priests, how by the light of a flickering lamp he had read out to him all about the visits which had been paid to Thanesar by his relatives and how having come to the sacred land, he could not well leave it until, even in the pitiless December rain, he had to enter a sacred tank and take sundry dips under the water, while the Brahman, standing on the bank in the shelter of some trees, repeated the *muntras* which gave, as it were, the approval of the church to this pilgrimage of his to Brahmavarta.

APPENDIX I.

THE BHAGVATGITA OR DIVINE SONG.

How much more admirable the Bhagvat-Gita than all the ruins of the East! H. D. THOREAU.

It is undoubtedly in religious speculation that the genius of the Indian people has risen to the highest level of its possibilities. And one of the noblest products and best specimens of this theological spirit is the *Bhagavatgita*, or Divine song. The date of this grand philosophical poem is very doubtful. European scholars generally consider that it has no claim to great antiquity, and that it was composed *after* the commencement of the Christian era; some of them even hold that it bears unmistakable traces of the influence of Christian doctrine and evidence of the acquaintance of its author with the Christian scriptures. On the other hand, some Indian scholars endeavour to assign a high antiquity to the poem, and suggest that what resemblance there may be between the ideas in the *Gita* and in the sacred books of the Christians, must have been borrowed by the latter from Hindu sources.*

The Bhagavatgita early attracted the attention of Europeans and was translated into English by Sir Charles Wilkins in the time of Warren Hastings, who himself wrote an introduction to it. Wilkins' translation has been followed by those of Thompson and Davis. The poem

* Vide Dr. Lorinser's Essay on the subject in the Indian Antiquary, Vol. II and the reply thereto prefixed to the translation of the Bhagavatgita by Kashi Nath Trimbak Telang M.A., L.L.B.

has been rendered into both Latin and Greek, and into most of the leading languages of Europe, and has secured the highest encomiums possible, from literary and philosophical men in all countries, on account of its lofty tone and striking conceptions.

The reader will remember that the *Bhagavatgita* is a dialogue between Krishna and Arjuna, on the eve of the tremendous struggle at Kurukshetra, and that the dialogue arose out of the refusal of the latter to take part in a contest destined to lead to such unprecedented slaughter of kinsfolk.

It appears from the Gita that Arjuna was not only moved by feelings of tenderness towards his kinsmen, but was appalled at the thought of the far-reaching consequences of the impending slaughter of so many men. His prescient mind foresaw that the wholesale destruction of the Kshatriyas would tend to serious immorality amongst their women, and thus lead to that most dreadful of all calamities *the mingling of different castes*! Such an evil was not to be contemplated, except with the extremest religious horror, since so great a sin as a *confusion of castes* would inevitably lead men to the hell prepared for the wicked and even entail the fall of ancestral spirits from the region of the blessed, "their rites of Pinda and water ceasing" through the defilement of their descendants. This was a terrible prospect to face, but a more immediate, if less weighty, objection presented itself to Arjuna in a doubt as to whether it was lawful for him to contend with his ancient relative Bhishma and his Brahman preceptor Drona, both of whom were eminently worthy of his highest respect.*

Krishna proceeds to overcome Arjuna's scruples, first by dwelling upon the indestructibility of the soul, and then by insisting that the duty of a Kshatriya being to fight, it was right and proper for Arjuna to take part in the battle, regardless of consequences. He further assumes the responsibility for the deeds that may be done by Arjuna at his suggestion. On these points Krishna says:—"Those that are really wise grieve neither for the dead "nor the living. It is not that I or you or those rulers "of men never were, or that all of us shall not hereafter "be. * * * * As a man casting off robes that are "worn out, putteth on others that are new, so the embodi-"ed (soul) casting off bodies that are worn out entereth "other bodies that are new. Weapons cleave it not, fire "consumeth it not, the waters do not drench it nor doth "the wind waste it. * * * There is no (objective) "existence of anything that is distinct from the soul, nor "non-existence of anything possessing the virtues of the "soul."

Plainly the life of the individual was, according to Krishna's teaching, of little account, and this is strictly in harmony with Brahmanical ideas. To comprehend such an attitude of mind it is absolutely necessary to guard carefully against the mistake of supposing that the Hindu conception of the indestructibility of the soul is the same as the Christian idea of the immortality of the individual spirit. In the opinion of the Hindu the individual soul is part of the world-soul, a sort of animating force which

* Arjuna had apparently forgotten that he had already encountered and defeated these venerable elders of his in the interests of the king of Panchala. (Supra, page 172.)

may be joined, on an unlimited number of successive occasions, to any corporeal frame, high or low, adapting itself to the conditions of its dwelling-house. Except when joined to matter of some sort, gross or subtle, it is void of self-consciousness.* Conscious existence in the estimation of the Hindu being a distinct and positive evil, the object and desire of every sentient being should be to obtain final and complete extinction of separate individual consciousness, by emancipation from the trammels of matter, through suppression of all the senses. Thus far in regard to Arjuna's objection to the impending wholesale slaughter of his Kshatriya kinsmen. But other subtle questions of theology arise in the course of the colloquy which Krishna proceeds to elucidate and settle for his dear friend and disciple.

We do not propose to follow, step by step, the intricacies of the dialogue, but merely to set forth, as far as we can disentangle them from the theological mysticism in which they are involved, the fundamental doctrines and precepts inculcated by Krishna on this occasion.

Work or labour, in any form, has always, in Brahmanical theology, been regarded as an evil. Krishna too recognises it as such, though he holds it to be tolerable and even unobjectionable in certain cases. Work for its own sake, or for the attainment of any object, is undesirable, though it is lawful to do such work as may be necessary for the performance of

* As in sacrifices the gods derived sustenance from the ethereal portion of the burnt-offering, so, no doubt, the corporeal frame (especially when cremated) supplied an ethereal one for the disembodied soul, which was not yet entirely freed from the trammels of *matter*, though released from the bonds [illegible] ts grosser forms,

sacrifices,* or the support of one's body; but even this work should be done without thought of reward. As to Vedic rites, *i.e.*, the old ceremonial observances, these duly carried out, lead, no doubt, to the attainment of pleasure and power, and even heaven itself for a time.† But the highest attainable good,—*absorption in the Supreme Being and consequent emancipation from re-births*—cannot be obtained by even Vedic rites. It is only to be reached by *Knowledge* or by *Faith*. Now both the terms *Knowledge* and *Faith* require special elucidation. What then is the nature of this *Knowledge* which is so efficacious for emancipation? Not assuredly what the western world understands by that term, but something very different, *viz.*, subjugation of the senses and a complete suppression of all affections and dislikes, all hopes and fears, all desires and aversions, all pride and humility. This condition of utter indifference to every thing, sensual or intellectual, is the state of *Knowledge* leading to absorption in the Supreme Being or World-soul.‡

* There is a most important reason in favour of the special exception in regard to the performance of work in the case of sacrifices, for, as Krishna explains: "From food are all creatures: from rain is the production of food: rain is produced from sacrifice: and sacrifice is the out-come of work."

† Neither the joys of Heaven, nor the pains of Hell, could, in the view of Hindu theologians, be *eternal*. When an embodied soul has, by good actions, austerities, &c., acquired sufficient merit, it is permitted to taste the joys of Heaven for a length of time proportional to its deserts. When these are exhausted it returns to be born again on this Earth. Similarly the embodied soul whose evil deeds deserve punishment serves its time in Hell and then returns to be re-born on the Earth. In either case there is *after re-birth* no recollection of previous existences or of former joys and sorrows. But, in Heaven or in Hell, a recollection would be retained of the last state on Earth, of which indeed, the celestial or infernal condition would be only a sort of continuation.

‡ "Absence of vanity, absence of ostentation, abstention from injury, forgiveness, uprightness, devotion to preceptor, purity, constancy, self-restraint, indifference to objects of sense, absence of egoism, perception of the misery and evil of birth, death, decrepitude and disease, freedom from attachment, absence of sympathy for son, wife, home, and the rest, and constant equanimity of heart on attainment of good and evil, unswerving devotion to me without meditation on anything else, frequenting of lonely places, distaste for concourse of men, con-

One method or arriving at this blissful condition, though not the shortest or most certain, is through the *Yoga system*, which meets with the approval of Krishna, who gives general directions as to how the devotee, eating little, should sit in some lonely place; how he should concentrate his gaze on the tip of his nose, how he should "mingle the upward and the downward life breath" and how finally "renouncing all desires without exception "that are born of resolves, restraining the entire group "of the senses on all sides by mind alone, he should by "slow degrees, become quiescent, (aided) by (his) "understanding controlled by patience and then directing "his mind to self should *think of nothing*." When the devotee arrives at *this* stage, he is emancipated, for surely he has found *true Knowledge*! While thus indicating the inefficiency of the Vedas for *final emancipation* and while bestowing only a qualified commendation upon the Yoga system, Krishna inculcates, very forcibly, the doctrine of the efficacy of *faith* and above all faith in himself, which, it would seem, it is the special object of the dialogue to bring into prominence. For himself Krishna claimed that he was "the productive cause of the entire Universe and also its destroyer." He asserted that he was "the beginning, the middle, and the end of beings," and that "there was nothing higher than himself." To give weight to his claims the god vouchsafed to show himself to Arjuna in "his Supreme Sovereign form, with many

"stancy in the knowledge of the relation of the individual self to the Supreme; "perception of the object of the knowledge of truth—all this is called knowledge- "all that which is contrary to this is ignorance. That which is the object of "knowledge I will (now) declare (to thee) knowing which one obtaineth im- "mortality. (It is) the Supreme Brahma having no beginning who is said to be "neither existent nor non-existent, &c., &c." (Krishna, in Bhagavatgita).

"mouths and eyes, many wondrous aspects, many celestial "ornaments, many celestial weapons uplifted, wearing "celestial garlands and robes (and) with unguents of "celestial fragrance, full of every wonder, resplendent, "infinite, with faces turned on all sides. If the splendour "of a thousand suns were to burst forth at once in the "sky (then) that would be like the splendour of that "mighty one. The son of Pandu then beheld there in "the body of that God of gods the entire universe divided "and subdivided into many parts, all collected together. "Then Dhananjaya (Arjuna) filled with amazement, and "with hair standing on end, bowing with (his) head, "with joined hands addressed the God.

"Arjuna said:—I behold all the gods, O God, as "also all the varied hosts of creatures (and) Brahman "seated on (his) lotus seat, and all the *Rishis* and the "celestial snakes. I behold thee with innumerable arms, "stomachs, mouths (and) eyes, on every side, O thou of "infinite forms. Neither end, nor middle, nor also beginning "of them do I behold, O Lord of the universe, O thou "of universal form. Bearing (thy) diadem, mace, and "discus, a mass of energy, glowing on all sides, do I "behold thee that art hard to look at, endued on all sides "with the effulgence of the blazing fire or the Sun, and "immeasurable. Thou art indestructible (and) the "Supreme object of this universe. Thou art without "decay, the guardian of eternal virtue, I regard thee to "be the eternal (male) Being. I behold thee to be "without beginning, mean, end, to be of infinite prowess, "of innumerable arms, having the Sun and the Moon for

" thy eyes, the blazing fire for thy mouth, and heating this " universe with energy thy own. For the space betwixt " Heaven and Earth is pervaded by thee alone, as also all " the points of the horizon! At sight of this marvellous " and fierce form of thine, O Supreme Soul, the triple " world trembleth. For these hosts of gods are entering " thee! Some afraid, are praying with joined hands. " Saying *Hail to thee*—the hosts of great *Rishis* and " *Siddhas* praise thee with copious hymns of praise. " The Rudras, the Adityas, the Vasus, they that are " (called) the Sáddhyas, the Viçwas, the Açwins, the " Maruts, also the Ushmapas, the Gandharvas, the " Yakshas, the Asuras, the hosts of Siddhyas, behold thee " and are all amazed. Beholding thy mighty form with " many mouths and eyes, O mighty-armed one, with " innumberable arms, thighs and feet, many stomachs, " (and) terrible in consequence of many tusks, all " creatures are affrighted and I also. Indeed, touching " the very skies, of blazing radiance, many-hued, mouth " wide open, with eyes that are blazing and large, behold-" ing thee, O Vishnu with (my) inner soul trembling " (in fright) I can no longer command courage and peace " of mind. Beholding thy mouths that are terrible in " consequence of (their) tusks, and that are fierce as the " (all destroying) fire at the end of the Yuga, I cannot " recognise the points of the horizon nor can I command " peace of mind. Be gracious, O God of gods, O thou " that art the refuge of the universe. And all these sons " of Dhritarashtra, together with the hosts of kings, and " Bhishma and Drona and also this *Suta's* son (Karna), "accompained by even the principal warriors of our "side, are quickly entering thy terrible mouths rendered "fierce by thy tusks! Some, with their heads crushed, "are seen striking at the interstices of (thy) teeth. As "many currents of water flowing through different "channels roll rapidly towards the ocean, so these heroes "of the world of men enter thy mouths that flame all "around. As moths with increasing speed rush for "(their own) destruction to the blazing fire, so also do "(these) people, with unceasing speed, enter thy mouths "for their destruction. Swallowing all these men from "every side thou lickest them with thy flaming mouths. "Filling the whole universe with (thy) energy, thy "fierce splendours, O Vishnu, are heating (everything). "Tell me who thou art of (such) fierce form. I bow to "thee, O chief of the gods, be gracious to me! I desire "to know thee that art the Primeval one, for I do not "understand thy actions."

After such an overwhelming argument addressed to the senses of his disciple, after such an astounding proof that he alone is not only the universal soul of Nature but the universe itself; Krishna discloses to Arjuna the efficacy of *faith* above both *works* and *contemplation*. Thus says the God: "Fix thy heart on me alone, place thy understanding on me. Hereafter then shalt thou dwell in me. There is no doubt (in this)" and again: "Exceedingly dear art thou to Me, therefore I will declare what is for thy benefit. * * * Forsaking all (religious) duties come to Me as thy sole refuge I will deliver thee from all sins."

To assert the doctrine of the efficacy of *faith* is obviously the special object of the Gita; but, with the conciliatory spirit of Hinduism, it is inculcated without too great a rupture with the orthodox notions in respect to those time-honoured props and refuges of the pious Hindu,—the Vedas and Yogaism. Both these are, however, shorn of a good deal of their importance by comparison with the *new* mode of attaining heaven and final emancipation—*through faith in Krishna.*

Though the caste-system is strongly upheld in the Bhagavatgita and the practices of the Yogis sanctioned, many of the most liberal and lofty sentiments find expression in this highly remarkable poem; as when Krishna says: "Whatever form (of godhead or myself) any worshipper desireth to worship with faith, that faith of his unto that form I render steady. Endued with that faith he payeth his adoration to that (form) and obtaineth from that all his desires, since all those are ordained by me. The fruits, however, of those persons endued with little intelligence are perishable. They that worship the divinities go to the divinities, while they that worship me come even to me." Again: "Even those devotees who, endued with faith, worship other godheads, even they, O son of Kunti, worship me alone, though irregularly." And in another place: "In whatever manner men come to me in the self-same manner do I accept them." Krishna also says: "I am alike to all creatures there is none hateful to me none dear. They, however, that worship me with reverence are in me and I also am in them."

In this serene and lofty impartiality of sentiment the

unknown author of the Gita has reached a level of generous and noble theology not to be surpassed and probably never before expressed. But, alas! it was impossible for him to stand, alone, upon this giddy height of calm philosophy, and he descends to a lower plain of sympathetic insight when his Krishna declares, that "there are two kinds of created beings in this world, *viz.*, the godlike and the demoniac. These latter are impure, given over to their desires and unholy, asserting that the universe is void of truth, and guiding principle, and even without a ruler. Wedded to vanity, power, pride, lust and wrath these revilers hate Me in their own bodies and those of others. Those haters (of Me), cruel, the vilest among men and unholy, I hurl continually down into demoniac wombs. Coming into demoniac wombs, deluded, birth after birth, they, O son of Kunti, without attaining to me go down to the vilest state."

In regard to divine incarnation, which is an old accepted idea in Hinduism, Krishna says: "Many births of mine have passed away, O Arjuna, as also of thine, those all I know, but thou dost not, O chastiser of foes! Though, I am unborn and of essence that knoweth no deterioration, though (I am) the lord of creatures; still, relying on my own (material) nature, I take birth by my own (powers) of illusion. Whensoever, O Bharata, loss of piety occurreth and the rise of impiety, on those occasions do I create myself. For the protection of the righteous, for also the destruction of evil-doers, for the sake of establishing piety I am born age after age."

Whether the author of the Bhagavatgita borrowed

ideas from Christianity or not, this, at least, is certain that Krishna-worship is a comparatively new phase of Hinduism, that its doctrine of salvation or final emanicipation by *faith* is also comparatively new, and that the tendency of this doctrine of *faith*, as taught in the Gita, is to wean men from rites and ceremonies and to discourage them from the practice of *Yoga*.

But since it seems to be a characteristic of each successive stage of Hinduism to keep on amicable terms with those that have preceded it, the Gita endeavours to lead men to the doctrine of *faith* in Krishna without more disparagement of orthodox ideas and practices than appeared absolutely necessary for the object in view—hence the qualified approval of Vedic rites and of Yogaism which we find in this treatise.

Of the Bhagavatagita, which has been extolled as a complete system of Indian *religious philosophy*, this brief note will, I believe, give a sufficient idea.* It is, as regards Hinduism, an eclectic system upon which has been grafted a new principle, the doctrine of salvation by faith, which may or may not be of foreign origin. Its lofty ideas and transcendental philosophy appeal with subtle force to the higher feelings of the thoughful Hindu. I have known a clever young student of the Gita so powerfully affected by its teaching as to lose mental balance to the extent of believing himself to be Arjuna. When this halucination

* Those who have a leaning towards esoterics and mysticism may read, "Discourses on the Bhagavatgita by T. Subba Row, B.A., B.L., F.T.S. (Bombay 1888) from which they will learn pp. 56—58, that the Pandavas represent in reality the five elements which constitute man or rather Humanity"; that "the Kauravas are no other than the evil propensities of man, his vices and their allies" and that "the philosophy of Krishna teaches Arjuna that he must conquer these, however closely related to him they may be, before he can secure the kingdom or the mastery over self."

passed away his one burning desire was to retire from the world, in order to live the life of the Rishis of old.

For my own part I leave this highest attainment of Indian religious philosophy with mingled feelings of admiration and sadness.

In every nation men have allowed their speculative imaginations to play around the great mystery of the Universe. The auther of the Gita has dreamed his dream as well as the others; and like Plato* and the rest, has presented, as a solution of the grand problem of existence, his own fancies and his own guess-work. And these dreams, fancies and guesses—labelled *theology* or *philosophy* as the case may be—have been accepted as eternal verities and passed down from generation to generation, only to be superseded, in their turn, by other equally substantial fancies, equally irrefragable verities.

In leaving the Gita, however, let us, at least, admit that the Indian poet's dream was not deficient in nobility of sentiment and grandeur of conception.

---

* Republic Book X, Chapter 614—621.

APPENDIX II.

THE CHURNING OF THE OCEAN.

Once upon a time the gods having practised penances, according to the prescribed ordinances, assembled in solemn conclave, on the golden summit of Mount Meru, to consider how they might obtain *Amrita*—the water of life. "Seeing the celestial assembly in anxious. consultation, Narayana* said to Brahma: "Do thou churn the ocean with the Suras (gods) and the Asuras By doing so, *Amrita* shall be obtained, together with all drugs and all gems."

In order to carry out these instructions the gods uprooted from its base, the towering mountain named Mandara† and placed it in the sea on the back of the Tortoise-king. This was their churning pole, and for a cord they used the mighty hooded-serpent, Vasuki. The Asuras taking hold of him by the head and the Gods by the tail commenced the churning of the ocean. As they laboured in their gigantic task of whirling Mandara round and round in the seething ocean, the serpent's body became heated by the friction to which it was subjected, and volumes of black vapour, mingled with red flames, issued from his awful mouth. These vapours were condensed in the upper regions and fell in refreshing showers upon the tired Gods. With the rain came

---

* "The name as commonly used applies to Vishnu and is that under which he was first worshipped."—Dowson's "Classical Dictionary of Hindu Mythology."

† Of Mandara the poet says. "Upwards it riseth eleven thousands *Yojanas* and descendeth downwards as much."

abundance of flowers shaken from the trees of rapidly revolving Mandara.

As the work proceeded, with more and more vigour, the inhabitants of the troubled ocean were destroyed in great numbers, and the forests on the sides of rotating Mandara took fire from the friction of the branches of the trees which were driven into conflict with one another. However, this conflagration was extinguished by Indra, and the churning was continued. Then the gums of various trees, and many gems began to mingle with the water, but the sought-for nectar itself did not appear. Almost spent with their exertions the gods appealed to Narayana for help, and he, renewing their vigour, directed them again to "insert the mountain and churn the waters."

Their fresh and vigorous efforts were crowned with success. First of all the Moon emerged from the waters, then "Lakshmi* dressed in white, and wine, the white "steed, and then the celestial gem Kaustuva which "graces the breast of Narayana. Lakshmi, wine and the "steed fleet as the mind all came before the gods on high. "Then arose the divine Dhanvantari himself with the "white vessel of nectar in his hand. And seeing him, "the Asuras set up a loud cry saying: 'Ye have taken "all *he* must be ours.'"

Although the object of their quest, the nectar of immortality, had been produced, the churning was continued, apparently in the hope of further treasures. Airavata, a huge elephant now emerged from the troubled waters and

* The goddess of fortune.

was at once appropriated by Indra. But after his appearance a baleful poison, the terrible Kalakuta, "blazing like a flame mixed with fumes," began to overspread the earth and to threaten the destruction of the Universe. In this perilous juncture, Mahadeva, at Brahma's solicitation, "swallowed the poison and held it in his throat," which acquired and ever after retained a blue colour. Hence Mahadeva is often known by the name Nilakantha, the blue-throated.

The Asuras having got possession of Dhanvantari with the vessel of nectar, were preparing to defend their acquisition by force of arms, but Narayana, assuming the bewitching form of lovely *Maya*, easily induced the Daityas, ravished with her charms, to part with their treasure.

As soon as the deception practised upon them became apparent, the Daityas and Danavas pursued the Gods, who, in the meantime, had been hurriedly taking draughts of this wonderful elixir of immortality. Along with them a Danava, named Rahu, in the disguise of a god, was also slyly partaking of the *Amrita*, but before the nectar had gone beyond his throat he was detected by the Sun and Moon and had his head severed from his body by the discus of Narayana.

The severed head of Rahu was, of course, immortal, and ascended into the sky with loud cries. And ever since that eventful day it has pursued the Sun and Moon with revengeful feelings, swallowing them up periodically, as is evident in the solar and lunar eclipses which have attracted the awed attention of mankind.

through the ages.

To these events succeeded the commencement of a terrible battle between the gods on one side, and the Asuras, Daityas and Danavas on the other. The gods being victorious carried the *amrita* to Heaven, and "offering due respect to Mandara placed him on his own base."

Thus far the wonderfully grand old myth which could have been conceived by no common mind, which is still believed in, and still gives rise to practices and ceremonies which are observed by two hundred millions of the Indian people, for whom it is still the malignant Rahu that periodically threatens the destruction of the greater and lesser lights of the firmament. On such occasions the Hindus beat their drums and blow their conchs to terrify away the demon. They throw away their earthen cooking pots, observe a rigid fast during the period of obscuration and crowd the bathing places for a purifying plunge, as soon as the light of Sun or Moon is once again fully restored to the delighted eyes of mankind.

APPENDIX III.

THE STORY OF NALA AND DAMAYANTI.

There was once a powerful king of the Nishadhas named Nala who was as beautiful as the god of Love himself. He was, moreover, an honourable man, highly accomplished and especially well-versed in the management of horses; but he had a weakness for dice.

Contemporary with Nala was Bhima king of the Vidharbas, a formidable monarch, and father of Damayanti the most lovely maiden in the world. Fame had carried to Nala the report of Damayanti's unrivalled charms and had made him quite love-sick. The fair lady, too, had often been told of the manly beauty and grace of the king of the Nishadhas, and had had a tender chord in her heart touched by what she had heard. Thus were these two young people actually in love with each other, although they had never met or even exchanged glances.

The enamoured king naturally sought solitude; and one day, while moodily lounging in the inner gardens of his palace, he saw some strange looking swans with golden wings. He caught one of then with his hands. The bird immediately addressed his captor, asking to be spared and promising to speak to Damayanti about him, "in such a way that she will not ever desire to have any other person for her lord." Of course the swan was liberated there and then, and, proceeding at once, along with his fellows, to the land of the Vidharbas, alighted in the gardens where Damayanti was sporting with her maids. The fair princess was eager to catch the strange birds as soon as she observed them; so she and her attendants began to run after the golden-winged swans, who fled in all directions without taking wing. One of these birds led the eager Damayanti away from her companions and then, seizing the opportunity, told the charming girl about Nala and his beauty, winding up with these words: "Thou also art a jewel among thy sex as Nala is the prime among men. The union of the best with the best is happy." To which the gratified princess replied: "Do thou speak thus unto Nala also."

The adventure with the swan had such an effcet upon the princess that she became melancholy, pale-faced and lean. Her thoughts were of Nala only, and she could find no pleasure in her surroundings. Her father noticed the change with much anxiety, and, after weighing the matter, concluded that the best thing he could do would be to find a husband for his daughter.

He accordingly gave notice, far and wide, to the kings and princes of the land that Damayanti would hold her *Swayamvara* on a certain date.

From every direction suitors thronged to Bhima's capital in the hope of winning the much-coveted beauty whose fame filled the whole earth. The celestial Rishi, Narada, on a casual visit to Indra's Heaven made passing reference to Damayanti's transcendent beauty and to her approaching *Swayamuara*. The gods excited by his words exclaimed in rapture: "We also will go there," and four of them, the *Lokapalas* or guardians of the world—Indra, Yama, Varuna and Kuvera—set out without delay for the country of the Vidharbas, accompanied by their attendents.

On the way they met the handsome and virtuous Nala bent on the same errand. Leaving their celestial cars in the sky they descended to the earth and entered into converse with the king. Without revealing themselves to him they cunningly got him to promise to help them, and when he had done so requested him to go to Damayanti and inform her that the *Lokapalas* were amongst the suitors for her hand, and to request her to choose one of them for her lord.

Poor Nala explained his own feelings with respect to the fair princess and the hopes with which he was hastening to the *Swayamvara*. He also protested that it would be impossible for him to have an interview with Damayanti in her well-guarded palace. But the gods removed this last difficulty, Indra simply saying: "Thou shalt be able to enter." And so it proved; for it was not long before Nala found himself in the inner apartments of the palace. His wonderful beauty created a great sensation amongst the astonished women of the zenana. Damayanti was the first to recover from the surprise of his unexpected presence in the inner apartments and smilingly addressed the intruder in these by no means harsh words. "What art thou O thou of faultless features, that hast come here awakening my love. O sinless one, O hero, of celestial form, I am anxious to know who thou art that hast come hither, and why thou hast come hither. And how it is that thou hast not been discovered by any one, considering that my apartments are well guarded* and the king's mandates are stern."

Nala, with a sad heart, told her who he was and honourably discharged the distasteful duty imposed upon him by the celestials. Undazzled by the prospect of having a god for her husband, Damayanti, with charming simplicity, said to Nala with a smile. "O king, love me and command me what I shall do for thee. Myself and what else of wealth is mine are thine. * * * * If thou forsake me who adore thee, for thy sake will I resort to poison or fire, or water, or the rope." Nala dwelt upon the danger of offending the gods and advised the princess to choose one of her celestial suitors for her lord and no blame would attach to him, But she told him to come himself to the *Swayamvara* and she would there give him her hand in the presence of the celestials.

Nala returned to the *Lokapalas*, who were eager in their enquiries about the details of his mission. He faithfully related what had passed between himself and Damayanti even so far as to tell them that the maiden had expressed her determination to choose him for her husband. Having discharged his obligations with strict fidelity Nala left the issue in the hands of the Gods.

On the day of the *Swayamvara* the astonished princess saw, on entering the hall, not one but five Nalas before her, all seated together. Unable to dis-

* If these poems are really ancient, I think we need not have any hesitation in concluding that the Zenana system was in force in India in early times and was not introduced, as many Hindus declare, after the conquest of India by the Muhammadans. Possibly the *purdah* was made more strict after the Muslims established themselves south of the Himalayas.

criminate from amongst them the king of the Nishadas, the fond maiden tremblingly prostrated herself before the five and, in an appeal full of sweet confidence, begged the gods to reveal themselves to her as she had in her heart chosen Nala for her lord. Touched by her simple prayer the *Lokapalas* resumed their celestial attributes and the fair maiden thereupon bashfully caught the hem of Nala's garment and placed the garland round his neck. The gods were pleased with the issue and generously bestowed many boons upon their successful rival, who appreciating the great honour that had been shown him addressed Damayanti in these words: "Since thou, O blessed one, hast chosen a mortal in the presence of the celestials, know me for a husband ever obedient to thy command. And, O thou of sweet smiles truly do I tell thee this that as long as life continueth in this body of mine I will remain thine and thine alone." The charming damsel, of course made a suitable response. Every thing was arranged satisfactorily, the wedding was duly celebrated and the king of the Nishadas returned home with his lovely bride.

But, as the course of true love never does run smooth, there was sorrow awaiting the young couple. It happened that as the gods were returning from Damayanti's *Swayamvara* they met Kali with Dwapara on the way to the capital of the Vidharbas. It was to seek Damyanti's hand that Kali* was journeying thither, and it was with great displeasure that he learned that the *Swayamvara* was over and that Nala had obtained the prize.

* This Kali is the Kali-yuga personified as the spirit of evil.—Dowson's "Classical Dictionary of Hindu mythology."

In his wicked heart he planned to ruin the happiness of Nala and with that object in view proceeded to his city. Watching his opportunity—which presented itself in the neglect by the king of some trifling ceremonial observance—Kali entered his person and took complete possession of him. The fiend also stirred up Pushkara to challenge Nala to play with him with dice. Nala could not refuse, and, being under the influence of Kali, gambled recklessly, and, needless to say, unsuccessfully ; for the dice were not ordinary dice, but *Dwapara* himself transformed. The gambling match lasted for months and Nala lost every thing he possessed including his kingdom. During the continuence of the match Nala was like one deprived of reason, so his wife sent her two children away to her parents in charge of a faithful charioteer. His successful opponent suggested that he might now stake Damayanti as he had lost everything else ; but Nala, his heart full of rage, rose with silent dignity and stripping himself of all his ornaments left the city. Damayanti, clad in a single piece of cloth—a *sari* no doubt,—followed him into exile.

Pushkara issued an order that no one should assist Nala under pain of death, so the ex-king and his consort were left to shift for themselves. In the hope of capturing some wild birds in the wood Nala threw his cloth over them, but they rose and flew away with it leaving him naked. He now shared Damayanti's single garment and the pair were soon in the greatest extremities of distress. He could not humble himself to seek the assistance of his wife's people, but thinking that if she were alone,

Damayanti might find an asylum with them, Nala, instigated still by vindictive Kali, abandoned his lovely wife one night in the lonesome forest. Her grief and despair upon finding herself deserted were most pathetic. With loud lamentations she wandered hither and thither like a maniac and came unexpectedly upon a huge serpent who quietly coiled himself about her gentle form and would have killed her very soon had not a hunter come to her rescue and with his sharp sword cut off the serpent's head. Enquiries and explanations followed with the result that "beholding that beautiful woman clad in half a garment with deep bosom and round hips and limbs delicate and faultless, and face resembling the full moon, and eyes graced with curved eyelashes, and speech sweet as honey, the hunter became inflamed with desire." But virtuous Damayanti, in great anger repulsed the wretch and cursed him so that he fell down dead at her feet.

Alone in the vast forests peopled by wild beasts and infested by thieves and *mlechchha-tribes*, poor bewildered Damayanti wandered about in quest of Nala, asking, in her trouble, the fierce tiger and the silent mountain to tell her where her lord had gone. After wandering about for three days and three nights the unfortunate queen came to the delightful asylum of some ascetics and entering it fearlessly, but with great humility, she was welcomed by the holy men, who, struck by her beauty, enquired whether she was the presiding deity of the forest, the mountain or the river. Damayanti explained her situation and received from the ascetics most comforting assurances of early reunion with Nala and great future happiness. After which "the ascetics with their sacred fires and asylum vanished from sight," to the great amazement of the queen.

Further wanderings in the denser parts of the forest brought Damayanti into a somewhat open space where she found a party of merchants encamped beside a stream with their horses, elephants and other beasts of burden. The merchants could give her no information about Nala, for, as the leader of the party assured her, she was the only human being they had met in those vast forests. However, as they were bound for the city of Suvahu, Damayanti attached herself to the caravan. The distance to be traversed was evidently a very long one and the forest very extensive; for after they had proceeded many days they were still in the woods and one evening encamped on the border of a lovely lotus-covered lake. In the dead of night a herd of wild elephants coming down to the lake discovered the tame elephants belonging to the merchants and instantly made a furious onslaught upon them. Indescribable confusion followed. Some members of the party were trampled to death under the feet of the mighty beasts, some perished by their huge tusks, others fled for safety in all directions. The fugitives concealed themselves in the thickets or took refuge in the branches of trees. Horses, camels and elephants, fighting with each other and rushing about in frantic terror added to the wild confusion of the dreadful scene of disorder and uproar, which was intensified by the outbreak of a terrible fire. Amidst the general panic—the shouts and cries of men and the noise of wounded and furious animals—Damayanti naturally awoke in the greatest alarm, but she soon had occasion for special fear for her own personal safety from an unexpected quarter.

"And those of the caravan that had escaped unhurt, met together, and asked one another—Of what deed of ours is this the consequence? Surely, we have failed to worship the illustrious Manibhadra, and likewise the exalted and graceful Vaisravana, the king of the Yakshas. Perhaps, we have not worshipped the deities that cause calamities, or perhaps, we have not paid them the first homage. Or, perhaps this evil is the certain consequence of the birds (we saw)! Our stars are not unpropitious. From what other cause, then, hath this disaster come? Others, distressed and bereft of wealth and relatives, said,—That maniac-like woman who came amongst this mighty caravan in guise that was strange and scarcely human, also, it is by her that this dreadful illusion had been pre-arranged. Of a certainty, she is a terrible Rakshasa or a Yaksha or a Piçácha woman. All this evil is her work, what need of doubts. If we again see that wicked destroyer of merchants, that giver of innumerable woes we shall certainly slay that injurer of ours, with stones, and dust and grass and wood and cuffs.* And hearing these dreadful words of the merchants, Damayanti, in terror and shame and anxiety, fled into woods apprehensive of evil."

Damayanti, however, managed to secure the protection of some Brahmans who had been travelling with the mer-

* I desire to draw special attention to this interesting passage which in its naive simplicity throws considerable light upon the ideas and sentiments which lie at the root of the practise of the worship of the Unseen Powers who are believed to govern the lives of men.

chants, and, in their company succeeded in reaching the city of Suvahu. Her strange, unkempt and almost maniac-like appearance, coupled with her scanty clothing, excited the curiosity of the citizens who rudely followed her about. Her painful situation in the street of the town, and her beauty which nothing could destroy, attracted the attention of the Queen-mother who was looking out of one of the windows of the palace. As a consequence Damayanti was sent for and installed in the household as a sort of humble companion to the princess.

We have now to trace the fortunes of Nala. After he had deserted Damayanti he came upon a mighty conflagration in the forests. From the midst of the fire a voice addressed him thus: "O righteous Nala come hither." Nala obeyed without fear or hesitation and found in the midst of the fire a mighty Naga or serpent, lying in great coils. The snake explained that he was suffering from the curse of a great Rishi "of high ascetic merit," whom he had deceived, and that he was doomed, under the conditions of the curse, to lie where he was until Nala should remove him to another place when he would be free again. The snake contracted his dimensions till he was no bigger than a man's thumb. Nala look him up and carried him to a place free from fire. Here the snake bit Nala and resumed his natural form. The effect on Nala of the snake's bite was startling indeed, for he underwent a strange transformation of person and assumed an unprepossessing appearance. The snake explained that what had occurred was for Nala's good and advised him to go to Ayodhya and offer his services to the King of that city as a charioteer and trainer of horses, on condition of receiving instruction in the art of gambling. The snake also presented Nala with a garment the wearing of which would immediately restore him to his proper form. Nala did as directed and was duly installed as King's charioteer and superintendent of the royal stables, under the name of Váhuka.

In the meanwhile Brahmans sent out by king Bhima, Damyanti's father, were searching the country, far and wide, for the lost couple. One of them met Damayanti and recognised her by a remarkable lotus-shaped mole which she had between her eyebrows. This discovery led to her return to her father's house, where her children were being reared in comfort, but nothing could console her for the absence of Nala. Through her mother she caused Brahmans to go forth into all countries, to cry in every assembly "O beloved gambler, where hast thou gone, cutting off half of my garment and deserting thy dear and devoted wife asleep in the forest, &c." Of course this appeal touched Nala—transformed into Vahuka.—to the heart, and certain remarks which he let fall, to the effect that a virtuous woman should not be angry with one who had been deprived by birds of his garments and so on, having been reported to Damayanti she suspected who that Váhuka really was, althongh so changed in person.

To bring him to her she had it proclaimed in the city of Ayodhya that Damayanti, unaware whether Nala was alive or not, had decided to hold the very next day another *Swayamvara* at which she would choose a second husband* for herself.

*This shows clearly that widow re-marriage was allowed.

King Ritupama of Ayodhya desired to be present on this occasion, but the distance to Kundina was over one hundred *yojanas*. However Nala in a most wonderful manner managed to do the distance within the appointed time, not without adventures on the way and the acquirement from his royal master of the whole science of dice-playing.

When they arrived at Kundina they found to their astonishment that no preparations were being made for Damayanti's *Swayamvara* and discovered that they had been deceived by a false report.

From the remarkable way in which Ritupama's chariot came rattling into Ayodhya, Damayanti suspected that it was driven by Nala and Nala only, but she was sore distressed when she saw Vahuka—so unlike her dear lord in appearance. Yet, as wonders were common in those days and the charioteer might after all be her dear husband in a natural disguise, she opened communication with him through a maid-servant and by various indications satisfied herself that Vahuka was no other than her lost Nala.

With the consent of her father and mother she caused Vahuka to be brought to her apartments. She received him clad in a piece of red cloth, wearing matt ed locks and covered with dirt and dust. Explanations followed. The Wind-god invoked by Damayanti testified that it was only to bring Nala to herself that the lovely queen had proclaimed her *Swayamvara* in Ayodhya and that she was faultless in the matter. Flowers descended from the air and celestial kettle-drums began to play.

Casting away all doubts about Damayanti, Nala put on the pure garment which had been given to him by the serpent and thus regained his own beautiful form. "And beholding her righteous lord in his own form Bhima's daughter of faultless limbs embraced him, and began to weep aloud. And king Nala also embraced Bhima's daughter devoted to him, as before, and also his children, and experienced great delight. And burying her face in his bosom, the beauteous Damayanti of large eyes began to sigh heavily, remembering her griefs. And overwhelmed with sorrow, that tiger among men stood for some time, clasping the dust-covered Damayanti of sweet smiles."

After these events Nala proceeded to his own country of the Nishadhas and challenged his brother to a game of dice, offering to stake all the wealth he had acquired, and lovely Damayanti as well, against the kingdom of which he had been dispossessed. He gave his brother the choice of an alternative—the dice or battle. Pushkara willingly accepted the offer, remarking insultingly: "It is evident that Damayanti, adorned with this wealth of thine that I will win, will wait upon me like an Apsara in heaven upon Indra." However, Fortune had changed sides. Nala recovered his kingdom, but generously shared it with his unworthy brother, and every one, of course, lived happily thereafter.

NOTES.

(1) *Date of the compilation of the Mahabharata.*—Like the Ramayana, the Mahabharata is based on popular legends of considerable antiquity, which, according to European scholars, appear to have been *collected together* into a more or less connected whole, at a comparatively recent date.

"The earliest direct evidence of the existence of an epic, with the contents of the Mahabharata, comes to us from the rhetor Dion Chrysostom, who flourished in the second half of the first century A.D.; and it appears fairly probable that the information in question was then quite new, and was derived from mariners who had penetrated as far as the extreme south of India. * * * * Since Megasthenes says nothing of this epic, it is not an improbable hypothesis that its origin is to be placed in the interval between his time and that of Chrysostom; for what ignorant sailors took note of would hardly have escaped his observation more especially if what he narrates of Herakles and his daughter Pandai has reference really to Krishna and his sister the wife of Arjuna, if, that is to say, the Pandu legend was actually current in his time. * * * * As to the period when the final redaction of the work in its present shape took place no approach even to direct conjecture is in the meantime possible, but at any rate it must have been some centuries after the commencement of our era.*

(2) *Translation of Mahabharata into Persian.*—The following account of the translation of the Mahabharata into Persian in the reign of the Mogul Emperor Akbar is worth reading, as it exhibits an estimate of the great epic from the standpoint of a

* The History of Indian Literature by Dr. Albrecht Weber, pp. 186—188.

bigoted Muslim:

"In the year 990 His Majesty assembled some learned Hindus, and gave them directions to write an explanation of the *Mahabharata*, and for several nights he himself devoted his attention to explain the meaning to Nakib Khan, so that the Khan might sketch out the gist of it in Persian. On a third night the King sent for me, and desird me to translate the Mahabharata, in conjunction with Nakib Khan. The consequence was that in three or four months I translated two out of the eighteen sections, at the puerile absurdities of which the eighteen thousand creations may will be amazed. Such injunctions as one never heard of—what not to eat, and a prohibition against turnips! But such is my fate, to be employed on such works. Nevertheless I console myself with the reflection, that what is predestined must come to pass.

After this, Mulla Shi and Nakib Khan together accomplished a portion and another was completed by Sultan Haji Thanesari by himself. Shaikh Faizi was then directed to convert the rough translation into elegent prose and verse, but he did not complete more than two sections. The Haji aforesaid again wrote it correcting the errors which had appeared in his first translation, and settling the conjectures which he had hazarded he had revised a hundred sheets, and nothing being omitted he was about to give the finishing touch, when the order was received for his dismissal, and he was sent to Bakar. He now resides in his own city (Thanesar.) Most of the scholars who were employed upon this translation are now with the Kauravas and Pandavas. May those who survive be saved by the mercy of God, and may their repentance be accepted.

The translation was called Razm-nama, and when fairly engrossed and embellished with pictures, the nobles had orders to take copies, with the blessing and favour of God. Shaikh Abul Fazl, who had already written against our religion, wrote the Preface, extending to two sheets. God defend us from his infidelities and absurdities."*

English Versions of the Mahabharata.—For full details of this epic the reader may be referred to "The Mahabharata of Krishna Dwaipayana Vyasa" translated into English prose by Pratab Chandra Roy (Calcutta) of which several volumes have been published.

A toterably detailed account of the poem, with a running commentary, occupies about 500 pages of Vol. I of the History of India by J. Talboys Wheeler.

A summary of all the eighteen sections of the epic is to be found in Sir Monier Williams "Indian Epic Poetry." (Williams and Norgate, 1863.)

* "Tarikh-i-Badauni" of Abdul Kadir Badauni, Elliot's Muhammadan Historians of India, Vol. V., pp. 537—538.

STRUGGLES IN THE DAWN.

CONCLUDING CHAPTER.

Having presented to the reader the foregoing condensed epitomes of the great Hindu epics, it only remains for me to offer a few brief observations upon some of the more abiding features of the national life and the religious and moral sentiments of the Hindus, as illustrated by these gigantic poems, in which we see, as in a mirror, an unconscious reflection of the ideas and tendencies, the intellectual cravings and the moral instincts of the age to which they belong.

It may seem superfluous to remind the reader that the Ramayana describes the adventures of Rama, including amongst them a war which he undertook in order to avenge an insult and to recover the person of his wife, who had been carried off by an unscrupulous enemy. The campaign against Ravana had not for its object extension of territory, but the punishment of an evil-doer and the righting of a personal wrong; while the protracted struggle which is the basis of the Mahabharata is purely a contest for supremacy between kindred families, each side being backed by friends and allies from amongst their own race, as well as from amongst alien tribes (the *mlechas*). In neither poem, be it noted, does any question of patriotism arise; for the contests in which the heroes are involved, are not against foreign invaders or national enemies.

The India known to the compilers of the Ramayana and Mahabharata,—the extensive theatre upon which their heroes played the stirring drama of their lives—was evidently a land covered with vast tracts of dense forest, whose mysterious gloom, pervaded with the aroma of incense and burnt-offerings, has cast a vague and mighty shadow over the hearts of the Hindu bards, as surely as the breezy atmosphere and the restless waves of the Ægean have imparted a healthy buoyancy to the Homeric rhapsodists.

The dreamy solitudes in which Valmiki and Vyasa love to linger have a restfulness about them which the European unsued to eastern lands can hardly comprehend. They have also a mystery only to be found in primeval forests, and they possess a dark background of horror, in the roar of the ferocious tiger, the hiss of the deadly serpent and the grip of the invisible fever-fiend, enough to awaken strange and gloomy imaginings.

The few who have lived, as I have done, through changing seasons, in the dense forests of Eastern India, can hover in spirit, through Valmiki and Vyasa's woodlands of the past:

First it is summer, and the hot sun-beams come filtering through the leafy covering, under the shadow of which man and beast listlessly repose through uneventful hours, while the shrill cricket chirps its monotonous song and the *cokil's* sweet note fills the hot and trembling air. Then the black clouds gather overhead. God Indra parts them with his flashing bolts. Loud thunder peals in the sky, the roaring hurricane enters into fearful conflict with the warring trees, and the rain descends, not in tiny drizzles, but in torrents, and its voice, as it buries itself in square miles of standing forest, is like the roar of many waters. Cascades, starting into life, leap gladly from the hill-side. The swollen streams, muddy and impassable, swirl and rush along carrying with them a burden of forest trees. A mantle of vivid green covers, as if by magic, the whole earth and climbs up till it almost hides the little cottage in which the proprietor takes refuge from the incessant drip, which descends from the leafy covering above.

To this succeeds a period when the steamy miasma rises in the green light from the rotton ground, and man and beast sicken in the malarious atmosphere, wherein the odour of decaying vegetation mingles with the exquisite perfume of orchids and strange flowers of the wilderness. In the glorious sky—in mystic cloudland—appear displays of light and colour, of subtile tints and gorgeous hues utterly beyond description, or the artist's cunningest skill. Watch, with fevered vision, from the neighbourhood of one of these dark forests, the rapidly shifting cloud-phantasms, arrayed in red and gold, upon the evening sky, then cease from marvelling at the exuberant and unbridled imaginings of the Indian Bard! Fix your attention at night upon the monstrous shapes which hover skulking in the background in the flickering firelight, listen to the unearthly wailing and stifled cries which steal through the hideous darkness, and doubt no more the existence and doings of gruesome Rakshasas who change their shapes at will! Learn also, at the same time, how indispensable a god is *Agni*, who protects you through the horrors of darkest night in the forests.

Later in the year winter smiles mildly over the enervated land and chills the tepid air. For hours after sunrise a dense fog wraps the primeval forest in its embrace, but when it, ghost-like, steals silently away, it reveals the white smoke of the cottages, curling upwards into a blue, unclouded sky. The sun hardly affords sufficient warmth to the labourer in the little patch of cultivation near the hut, and the moon looks cold and pallid. The streams begin to dwindle away, the cascades are silent.

Such is the succession of seasons in a tropical forest-land like the India of the epics. And throughout all the seasons the forest is enveloped in a dreamy air of depression and despondency which peoples the solitudes with hideous Rakshashas; but leaves no place for sporting nymphs or dancing fairies. Life in such woodlands is real forest-life, not like Thoreau's delightful playing at hermit in Walden, within a couple of miles of Concord and in sight of a railway.

Thus far the forests: but the sublime Alps of the Indian world, tallest and most majestic of mountains, have not been without influence upon the feelings of the Indian poets, elevating them to lofty heights of contemplation. And when we read what the few travellers who have penetrated those regions have to tell us of the ineffable grandeur and sublimity of the lone mountains, the glittering ice-fields and the untrodden snows of the interior;

when we consider the solemn silence of those uninhabited solitudes, we cannot wonder that the Indian poets who had heard of them, and perhaps visited their rocky fastnesses, made of them a land of mystery and the sporting place of their Gods and Apsaras.

Not only from the woods of *Dandhaka* and the vales and crests of mighty *Himavat* did the epic poets of India gather inspiration; but also from the noble and lovely rivers of their fair land, winding beneficently through many hundreds of miles of fertile country, from their birth places above the clouds to the bosom of the all-embracing ocean, while determining in their course the march of migration and conquest.

Mountains, forests and rivers, all of colossal proportions, have served to impress a grandiose if bewildering character upon the great epics of India, which the reader, even of this volume, can hardly fail to observe.

Religion being the dominant note of these voluminous poems claims our first consideration. In this connection I would draw attention to the fact that India is very far from that stage of intellectual development in which literature, science, art and politics become secularised. In Europe secularisation has taken place gradually, under the influence of the spirit of rationalism, as Mr. Lecky has so admirably explained. In India a beginning has been made in the secularisation of knowledge. It is yet only a *mere beginning* which owes its origin to the influence of English education; but the effects being confined to a *very small class indeed*, it may still be said, with truth, that all departments of knowledge which form the intellectual heritage of the Indian people—

even law, poetry and the drama—fall within the domain of theology. And certainly, there is no indigenous science amongst the Hindus which is not subject to priestly influence and interpretation.

Throughout the epics we find the supernatural beings who influence the destinies of mankind arrayed in two distinctly hostile camps. On one side are the Gods with the Gandharvas and Apsaras. On the other side the Asuras including Daityas and Danavas, Rakshasas and Pisachas. The contest lies, be it noted, between the lesser Gods and the Asuras with their allies. The superior gods interpose, from time to time, in the interests of the celestials ; but behind and above the turmoil of existence the shadowy form of inexorable *Destiny* reveals its overwhelming presence.

The part of man in the perpetual strife carried on between the two orders of superhuman beings is neither an ignoble nor a passive one. Man is not, as in most other religions, either the abject and unworthy recipient of gracious favours from the gods, or the unhappy victim of the malice of devils and demons. His position in the universe, as conceived by the authors of the Indian Epics, reflecting, no doubt, the prevailing ideas of their time, was a far higher one. Man is no nonentity in the struggle between the good and the evil forces of nature, but is rather a very important factor ; for it is his especial duty to piously assist and *nourish* the celestials by perpetual sacrifices, so that they, on their part, might have the strength to perform their respective duties in the government of the universe, and ensure the repression of the forces of evil. Neither is man a merely useful but servile auxiliary of the celestials; since he may by austerities, sacrifices, and ceremonies, earn and acquire rights and power for himself, and use his accumulated store of energy at his own will and for his own purposes.

Now it is a noteworthy fact that this high ideal of man's dignity in the scale of beings has led in India to a degradation of the gods. It would seem as if you could not raise man without pulling down the deity; as if you could not exalt the human race without abasing the celestials. Hence we see the irreverent familiarity with which the highest gods, even Mahadeva, is personated by the Hindus in religious processions, or even on the occasion of the wild saturnalia of the *Holi* festival, when a man painted white with a wig of long yellow hair on his head, a string of huge beads about his neck and a trident in his hand—*the Supreme Deity personified*—is borne aloft amidst a crowd of excited men who are indulging in the grossest license of obscene speech and gesture.

In regard to a future life beyond the grave the writers of the Epics hold very decided opinions, a fact of great interest if we remember that the Jews acquired their ideas about existence after death and of good and evil spirits, for the first time in their Babylonian captivity and passed them on as a heritage to Christianity; the conceptions of our great Christian poet Milton being strongly coloured by ideas which undoubtedly had their roots in Persian *Mazdeism*.

The Heavens of the Hindu gods are essentially material and sensuous, with their palaces and gardens, music and dancing, their lively Gandharvas and frail

Apsaras. Yet the goddesses play a very subordinate part, indeed, in India's heroic age. We find in the epics, no powerful Hera, no wise Pallas Athene, no lovely Venus, no silver-footed Thetis—bright creations which lend such a charm to the myths of Hellas. Ganga, it is true, acts a minor and appointed part in the great drama, and Parbati is mentioned, while Durga and Kali only flit across the stage. But it is quite evident that in the Olympus of the Aryan Indians the goddesses had not attained the power and dignity they enjoy to-day. The frequent boasts in the Epics against the celestials with Indra at their head; the way in which every chief or leader, even of the Venars, is said to be a match for Indra's self, seem to indicate an unmistakable, if covert, hostility to the old gods of the Aryan invaders, which is well worthy of notice as indicating a transition period in the religious development of the Hindus, a period of doubt and confusion, which is emphasised by the fulsome flattery addressed to any one of whom a favor is desired, be he man or god. He is the *best* of men, the greatest of kings, equal to gods, he is a god, he is Indra, he is Yama, he is Prajapati, he is superior to all the gods, he is the ruler of the three worlds, he is in fact anything and all things to the uncertain suppliant who craves his help. And in these perplexities we seem to have a share too; for under the influence of the pantheistic notions of the writers, combined with their conceptions of endless transmigrations and utter indifference to permanent shapes of any kind, individuality seems lost (as when we find Krishna addressed as the younger brother of Indra*), and a world of

* Mahabbharata, Bhisma Parva Section LIX, page 224.

confused phantasmagorial forms seems to dance before us, till we feel dizzy contemplating this distracting and impermanent universe.

But amidst the ever-shifting pageant of existence the Hindu seems to have arrived at and firmly grasped the idea of a periodic law which has given a certain grandeur to his speculations about both the past and the hereafter.

From the orderly sequence of natural phenomena, as in the succession of day and night, in the measured march of the seasons of the revolving year, in the periodic movements of the heavenly bodies, the Hindu recognised an appointed, unvarying and endless cycle of changes. Genearalizing from these facts he concluded that this law must hold for the entire *Cosmos* as well, which would pass through its grand but destined cycle of changes, over and over again, in the æons of Eternity.

How the Hindu thinker accounted, by his doctrine of *Karma*, for the striking inequalities and apparent injustice inseparable from mundane existence the reader has learned in sufficient detail already. As to the *moral* responsibility of man for his actions, the poets of the epics had thought out the problem in its various aspects and despairingly left it unsolved. For as Sanjaya, the envoy of the Pandavas to their cousins, sadly says, in the true spirit of agnosticism: "In this respect three opinions are entertained; some say that every thing is ordained by God,* some say that our acts are the results of free will, and others say that our acts are the results of

* What god can Sanjaya refer to? Surely it must be Fate, inexorable Destiny, of which he is thinking.

those of our past lives."*

The attribution of righteousness to the gods does not seem to be insisted upon; for Krishna, as we have seen, is particularly prone to guileful arts in order to compass his objects, like the Pallas Athene of Homer, at whose suggestion Pandaros treacherously and unjustifiably wounded Menelaus with an arrow.

In regard to the political condition of India in those early times we may, I think, gather from the epics that the petty rulers who shared the land amongst themselves were very numerous—thousands,† indeed, if the poet's statements could be relied upon—, and we need not doubt that it was the perpetual endeavour of the more able and ambitious of these kings to get as many as possible of their fellow chiefs to acknowledge their supremacy.

No one who studies the narratives attributed to Valmiki and Vyasa will fail to catch glimpses of the simple sagas which formed the ground-work of the great edifices raised by the Indian poets; but, as I have observed in the Introductory Chapter, the value and extent of what is usually considered historical matter to be traced in the Ramayana and Mahabharata is so small and so doubtful that it fails to command either my interest or my confidence. It may be due to perversity of character, or to want of historical acumen on my part; but when I am expected to believe that the progress of the *Bhojas* and their allies eastward may be traced in the legend of Karna, given in the Mahabharata, with which the reader

* Mahabharata, Udyoga Parva, section CLIX.

† Mahabharata, Bhishma Parva, section LIX page 217 and section LXXXII, page 295.

of the foregoing pages is familiar, I do not feel inclined to acquiesce. And when I am gravely assured that the romantic story of Satyavati, the fisherman's daughter, her marriage with Santanu and her previous amour with the father of Vyasa, *although absurd in Vyasa's own poem*, becomes intelligible, if we will only put the individual fisherman out of court altogether, *forget* what the poet tells us about Satyavati, and *imagine* that the young lady in question was a personage of some importance in the family of the *king of the fishing people*, I feel such efforts towards constructive history are somewhat beyond my abilities.*

While writers of one class strain after the hidden historical elements in the Ramayana and Mahabharata, those of another class (represented by both Europeans and Indians), ingeniously discover in these narratives merely solar myths or moral allegories. It were needless to enlarge upon this topic here, and I have already given instances of such interpretations in the Note appended to the Ramayana (page 96) and in the summary of the Bhagavat-Gita (page 321). I would merely add that if it be the true function of history to reveal to us living pictures of bygone times, to disclose to us the social life of earlier days, and to make us acquainted with the thoughts, ideals and aspirations of former generations, then the Indian Epics are a solid contribution to historical literature, even if they do not happen to chronicle actual events.

---

*However, the reader who considers such historical inferences sufficiently interesting and important may consult the articles entitled "Early History of Northern India" by F. W. Hewitt in the Journal of the Royal Asiatic Society 1888-89-90.

The heroes of the epics being mostly demi-gods with a long previous history, an appointed destiny, and subject, like mortal men, to pass through many future existences in other forms, do not, I confess, engage my sympathies very much. Even human beings upon this epic stage lose their distinctive character, and cease to interest us if we regard them merely as souls masquerading, as it were, for a certain time in particular forms assumed for the occasion, different from the many they have worn in former states and unlike those which they will wear in future lives. Indeed the doctrine of metempsychosis, with its fluxional succession of beings, human and divine, undermines the conceptions of definite and permanent individuality so thoroughly that I do not wonder that sober human history, with its limited stage and narrow chronology, has had but little charm for the Hindus.

More remarkable than the heroes of Kurukshetra, however, are the Rishis and Hermits, who stand out upon the canvas of the Epic poets with startling distinctness. These sages with their austerities, their superhuman powers, their irascibility and their terrible curses, are the Hindu representatives of the magicians and sorcerers of other countries, and form a remarkable feature in the life of even modern India. As a rule the saints of Christendom are of another type, yet, strange to say, there are a few of them, St. Renan for example, to whom have been attributed characteristics not unlike those of the Indian Rishis.* Elsewhere a large share, perhaps the greater share, of magical power has been credited to the fair sex;

* Renan's "Recollections of my Youth," pp. 72—75.

but the Hindu has, characteristically, made no such concession to women, who never at any time in India were granted the free and honoured position accorded them amongst the Germans of Tacitus or the Norsemen of the Eddas, and never enjoyed even the restricted liberty which Greek women were privileged to exercise. Nevertheless, there is undoubtedly a substratum of chivalrous feeling towards the weaker sex manifested throughout the epics, often in a distinct and pronounced manner.

As to the social life of the early heroic age, of which we get so many interesting glimpses in the Epics, it is certain that it was extremely simple and rude; as, for instance, to cite a single example, the life of the Pandavas in their primitive "house of lac," where their mother ministered to them without the assistance of any servants at all, although, be it remembered, the young princes were supposed to be enjoying themselves away from home on a sort of holiday excursion. There is, however, ample evidence to show that by the time the poems were actually compiled, or at any rate cast into their present forms, a complicated society had been evolved and a life of luxurious ease and refinement was not unknown. Throughout the period embraced in the epics the caste-system was well established, animal food commonly used,* and spirituous drinks not prohibited. Polygamy was common, and polyandry a recognised institution, while the practice known as *Niyoga*—of raising up offspring to deceased relatives, or childless men—was, undoubtedly, fully established.

Now *caste*, with its baleful influences, still dominates

* "All creatures support life by living upon one another."—Mahabharata, Bhishma Parva, page 16.

Hindu life ; polygamy continues to be common in some parts of India ; polyandry is still practised, here and there, in backward places ; and Niyoga, which has never ceased to be orthodox doctrine, has, in these days, had special prominence given to it by Swami Dayanand, and the sect recently founded by him. The practice in question—which is known in a modified form as *levirate** amongst the Jews—has been established in India since time immemorial, and we have had important instances of it in the foregoing pages.

What Manu, the great Indian *lawgiver*, says on the subject of *Niyoga* is as follows: "On failure of issue by the husband if he be of the servile class, the desired offspring may be procreated, either by his brother or some other *sapinda*, on the wife, who has been duly authorized. Sprinkled with clarified butter, silent, in the night, let the kinsman thus appointed beget one son, but a second by no means, on the widow or *childless wife.* By men of twice-born classes no widow or childless wife must be authorized to conceive by any other man than her lord."†

Swami Dayanand, however, does not limit the practice of *Niyoga* to the inferior castes, nor to the cases referred to by Manu. The modern *reformer* goes much further, teaching a doctrine, *said to be founded on the Vedas,* which allows a latitude in respect to the relations between the sexes that, to say the least, is extremely startling in this nineteenth century.‡ I am bound to add that I have

---

* Deut: XXV—5—10 and Gen: XXXVIII.

† Manu chapter IX 59, 60 and 64.

‡ On the subject of Niyoga the reader may consult Sir Henry Maine's Dissertation on Early Law and Custom, pp. 100 and 107, and A Treatise on Hindu Law and Usage by John D. Mayne, Chapter IV.

been very positively assured that Swami Dayanand's precepts in respect to Niyoga are not actually practised by his followers; but their dangerous tendency is, I presume, undeniable.

From the earliest ages known to the writers of the Ramayana and Mahabharata cremation of the dead has been the practice in India. Hence in Indian archæology we are deprived of those sources of information—graves, tumuli, cromlechs and sepulchres—which elsewhere, as in Egypt, have furnished such a wealth of facts regarding the earlier races of mankind.

The sacred character of the Brahmans receives abundant recognition in the Epics. And it is noteworthy that except in the relinquishment of animal food and vinous drinks by a great majority of the Hindus, little change has taken place in the social habits of the people since the heroic age depicted in the Epics. We need not doubt, however, that the abstention from animal food and with it from wine and spirits of all kinds, has, in the course of many generations, profoundly modified the national character, and has, perhaps more than anything else, gradually converted the turbulent, aggressive Aryan into the mild and contemplative Hindu.*

A high degree of culture had doubtless been attained by the Indians before the epics were cast into their present forms. The industrial arts would seem to have flourished, and we have seen how highly the poets appreciat-

*The abandonment of animal food and ardent spirits was probably due to Buddhistic influence, though Buddha himself, as is well known, ate pork. I have been assured by well-informed Indian gentlemen that within the last few years there has been a marked tendency amongst many sections of the people to take to a flesh diet and alcoholic stumlants—in fact to revert to the old Aryan habits in these respects.

ed and enjoyed the beauty of the woodlands, and how much they were impressed with the scenery of their grand mountains. This in itself is a remarkable fact; as the charms of landscape beauty do not seem to have been realized in the West until a somewhat later time.

The ideal of human, (particularly female) beauty which possessed the minds of the Hindu Bards has been indicated by several allusions and quotations in the preceding chapters. It is certainly not that embodied in the Venus of Melos, or the Apollo Belvedere; but every age and country has its own ideals.

Throughout the foregoing brief narrative there has been ample evidence of the height to which the speculative imagination of the Hindus had carried them in endeavouring to read the riddle of human destiny, and notably so in the subtle pantheism of the Bhagavatgita, a work which even if the date assigned to it by European scholars be accepted, and with that its authors supposed acquaintance with Christian ideas, must still excite our admiration by its largeness of conception and liberality of sentiments—expressed many centuries before Luther nailed his famous ninety-five theses upon the door of the church at Wittenberg.

The imaginative faculty never fails the bards of the Indian epics who too often indulge in a very delirium of exaggeration. Yet, notwithstanding their supreme contempt for probabilities or consistency, and their lofty scorn of numerical limitations, it cannot be denied that these Hindu poets, with their lawless imaginations, take us completely captive and carry us along with them, surprised and delighted, through the wonderful scenes of their creation; while one cannot but feel in their company that the intellectual atmosphere which surrounds them is a stronger one and more spiritual than that which was breathed by the Greaks of Homer or the Teutons of the Eddas.

On the whole it may be said that the Indian Epics, as they have reached us, reveal to the careful student an ancient free and vigorous primitive social life and turbulent times, overlaid by a later and less healthy, if more refined, civilization which was permeated with ecclesiasticism; and that they exhibit a strange mixture of what Mr. Herbert Spencer would call the "ethics of enmity" and the "ethics of amity." The later stage of Indian history—the age of Brahmanism, succeeding the heroic age and continuing to the present day—may, I think, be well compared with the Middle Ages in Europe, when priestly influence was predominant and national life at a low ebb. Europe, under the influence of the spirit of industrialism and modern science, has emancipated itself from the numbing influences of the Dark Ages. When will India do the same? For how many more centuries is she destined to wrangle over unprofitable theological questions, as did the Byzantine Greeks while the conqueror was thundering at their gates?

My pleasant undertaking has occupied more time than I had anticipated when I took it in hand; but I leave it now with a profound appreciation of the capabilities of a people who have produced such works as the Ramayana and Mahabharata.

In every age,—even in an industrial age of busy scientific progress and mechanical triumphs like our own —the human mind turns with fond interest to any picture which shows how men in the fore-time lived and thought, and it listens eagerly to any song which echoes through the vanished years the fervent hopes and lofty aspirations of buried generations. Therefore I trust that my little work, though it be but a sketch of a great picture and the echo of a grand old song, may find favor with the reading public.